Temptations

A New Dimension in Delta Cooking

Presbyterian Day School
Cleveland, Mississippi

The purpose of the Presbyterian Day School is to provide a superior education in a Christian atmosphere.

Printed in the USA by
WIMMER BROTHERS
P.O. Box 18408
Memphis, Tennessee 38181-0408

FOREWARD

The Delta is a treasure trove of delectable taste temptations provided by man and nature.

With these recipes we plan to entice the amateur as well as the experienced cook. Each recipe has been selected to allure, to enchant, and to fascinate with the possibilities of what can be accomplished in the reader's own kitchen.

Hopefully, this collection of recipes will be an inducement, an attraction, an inspiration to those who prepare and those who partake. We intend to whet your appetite and to tantalize your imagination with the charm of this wonderful land that casts its spell in so many ways—but especially in food.

The culinary enchantment of some of the best cooks in the Delta will captivate you through the following pages and tempt you into savory delights that we hope will be totally irresistible.

Enjoy!

Mary Ann Odom

Editors Note

Our deepest gratitude goes to Mrs. Mike Sanders whose artistic talent has made our cookbook a work of art within itself.

Editors

Chairman: Mrs. Don Blackwood
Co-Chairman: Mrs. H.L. Dilworth

Co-Editors

Mrs. Don Aylward   Mrs. Bill Parker
Mrs. Howard Grittman, Jr.   Mrs. Mark Routman
Mrs. Billy Tabb

Acknowledgements

We deeply appreciate the contributions of the following:

Recipe Committee

Collection chairmen: Mrs. Tommy Naron
Mrs. Hugh Smith, Jr.

Section chairmen:

Mrs. Michael Burchfield	Mrs. Mike Robbins
Mrs. Roy Cole	Mrs. Terry Russell
Mrs. Allen Findley	Mrs. Ken Strong
Mrs. Keith Griffin	Mrs. Barry Sullivan
Mrs. Dan Hammett	Mrs. David Taylor
Mrs. Jim Meyer	Mrs. James Taylor
Mrs. Troy Odom	

Men's section—Wilson Sledge

Promotion and Marketing
Mrs. Kirkham Povall
Mrs. Mark Koonce

Art
Mrs. Mike Sanders

Special writer
Mrs. Lee Odom

Typists

Mrs. Robert Fillingham	Mrs. Wilson Sledge
Mrs. Keith Griggin	Mrs. Ken Strong
Mrs. Jerry Hollingsworth	Mrs. Paul Warrington

Finance
Mrs. John Denton   Mrs. Billy Nowell   Mrs. Allen Pepper

TABLE OF CONTENTS

MANY THANKS

To the many people who shared their recipes and gave their time in making TEMPTATIONS a reality, we owe a debt of gratitude. Without your help, this project would not have reached a successful completion. Our only regret is that many tasty recipes could not be used due to a limited space.

Delta cooking, like its people, has always been unique; TEMPTATIONS, we hope, not only captures that uniqueness, but also adds a new dimension.

Suzan and Anne

Appetizers,
Beverages

AUNT JESSIE'S BLOODY MARY

4 Servings

2 cups tomato juice
1 cup vodka
Juice of 2 lemons
4 teaspoons steak sauce

Salt
Pepper
Tabasco, to taste

Mix all ingredients and serve.

Mrs. Jeff Levingston (Barbara)

FROZEN MARGARITAS

4 Servings

1 (6-ounce) can frozen
limeade, thawed

¾ cup tequila
¼ cup Triple Sec

Rub rim of glasses with fresh lime juice then place in salt. Set aside, combine limeade, tequila, Triple Sec in blender, add enough crushed ice to fill ¾ full. Blend and serve in prepared glasses.

Mrs. Don Blackwood (Susan)

BANANA DAIQUIRI

2 Servings

1 large banana
2 ounces orange juice

1 teaspoon sugar
1½-ounces rum

Combine and blend—add 4 ice cubes and blend in blender.

The Editors

SANGRIA   2 Quarts

1 bottle Spanish red wine
1-ounce Triple Sec or Cointreau
1-ounce Grand Marnier
½ cup lemon juice
½ cup sugar
1½ cups chilled carbonated soda water

Slices of 1 lemon, 1 orange, 1 lime
Fresh strawberries or fresh peach slices
2 cinnamon sticks (optional)

One hour before serving, sprinkle fruit with Grand Marnier and put the cinnamon sticks in the wine. Just before serving, remove cinnamon sticks and combine brandied fruit, wine, and all ingredients in a pitcher with ice.

Mrs. Jim Brown (Pat)

WHITE WINE PUNCH   25 (3-ounce) Servings

1 fifth of white wine, chilled
1 fifth champagne, chilled

1 fifth ginger ale, chilled

Combine and serve.

Mrs. Mark Routman (Terry)

BRANDY ALEXANDER   8 Servings

⅓ cup brandy
⅓ cup Crème de Cocoa

Vanilla Ice Cream
Nutmeg

Put brandy and Crème de Cocoa in blender. Gradually add ice cream until blender is filled to 4 to 5 cups. Serve in small glasses and sprinkle with nutmeg.

The Editors

Variation: Omit Crème de Cocoa and use 1 cup coffee ice cream instead of vanilla ice cream.

BULLSHOTS
12 cups

6 cups beef consommé
6 cups commercial bloody mary
 mix
Dash of hot sauce
Dash of Worcestershire sauce

Dash of celery salt
Dash of lemon-pepper
 seasoning
Celery Tops

Combine first 6 ingredients; mix well. Chill at least 1 hour. To serve, pour in individual glasses and garnish each serving with a celery top. Vodka may be added if desired.

Mrs. Tom Sullivan, Jr. (Teri)
Denham Springs, Louisiana

COFFEE PUNCH
24 cups

1 quart strong coffee
1 pint heavy cream, whipped
5 Tablespoons sugar

5 teaspoons vanilla
½ gallon vanilla ice cream
1 pint bourbon

Cool coffee and add sugar and vanilla. Mix in bourbon and pour into punch bowl. Add ice cream and stir. May serve whipped cream on top.

The Editors

CAPPUCCINO
4½ Cups

2 cups coffee
2 cups milk
1 Tablespoon sugar
1 Tablespoon cocoa

1 shot brandy
1 shot dark Cream de Cocoa
Whipped cream
Whole cinnamon sticks

Mix and bring to a boil. Top with whipped cream and a cinnamon stick. Double or triple this recipe and serve around a fire after a winter dinner party.

Mrs. Bill Profilet (Mary Love)

FROZEN FRUIT PUNCH
100 (4-ounce) Servings

3 (46-ounce) cans pineapple
    juice
2 (46-ounce) cans orange juice
2 (6-ounce) cans frozen
    lemonade

3 packages unsweetened
    strawberry drink mix (add 3
    quarts water)
2 pounds sugar

Prepare lemonade as directed on can. Add drink mix and 3 quarts water. Add sugar, pineapple juice and orange juice. Put punch in freezer and as it starts to freeze stir occasionally until slushy.

Mrs. W. G. Jefcoat (Melissa)

CHRISTMAS PUNCH
4½ Quarts

4 cups cranberry juice
2 cups pineapple juice
3 quarts cold ginger ale

1 Tablespoon almond extract
½ cup sugar
1 teaspoon red food coloring

Combine all ingredients. Stir until sugar is dissolved and thoroughly mixed.

Decorative Ice Ring
Freeze 1 inch water with red cherry halves and green holly leaves arranged in bottom of a bundt pan. After this has frozen add enough water to make a 2 to 3 inch ring. Freeze until ready to serve.

Mrs. J. T. Pannell (Patti)

CHOCO-BOURBON SNORT
10 Servings

6 chocolate bars with
    almonds
1 cup cold coffee

½ cup (or less) bourbon
1 quart vanilla ice cream

Pulverize chocolate bars and coffee in blender. Add ice cream and bourbon and blend. Serve as an after dinner drink.

Mrs. Bob Buchanan (Sharon)

CREAM CHEESE AND CONSOMME PIE

1 can (10¾-ounce) consomme
1⅓ package gelatin
1 (8-ounce) package cream cheese, softened

1 (8-ounce) can smoked oysters, chopped

Season consomme with Worcestershire sauce, lemon juice and tabasco to taste. Heat with gelatin until dissolved. Pour into glass pie plate and congeal. Combine cream cheese and oysters. Season again with Worcestershire sauce, and season salt to taste. Spread over congealed consomme and refrigerate. When ready to serve, run a knife around plate and turn out on serving platter. Serve with crackers.

Mrs. W. C. Cox, Jr.
Jackson, Mississippi

STUFFED SNOW PEAS

50 to 60 appetizers

½ pound snow pea pods
1 (2½-ounce) jar thinly sliced, dried beef
1 teaspoon horseradish

1 cup sour cream
½ teaspoon mustard
⅛ teaspoon pepper

Trim tips and ends from pea pods. In a medium saucepan, bring 3 cups lightly salted water to boil. Carefully put pea pods in boiling water. Simmer for about 1 minute. Immediately immerse in cold water. Drain and refrigerate until chilled. Chop beef very fine in food processor. Combine beef and other ingredients in small bowl. Take pea pods and using small sharp knife, carefully slit one side of pea pod, making a small boat. With small spoon (demitasse) fill pea pods with beef mixture. Store upright in refrigerator for 1 hour.

Mrs. H. L. Dilworth (Anne)

AVOCADO BUTTER

2 avocados, peeled
¼ cup lemon juice
⅓ cup butter, softened
1 envelope gelatin

½ cup half-and-half
½ teaspoon each, salt, garlic
   powder, paprika
¼ teaspoon red pepper

Mash avocados with lemon juice. Cream thoroughly into softened butter. Soften gelatin in half-and-half and dissolve over hot water. Add this to avocado mixture and add seasonings. Adjust seasonings, if necessary. Prepare a 1½ cup mold or pack into a 2 cup crock. Use for a spread on crackers. Six to eight finely minced shrimp may be added.

Mrs. Marie Ashley

EGGPLANT CAVIAR

1 medium eggplant
1 large onion, chopped
1 green pepper, chopped
2 large garlic cloves, chopped
½ cup olive oil
2 tomatoes, peeled and
   chopped

2 teaspoons salt
1 teaspoon pepper
¼ teapsoon cayenne pepper
¼ teaspoon Worcestershire
   sauce
1 teaspoon MSG
2 Tablespoons dry white wine

Punch several holes in eggplant. Place in shallow pan with small amount of water. Bake at 400° until soft (about 1 hour). Sauté onion, pepper and garlic in olive oil. Peel eggplant and chop. Mix with sautéed vegetables, tomatoes, salt, peppers, Worcestershire sauce, MSG, and white wine. Cook until thick. Refrigerate. Serve cold.

Mrs. Leo McGee, Sr. (Martha)
Gunnison, Mississippi

JACKIE'S STUFFED MUSHROOMS

2 (12-ounce) packages fresh
  mushrooms
3 Tablespoons butter
½ cup chopped green onions
½ cup chopped green pepper
1 clove garlic, pressed

3 Tablespoons all-purpose flour
½ cup milk
1 (6-ounce) can crab meat
Worcestershire sauce to taste
Pepper to taste

Wash mushrooms and remove the stems. Dice the mushroom stems and sauté in 3 tablespoons of butter along with the onions, green pepper and garlic. Add flour and milk, stirring well. Add crab meat. Season with Worcestershire and pepper to taste. Stuff mushroom caps and bake on a cookie sheet for 20 - 25 minutes at 350°.

Mrs. W. F. Tate (Rachel)

HOT MUSHROOM TURNOVERS   3½ dozen

1 (8-ounce) package cream
  cheese, softened
2 to 2½ cups all-purpose flour
¾ cup butter or margarine,
  softened
½ pound mushrooms, minced

1 large onion, minced
¼ cup sour cream
1 teaspoon salt
¼ teaspoon thyme leaves
1 egg, beaten

About 2 hours before serving: In a large bowl with mixer at medium speed, beat cream cheese, 1½ cups flour and ½ cup butter until smooth. Shape into a ball, wrap, refrigerate for 1 hour. Meanwhile, in 10-inch skillet over medium heat, in 3 tablespoons hot butter, cook mushrooms and onion until tender, stirring occasionally. Stir in sour cream, salt, thyme and 2 tablespoons flour. Set aside. On floured surface with floured rolling pin, roll ½ of dough ⅛-inch thick. With floured 2¾-inch round cookie cutter, cut out as many circles as possible. Repeat. Preheat oven to 450°. Onto one half of each dough circle, place a teaspoon of mushroom mixture. Brush edges of circles with some egg, fold dough over filling. With fork, firmly press edges together to seal, prick tops. Place turnovers on ungreased cookie sheet, brush with remaining egg. Bake 12 to 14 minutes until golden.

Mrs. Steve Davis (Debbie)

STUFFED MUSHROOMS

12 servings

12 large fresh mushrooms
2 Tablespoons butter
1 medium onion, finely
  chopped
2-ounces (½ cup) pepperoni,
  diced
¼ cup green pepper, finely
  chopped
1 small clove garlic, minced

1 Tablespoon snipped parsley
¼ teaspoon dried oregano,
  crushed
½ cup finely crushed butter
  round crackers (12)
½ teaspoon seasoned salt
Dash pepper
½ cup chicken broth

Wash mushrooms. Remove stems; finely chop stems and reserve. Drain caps on paper towels. Melt butter in skillet; add onion, pepperoni, green pepper, garlic and chopped mushroom stems. Cook until vegetables are tender, but not brown. Add cracker crumbs, cheese, parsley, seasoned salt, oregano and pepper. Mix well. Stir in chicken broth. Spoon stuffing into mushroom caps, rounding tops. Place caps into a shallow baking pan with about ¼ inch of water covering bottom of pan. Bake uncovered in 325° oven for 20 to 25 minutes.

Mrs. James Taylor (Bev)

MUSHROOMS LOGS

4 dozen

2 (8-ounce) cans refrigerated
  crescent dinner rolls
1 (8-ounce) package cream
  cheese, softened
1 (4-ounce) can mushroom
  stems and pieces, drained
  and chopped

1 teaspoon seasoned salt
1 egg, beaten
1 to 2 Tablespoons poppy seeds

Separate crescent dough into 8 rectangles; press perforations to seal. Combine cream cheese, mushrooms and salt, mixing well. Spread cream cheese mixture in equal portions over each rectangle of dough. Starting at long sides, roll up each rectangle jelly-roll fashion; pinching seams to seal. Slice logs into 1-inch pieces. Place seam side down on an ungreased baking sheet. Brush each log with beaten egg, and sprinkle with poppy seeds. Bake at 375° for 10 to 12 minutes.

Mrs. Don Aylward (Lee)

SPANISH MUSHROOMS

Olive oil
4 cloves garlic, finely chopped
1 (12-ounce) box fresh
  mushrooms, sliced
2 to 3 Tablespoons fresh
  chopped parsley

Whole red pepper flakes
Salt
MSG
French bread

Pour olive oil in skillet to cover bottom. Sauté garlic; add mushrooms, parsley, and red pepper flakes to taste; sauté briefly. Sprinkle with salt and MSG. Spoon mushrooms on French bread chunks. Serve immediately.

Mrs. H. L. Dilworth (Anne)

CURRY DIP
2½ cups

1 cup sour cream with chives
1 cup mayonnaise
½ Tablespoon lemon juice
½ teaspoon salt
¼ teaspoon paprika
¼ cup chopped parsley

1 Tablespoon grated onion
⅛ teaspoon curry powder
½ teaspoon Worcestershire
  sauce
Garlic salt to taste

Mix all ingredients and refrigerate. Serve with chips, celery or carrot sticks.

Mrs. Phillip Rizzo (Ramona)

SPINACH DIP

2 (10-ounce) frozen chopped
  spinach
5 green onions, chopped
1 (1.4-ounce) package Knorr's®
  vegetable soup mix

1 cup mayonnaise
1 (8-ounce) can water
  chestnuts, chopped
1 cup sour cream

Thaw spinach. Squeeze moisture out until drained thoroughly. Mix remaining ingredients. Blend well. Scoop out center of Hawaiian Bread and fill with dip. Use pieces of bread to dip.

Linda Horton

CHICKEN-CUCUMBER SURPRISE

5 dozen servings

1 (5-ounce) can white chicken, drained and flaked
1 hard-boiled egg, finely chopped
½ cup mayonnaise
¼ cup finely chopped onion
¼ cup finely chopped green pepper

2 Tablespoons finely chopped pecans, toasted
Dash of salt
Dash of pepper
5 cucumbers thinly sliced
Paprika

Combine first 8 ingredients; cover and chill for at least 2 hours. Spread 1 teaspoon of chicken mixture on each cucumber slice; top each with dash of paprika.

Mrs. Howard Grittman (Ann)
Drew, Mississippi

CHICKEN ROLL CANAPES

5 dozen

3 large chicken breasts (six pieces), skinned and boned
2 Tablespoons soy sauce
2 Tablespoons oil
¼ cup dry Sherry
1 garlic clove, finely minced

1 teaspoon finely minced ginger root (or powdered ginger)
3 Tablespoons butter, melted
White bread rounds
Butter
Mustard

Flatten breasts between wax paper. Combine soy sauce, oil, Sherry, garlic and ginger. Pour over chicken and marinate overnight, turning occasionally. Take chicken and roll tightly, lengthwise, jelly roll fashion and tie with enough string to hold in place. Put in shallow baking dish, add marinade and melted butter. Bake in pre-heated oven (325°) for 30 minutes, basting and turning often. Cool and refrigerate. Slice chicken rolls thinly. Spread bread rounds with soft butter and mustard to taste. Top with chicken slice. Garnish with pimiento and tiny springs of parsley. May be assembled ahead of time and covered with damp cloth.

Mrs. Robert Tibbs (Pat)

CHICKEN NUGGETS AND SAUCES   30 appetizers

**6 whole chicken breasts,
  skinned and deboned
1 cup water
1 cup all-purpose flour**

**1½ teaspoons salt
2 eggs, beaten
1½ cups cooking oil**

Cut chicken into 1½-inch chunks. Add water, flour and salt to beaten eggs. Dip chicken pieces into this batter and fry in hot oil until golden brown. Drain on paper towels; serve with dunking sauces.

Sauce Number 1   1½ cups
**1 (12-ounce) jar pineapple
  preserves**

**¼ cup horseradish
¼ cup prepared mustard**

Heat all ingredients together in a small saucepan until smooth.

Sauce Number 2   2 cups
**1 cup catsup
1 Tablespoon brown sugar
6 Tablespoons margarine**

**1 teaspoon dry mustard
2 teaspoons vinegar**

In small saucepan, mix all ingredients together; cook 5 minutes, stirring constantly.

Mrs. W. P. Skelton (Louise)

CHEESE STRAWS

**½ pound sharp Cheddar
  cheese
½ cup butter (not margarine)**

**1½ cups all-purpose flour
½ teaspoon salt
Red pepper to taste**

Use food processor and microwave for speedy production. Grate ½ pound cold cheese. Put on wax paper and microwave for 12 seconds on full power. Microwave ½ cup butter for 10 seconds on full power. Use steel blades in processor to blend softened cheese and butter. Add 1 cup flour, ½ teaspoon salt and red pepper to taste. Process until mixed and then add ½ cup flour. Process until it forms a big ball. Put through cookie press to make straws. Bake on cookie sheet for 13 minutes at 400°.

Mrs. Billy Latham (Sue)

LAYERED NACHO DIP
6 cups

1 (16-ounce) can refried beans
½ (1.25-ounce) package taco seasoning mix
1 (6-ounce) carton avocado dip
1 (8-ounce) carton sour cream
1 (4½-ounce) can chopped ripe olives

2 large tomatoes, diced
1 small onion, finely chopped
1 (4-ounce) can chopped green chilies
1½ cups (6-ounces) shredded Monterey Jack cheese

Combine beans and seasoning mix; spread bean mixture evenly in a 12x8x2-inch dish. Layer remaining ingredients in order listed. Serve with large corn chips.

Note: 1 can of Rotel tomatoes may be substituted for the tomatoes and green chilies.

Mrs. Jimmy Goodman (Carolyn)
Mrs. Robert Neal (Vail)

Variation: May use 1 large avocado mashed with 1 Tablespoon lemon juice added for the avocado dip.

DIP IN BREAD BOWL

1 loaf round bread
16-ounces cream cheese
2 cups sour cream
2 bunches green onions and tops, chopped

8-ounce thin ham, chopped
MSG

Slice the top off loaf of round bread. Hollow out middle, cube pieces to use for dipping. Soften cream cheese. Combine with sour cream, onions, ham and sprinkle with MSG. Put dip into bread bowl with bread cubes surrounding it.

Mrs. Leo McGee (Judy)

CURRY CHEESE LOAF

15 to 20 servings

1½ pounds Cheddar cheese,
  shredded
1 (8-ounce) cream cheese,
  softened
2 to 3 Tablespoons mayonnaise

2 teaspoons curry powder
Garlic salt
Tabasco
Salt

Mix cheese, cream cheese, mayonnaise and curry. Add garlic salt, Tabasco, and salt to taste. Shape into loaf and chill.

Toppings
First topping: Chutney
Second topping: Green onions, finely chopped
Third topping: Peanuts, finely chopped

Spread evenly over loaf.

Mrs. Jimmy Sanders (Hazel)

OLDE ENGLISH CHEESE BALL

16-ounces cream cheese
1 (5-ounce) Olde English sharp
  cheese spread
2 Tablespoons mayonnaise
1 Tablespoon Parmesan cheese
1 Tablespoon grated onion
1 Tablespoon chopped pimiento

1 Tablespoon lemon juice
Generous dash of
  Worcestershire sauce
Garlic salt and black pepper
1 cup chopped pecans
½ cup finely chopped parsley

Mix first nine ingredients in food processor. Chill on waxed paper until firm. Shape into ball and roll in mixture of pecans and parsley. Freezes well.

The Editors

CHEESE RING

1 pound sharp Cheddar
 cheese, shredded
1 cup pecans, finely chopped
1 cup mayonnaise

Chopped onion to taste
Garlic powder to taste
1 jar strawberry preserves

Combine all ingredients except strawberry preserves. Mix well and place in greased mold (grease mold with a little mayonnaise). Chill overnight in refrigerator. To loosen cheese ring, place in warm water for a few seconds and the cheese will come out. When serving, put strawberry preserves into center of ring.

Mrs. Tommy Naron (Memorie)

TASTY CHEESE ROUND

2 (8-ounce) packages cream
 cheese, softened
2 cloves garlic, crushed
2 teaspoons caraway seeds
2 teaspoons basil

2 teaspoons dried dillweed
2 teaspoons chopped chives
2½ Tablespoons lemon-pepper
 seasoning

Combine first 6 ingredients; mix well. Shape into a 5-inch round patty; coat top and sides with lemon-pepper seasoning. Cover and chill overnight. Serve with assorted crackers.

Mrs. Howard Grittman (Ann)

INTRIGUING DIP   3½ cups

2 cups sour cream
8-ounces cream cheese
 (whipped until smooth)
¼ pound blue cheese
 (crumbled)
1 Tablespoon wine vinegar

1 Tablespoon horseradish
1 teaspoon salt
2 Tablespoons onion juice
1½ teaspoons dry mustard
1 teaspoon paprika
½ teaspoon pepper

Combine all ingredients and refrigerate at least 4 to 6 hours to allow flavors to mellow. Serve with raw vegetables.

Mrs. Robert Tibbs (Pat)

CHEESE PETIT FOURS ✓

84 servings

3 loaves of very thin
   sandwich bread
2 cups margarine
4 jars of Olde English cheese
   spread
1½ teaspoons Worcestershire
   sauce

1 teaspoon hot sauce
1 teaspoon onion powder
1 teaspoon garlic salt
Dash of cayenne pepper
Dill weed for topping

Cut crust off two and a half loaves bread, three slices at a time. Cream margarine, cheese spread, Worcestershire sauce, hot sauce, onion powder, garlic salt and pepper with rotary beater until consistency of icing. Spread mixture between layers of bread. Quarter and spread mixture over sides and top. (Each petit four is three slices thick). Freeze on cookie sheets, then put into plastic bags in freezer. Do not defrost until ready to use. Bake 15 to 20 minutes at 350°. Sprinkle with dill weed on each petit four.

Mrs. Clint Wood (Laura)

MARINATED CHEESE CUBES

1 (16-ounce) package
   Mozzarella cheese (cut in ½
   inch cubes and pricked with
   a fork)
2 cups olive oil
1 medium bell pepper, cut in
   strips
¼ cup wine vinegar

1 Tablespoon crushed red
   pepper
1 Tablespoon oregano
1 Tablespoon green
   peppercorns
1 teaspoon thyme
2 cloves garlic

Heat all ingredients, except cheese until hot. Cool and pour over cheese. Refrigerate for 2 weeks. Let come to room temperature before serving. This will keep 6 more weeks.

Mrs. Howard Grittman (Ann)
Drew, Mississippi

ROQUEFORT GRAPES

10-ounces almonds, pecans or
  walnuts
1 (8-ounce) package cream
  cheese

⅛ pound Roquefort cheese
2 teaspoons heavy cream
1 pound seedless grapes (red
  or green)

Toast nuts at 275° and chop coarsely. Combine cheese and cream until smooth. Coat grapes and roll in nuts. These can be arranged to look like a cluster of grapes with a sprig of ivy.

Mrs. H. L. Dilworth (Anne)

BACON-ALMOND CHEESE SPREAD

1 pound Cheddar cheese,
  shredded
12 green onions, chopped
1 pound bacon, cooked crisp
  and crumbled

2 cups mayonnaise
1 cup slivered almonds, toasted
Salt to taste

Mix all ingredients and chill. Shape into ball or spoon into serving bowl. Serve with crackers.

The Editors

HOT CHEESE SQUARES

1 pound sharp Cheddar
  cheese, shredded
1 pound Monterey Jack cheese
  with peppers, grated
2 (4-ounce) cans green chilies,
  chopped

1 (14-ounce) can evaporated
  milk
1 cup all-purpose flour
1 cup butter, room temperature

Grate cheeses and sprinkle in a lightly greased 10x15-inch glass baking dish. Sprinkle all over with green chilies. In blender, mix evaporated milk, flour and butter and pour over other ingredients. Bake at 350° for 35 to 40 minutes or until set. Let cool about 20 minutes; cut into squares.

Mrs. Jimmy Yeager (Neysa)

APPETIZER CHEESE CAKE
10 to 12 wedges

*1 (6-ounce) box cheese
  crackers*
*½ cup finely chopped stuffed
  olives*
½ cup finely chopped celery
*1 medium green pepper, finely
  chopped*
1 small onion, finely chopped
2 Tablespoons lemon juice

1 teaspoon salt
*1 teaspoon Worcestershire
  sauce*
¼ teaspoon paprika
Dash of Tabasco
2 cups sour cream
Ripe olives, sliced
Pimiento strips
Melted butter

Brush sides and bottom of 9-inch spring form pan with melted butter and press half the crushed cracker crumbs on bottom to form base. Combine stuffed olives, celery, green pepper, onion, lemon juice, salt, Worcestershire, paprika and Tabasco with sour cream; blend well. Spread this mixture over cracker base. Scatter remainder of crumbs over top. Cover with wax paper and refrigerate for at least 24 hours. Remove pan side and place cake (still on pan bottom) on serving platter. Garnish top with ripe olive rings and pimiento.

Martha L. Norman
Jackson, Mississippi

BAKED BRIE

*1 (9-inch) whole wheel of brie
(60% double cream)
Brown sugar*

*¾ cup chopped nuts (pecans,
walnuts or sliced almonds)*

Remove the rind from the top of brie, leaving a ⅛ to ¼ inch rim all the way around the top. Put whole brie on a greased cookie sheet. Sprinkle brown sugar liberally on top and cover with chopped nuts. Place under broiler and watch for nuts to brown, about 3 to 5 minutes. Brie should slide off cookie sheet with the help of a spatula. Serve with plain crackers.

Mrs. H. L. Dilworth (Anne)

COCKTAIL MEAT BALLS   40 meatballs

Meat Mixture
1 pound ground beef   *1 teaspoon salt*
1 egg, beaten   *⅛ teaspoon pepper*
½ cup fine dry bread crumbs

Sauce
1 clove garlic, quartered   *2 Tablespoons catsup*
⅔ Tablespoon oil   *⅛ teaspoon black pepper*
1 cup cola soft drink   *1 Tablespoon vinegar*
¼ teaspoon dry mustard   *1 Tablespoon soy sauce*

Combine all ingredients for meat mixture. Shape into bite size balls. Set aside. Over very low heat, sauté garlic in oil until pieces are tender, but not brown. Discard garlic. Brown meat balls in the oil and remove. Add the remaining sauce ingredients and bring to a boil. Add meat balls. Cook over low heat until most of the sauce is absorbed.

Mrs. Curtis Lofton (Janice)

BACON-WRAPPED, HOT SAUSAGE COCOONS   36 appetizers

¼ cup butter or margarine   *1 egg, beaten*
½ cup water   *¼ pound hot bulk sausage*
1½ cups packaged   *¾ pound sliced bacon*
   herb-seasoned stuffing

Melt butter in water in saucepan. Remove from heat; stir into stuffing; then add egg and sausage. Mix with hands thoroughly. Chill about ½ hour for easier handling; then shape into small cocoons about the size of pecans. Cut bacon strips into thirds; wrap bacon around sausage cocoons and fasten with a toothpick. These can be baked in an oven or microwaved. For oven-baking, place on shallow pan and bake at 375° for 35 minutes. Bake until crisp, turning at halfway point in cooking. Drain on paper towels and serve hot. For microwave cooking, place ½ of recipe on paper towel-lined container; microwave on high for about 8 minutes or until bacon is brown and crisp. Blot with more paper towels and serve hot.

Note: I prefer these cooked in the microwave. This recipe may be doubled or tripled; also they freeze well before baking.

Mrs. Mark Routman (Terry)
Mrs. Larry Boozer (Sandra)

MARINATED SMOKED SAUSAGE

3 pounds smoked sausage   **5-ounces soy sauce**
16-ounces Italian dressing

Cut sausage into bite-sized pieces and bake in 350° oven on broiler pan. Drain. Mix dressing and soy sauce and pour over sausage. Let stand in refrigerator for 2 or 3 days. Heat and serve with toothpicks.

Mrs. Billy Nowell (Ann)

EGG ROLLS   2 dozen

1 pound uncooked shrimp,   **3 Tablespoons sherry**
**   peeled**   **1½ Tablespoons soy sauce**
1 pound boneless lean pork,   **2 teaspoons fresh grated ginger**
**   uncooked**   **1 teaspoon sugar**
4-ounces fresh mushrooms   **½ teaspoon salt**
8 green onions   **¼ cup water**
1 red pepper, seeded   **1½ Tablespoons cornstarch**
1 (8-ounce) can water   **24 egg roll wrappers**
**   chestnuts, drained**
8-ounces Chinese cabbage
**   (about ½ head)**

Finely chop shrimp, pork, mushrooms, onions, pepper, cabbage, and water chestnuts. May use food processor. Place in large bowl and add sherry, soy sauce, ginger, sugar and salt. Mix well. Mix water and cornstarch. Place ¼ cup of meat mixture evenly across corner of wrapper. Brush cornstarch mixture around edges. Carefully roll wrappers around filling; fold in corners. Fry egg rolls in hot oil until golden brown, about 5 minutes. Drain and serve warm.

Mrs. Howard Grittman (Ann)
Drew, Mississippi

GREEK MEAT AND SPINACH PASTIES

8 to 10 appetizers

½ pound ground pork
½ pound ground chuck
½ teaspoon oregano
½ teaspoon salt

½ teaspoon pepper
1 (10-ounce) package chopped
spinach, cooked and drained
1 package puffed pastry

In a large heavy skillet, brown pork and beef; drain well. Place meat, oregano, salt, pepper and spinach in a large bowl and mix well. On a floured surface, roll out pastry dough ⅛ inch thick. Cut into 8 to 10 4x2-inch rectangles. Place small portion of meat and spinach mixture in center of rectangle. Brush edges of dough with egg yolk. Fold over and press together firmly. Brush surface of pasties with egg yolk. Cut very narrow strips from dough trimmings; place in a cross on pasties. Brush with egg yolk. Sprinkle baking sheet with cold water; place pasties on dampened baking sheet. Preheat oven 425° and bake pasties 15 to 20 minutes or until puffed and golden. Serve hot.

Note: Make ahead of time and freeze.

Mrs. John Nolen Cannon, Jr. (Toni)
Tunica, Mississippi

SEAFOOD DIP

1 bunch chopped green onions
4 Tablespoons parsley flakes
½ cup margarine
2 Tablespoons all-purpose flour
1 pint half-and-half cream
8-ounces grated Swiss cheese
1 teaspoon Worcestershire
sauce

½ teaspoon liquid hot pepper
sauce
¼ teaspoon red pepper
Salt and pepper to taste
2 (6-ounce) cans crab meat,
drained
1 (4½-ounce) can shrimp,
drained

Sauté onions and parsley over medium heat in margarine until onions are clear. Add flour, stir, add half-and-half, then cheese. Add all seasonings. Then add crab meat and shrimp. Serve warm with favorite chips. This dip freezes well and can be heated before serving.

Mrs. James McLelland (Carolyn)

CHAFING DISH SEAFOOD DIP 50 servings

2 (10¾-ounce) cans cream of
mushroom soup
1 (10¾-ounce) can cream of
shrimp soup
1 (8-ounce) package cream
cheese
3 (6½-ounce) cans shrimp,
drained
2 (8-ounce) cans water
chestnuts, sliced

1 pound crab meat (canned,
frozen or fresh)
3 (8-ounce) cans mushrooms,
drained
1 teaspoon Tabasco
2 teaspoons dry mustard
2 teaspoons curry powder
4 Tablespoons Worcestershire
Salt and pepper to taste

Heat soups slowly, stir in cream cheese until melted. Add remaining ingredients. Serve hot with melba toast rounds.

Mrs. Steve Davis (Debbie)

SEAFOOD STUFFED MUSHROOMS

15 large fresh mushroom caps
(stems removed and finely
chopped)
1 bunch green onions
(chopped-including tops)
½ cup butter (no margarine)
½ bag seasoned bread crumbs
1 teaspoon garlic powder

1 (8-ounce) package cream
cheese, softened
1 (6-ounce) can crab meat,
drained
1 (4½-ounce) can shrimp,
drained (optional)
½ cup butter

Sauté mushroom stems and chopped onions in butter. Pour over bread crumbs in a bowl and mix well. Add garlic powder. Stir. Add cream cheese. Stir well. Add crab meat and/or shrimp. Mix well. Add a tablespoon of milk if mixture is too thick. Spoon generous portion of mixture into mushroom caps and arrange in a large glass dish sprayed with vegetable oil spray. Bake in 350° oven until tops are slightly brown. Be sure to brush with melted butter several times during cooking time.

Note: Mixture can be prepared and frozen for later use in stuffing fresh mushrooms.

Mrs. Bert Hayes (Cindy)

CRAB ROLLS
6 dozen rolls

1 pound soft processed
 cheese
1 pound butter
2 (7¾-ounce) cans crab meat
 or 1 pound fresh crab meat

1½ loaves very thin sliced
 bread
2 cups sesame seeds

Melt cheese and ½ pound butter in double boiler; cool. Add crab meat and stir until spreadable. (Butter and cheese tend to separate but continue stirring). Remove crusts from bread and roll until flat. Spread with cheese mixture and roll up. Melt remaining butter and add sesame seeds. Roll bread rolls in sesame seed mixture. Lay seam down in baking dish and freeze. To serve, cut into thirds and broil about 5 minutes. Watch closely.

Mrs. Howard Grittman (Ann)
Drew, Mississippi

CRAB BITES

1 (7¾-ounce) can lump crab
 meat
5-ounces Olde English cheese
¼ cup softened butter

2 Tablespoons mayonnaise
½ teaspoon garlic salt
½ teaspoon season salt
English muffins

Mix and spread first six ingredients onto English muffin halves. Cut into wedges. Heat on cookie sheet at 350° until warm. Freezes well.

Mrs. John Thornell (Nita)

CRAYFISH BALLS
20 appetizers

1 pound crayfish, ground
1 medium sized onion, chopped
1 egg
2 Tablespoons parsley,
 chopped

Salt, red pepper and black
 pepper to taste

Mix together all ingredients and roll into the shape of meat balls. Bake at 350° for 15 to 20 minutes.

Mrs. Mark Routman (Terry)

BREAUX BRIDGE CRAYFISH DIP

1 medium onion, chopped
1 medium bell pepper,
  chopped
1 rib celery, chopped
2 cloves garlic, crushed
¼ cup butter
1 (10-ounce) can Rotel
  tomatoes

1 (10¾-ounce) can cream of
  mushroom soup
1 teaspoon Worcestershire
  sauce
Salt and pepper to taste
2 pounds shelled raw crayfish
  tails

Sauté onion, bell pepper, celery and garlic in butter. Add Ro-Tel tomatoes and cook for 10 minutes. Add mushroom soup, lemon juice, Worcestershire, salt and red pepper. Cover, and cook for 25 to 30 minutes. Add crayfish tails. Cook until tails are tender. Do not overcook crayfish. Serve with crackers. This dip can be made ahead and frozen until ready to use.

Bayou Land Seafood
Breaux Bridge, LA

SALMON LOAF

1 (1-pound) red salmon
  (refrigerated 24 hours in can)
  drained, skinned, bones
  removed
1 cup mayonnaise

1 large dili pickle, chopped
1 small onion, chopped
2 Tablespoons fresh lemon juice
Black olives

Flake cold salmon on plate. Mix other ingredients and pour over salmon. Garnish with olives. Serve with crackers. May also be served at a light summer supper.

Mrs. Bob Buchanan (Sharon)

Appetizers

BACON-WRAPPED SCALLOPS
24 appetizers

½ cup all-purpose flour
1½ teaspoons salt
1½ teaspoons paprika
½ teaspoon ground white pepper
½ teaspoon ground garlic powder

1 egg
1 cup milk
24 sea scallops
1 cup unseasoned bread crumbs
8 bacon strips, cut into thirds

Combine flour, salt, paprika, pepper, and garlic powder in shallow dish. Beat egg with milk. Roll each scallop in seasoned flour, shaking of excess; dip in egg mixture; coat with bread crumbs, covering completely. Wrap each breaded scallop in bacon; secure with toothpick. Place on lightly greased baking sheet. Bake at 400° until bacon is crisp and scallops are cooked through, about 20 to 25 minutes.

Note: Good as an entrée or as an appetizer. Serves 6 as an entrée.

The Editors

CRUSTLESS SHRIMP QUICHE
16 squares

4 eggs, beaten
1 cup sour cream
½ teaspoon Worcestershire sauce
1 cup shredded Cheddar cheese

2 (4½-ounce) tiny canned shrimp, rinsed and drained
1 (2.8-ounce) can fried onions

Heat oven to 300°. Combine eggs, sour cream and Worcestershire. Stir in cheese, shrimp and onions. Pour into a greased 9-inch square pan. Bake 60 minutes or until set. Cool and cut into squares.

Mrs. Don Blackwood (Suzan)

COLD SHRIMP WITH HERB DRESSING — 10 servings

2½ Tablespoons salt
3½ pounds large shrimp,
   shelled, with last section of
   tail left intact
1 egg yolk
¼ teaspoon Dijon-style mustard
1½ Tablespoons lemon juice
1 Tablespoon white wine
5 to 6 drops Tabasco
Pinch of sugar

1 teaspoon anchovy paste
¾ cup vegetable oil
¼ cup olive oil
1 Tablespoon warm water
3 Tablespoons minced chives
2 Tablespoons minced parsley
3 Tablespoons minced tarragon
   or 2 teaspoons dried tarragon
2 Tablespoons minced fresh
   basil

Bring large pot of water to boil with 2 tablespoons salt. Add shrimp, let water come back to boil and cook until shrimp curl, 2 to 3 minutes for large shrimp. Drain under cold running water; pat dry. Cover and refrigerate until serving time. In medium bowl, combine egg, mustard, lemon juice, wine, hot sauce, sugar, anchovy paste and ½ teaspoon salt. Whisk until thoroughly blended. Gradually whisk in oils, drop by drop at first, then in a thin stream. When all oil is used, whisk in warm water. Stir in all the herbs. Can serve immediately or cover and refrigerate for up to 6 hours. Place shrimp on serving plate with vien side down and tails curled up.

Mrs. Howard Grittman (Ann)
Drew, Mississippi

SHRIMP DIP

½ cup chili sauce
1 (8-ounce) package cream
   cheese, softened
½ cup mayonnaise

¼ cup chopped onion
2 teaspoons horseradish
1 (4½-ounce) can small shrimp,
   rinsed and drained

Combine all ingredients. Mix well. Chill and serve.

Mrs. Joe Smith (Suellen)

PICKLED SHRIMP

5 pounds shrimp (30 to 36 count
   per pound)
1/4 cup mixed pickling spices
1 cup celery and leaves
2 onions sliced
Bay leaves
1 1/4 cups salad oil

3 cups white vinegar
2 teaspoons salt
1/2 teaspoon celery seed
2 1/2 Tablespoons capers and
   juice
Dash of Tabasco

Cook shrimp with pickling spices and celery. Bring to a boil and cook 3 to 4 minutes. Drain, peel and cool. Alternate shrimp, onions, and bay leaves in shallow dish. Mix next six ingredients and pour over shrimp. Refrigerate. Can be made up to a week ahead of time. Drain before serving.

Mrs. H. L. Dilworth (Anne)

SPINACH OYSTER DIP
2 1/2 quarts

1 cup chopped green onions
1 cup finely chopped celery
1 cup chopped parsley
1 cup chopped lettuce
1 cup margarine
4 (10-ounce) packages
   chopped spinach (thawed)
1 1/2 teaspoons garlic salt
1/2 teaspoon black pepper
2 Tablespoons anchovie paste
   (in a tube)

2 to 3 Tablespoons
   Worcestershire sauce
4 Tablespoons all-purpose flour
1/2 cup water
8-ounces evaporated milk
2 (6-ounce) rolls of jalapeño
   cheese, chopped
2 pints oysters

Sauté vegetables until tender; add spinach. Add next 4 ingredients and blend together. Add flour to water. Blend until smooth; stir into spinach mixture. Simmer and stir. Add milk and heat; add cheese and blend until melted. Remove from heat. Before ready to serve, heat oysters in own juice until they curl. Drain and chop. Add oysters to spinach mixture, when mixture is hot, serve in chafing dish with melba toast.

Mrs. Howard Grittman (Ann)
Drew, Mississippi

MURLE'S OYSTER DIP

1/4 cup butter
2 green onions and tops,
  chopped
2 Tablespoons chopped green
  pepper
2 Tablespoons all-purpose flour
Milk as needed
1 (4-ounce) can mushrooms
  and juice
Red pepper to taste

Salt to taste
Black pepper, to taste
1 Tablespoon paprika
Worcestershire, to taste
2 1/2-ounces mellow Cheddar
  cheese, shredded
Lemon juice, to taste
Sprinkle of MSG
1 pint oysters, drained (save
  juice)

Melt butter; add green pepper and onion. Cook over medium heat until tender. Add flour and stir. Add enough milk to make a smooth thick sauce. Add mushroom juice, salt, red pepper, black pepper, paprika, Worcestershire, cheese, lemon juice, and MSG. Stir until melted and blended. Slowly add juice of oysters as needed until sauce is of proper consistency. Add oysters which have been cut into 2 or 3 pieces. Simmer for 20 minutes. Refrigerate overnight if possible. Before serving, heat over low heat, adding a bit more milk if too thick. Serve from chafing dish on melba rounds or corn chips.

Mrs. Murle Parkinson
Drew, Mississippi

HOT BEEF DIP IN RYE BREAD

Filling
1 (8-ounce) package cream
  cheese
1 (8-ounce) carton sour cream
2 (2 1/2-ounce) jars dried beef,
  chopped

1 (4-ounce) can green chilies,
  diced
4 green onions, chopped
1 round loaf rye bread, top cut
  off, center removed

Mix all ingredients and put in hollowed loaf. Save the center and cube for dipping. Wrap loaf in heavy duty foil. Bake 1 hour at 350°. Serve with rye and French bread cubes.

Mrs. Billy Latham (Sue)

GRAND MARNIER DIP   2½ cups

3 egg yolks
½ cup plus 2 Tablespoons sugar
¼ teaspoon salt

¼ cup Grand Marnier
2 cups whipping cream

Combine egg yolks, sugar and salt in a small saucepan; mix well. Cook over medium heat, stirring constantly 2 or 3 minutes or until sugar dissolves. Remove from heat, stir in Grand Marnier. Let cool. Beat whipping cream until stiff peaks form; fold into Grand Marnier mixture. Cover and chill 1 to 2 hours. Serve with fresh fruits.

The Editors

FRESH FRUIT DIP

½ cup sugar
2 Tablespoons all-purpose flour
1 cup pineapple juice

1 egg, beaten
1 Tablespoon butter
1 pint whipping cream, whipped

Combine first 5 ingredients. Cook over medium heat while stirring until thickened. Remove from heat and cool. Add whipped cream. Store in refrigerator.

Mrs. Jeff Levingston (Barbara)

MELON BALLS IN SWEET WINE

1 ripe cantaloupe, seeded and scooped into balls
1 ripe honeydew melon, seeded and scooped into balls

2 cups sweet wine (Barsac, Sauterne, or Anjou)
1 teaspoon minced candied ginger

Place melon balls in bowl and add wine and ginger. Toss well. Cover and refrigerate overnight. Serve with toothpicks.

The Editors

Soups,
Sandwiches

ASPARAGUS SOUP
6 servings

2 pounds fresh asparagus
Salt, black pepper
2 cups milk
1 teaspoon tarragon
1 cup white wine

1 extra teaspoon dried tarragon
6 Tablespoons unsalted butter
6 Tablespoons all-purpose flour
6 cups canned chicken broth

Wash asparagus and cut off tough ends. Break in pieces and boil in salted water 12 to 15 minutes until tender. Drain and purée. Return purée to saucepan with milk and simmer, stirring until smooth. Put tarragon into a saucepan with the white wine and add some pepper, bring to simmer and cook until it reduces to about one tablespoon. Set aside. In a saucepan melt 4 tablespoons butter. Stir in flour and continue cooking and stirring a few seconds. Add chicken broth and simmer several minutes, then add asparagus purée. Pour a cup of soup into the saucepan which contains reduced wine and tarragon. Stir over heat, then pour back into asparagus mixture. Bring to a boil. Taste and correct seasoning. Stir the remaining butter and tarragon into the soup.

Mrs. John Tatum (Carol)

ASPARAGUS-POTATO SOUP
4-6 servings

1 (13¾-ounce) can chicken
  broth
3 cups chopped potatoes
⅓ cup chopped onion
1 teaspoon salt

1 or 2 (14½-ounce) cans
  asparagus tips
1½ cups half-and-half
1 (5-ounce) jar neufchatel
  cheese with pimento

Combine broth, potatoes, onion and salt. Bring to boiling. Then simmer until potatoes are tender—then add cut-up asparagus tips. Blend together cream and cheese. Stir into soup mixture until melted. DO NOT BOIL! If you like a smooth soup, it may be blended.

Mrs. John Tatum (Carol)

BEET SOUP WONDERFUL

5½ cups

2 Tablespoons butter
1 medium onion, chopped
4 cups chicken broth
1½ pounds beets, peeled and
  quartered

3 Tablespoons red wine vinegar
½ teaspoon salt
Freshly ground pepper
1 cup buttermilk
Sour cream

Melt butter in saucepan. Sauté onion for 3 or 4 minutes. Add stock, beets, vinegar, salt and pepper. Cook slowly, covered, until beets are tender. Process beets and cooking liquid, in batches in food processor to thick purée; transfer to large bowl and stir in buttermilk. Refrigerate soup, covered, until cold, about 4 hours. At serving time, taste for seasoning and adjust if necessary. Garnish each serving with a dollop of sour cream and sprig of dill. Wonderful!

Mrs. Stanley Levingston (Sylvia)

CHEESY BROCCOLI SOUP

8 servings

2 (13¾-ounce) cans chicken
  broth or 3½ cups homemade
  chicken stock
2 pounds fresh broccoli,
  trimmed and scraped
3 cups milk
1 cup finely diced ham
1 teaspoon salt (or to taste)

Pinch onion salt
¼ teaspoon black pepper
¼ teaspoon dried thyme
1 cup light cream
½ pound shredded Cheddar
  cheese
¼ cup butter, softened

Combine chicken broth and broccoli in large saucepan. Bring to a boil and cook for 7 to 8 minutes, or until broccoli is tender. Strain the broth into another saucepan. Purée broccoli in blender or food processor and set aside. Add the milk, ham, salt, onion salt, and pepper to the broth. Bring to a boil. Lower the heat and simmer for 5 minutes. Stir in thyme, cream, cheese, butter, and broccoli purée. Cook until heated through, but do not boil. Garnish with lightly blanched broccoli florets, if desired.

Mrs. Don Aylward (Lee)

CORN CHOWDER
4 servings

4 cups milk
4 slices bacon
1 small onion, chopped
1 stalk celery, chopped

Salt and pepper to taste
1 (17-ounce) cream style corn
Instant mashed potatoes
Dash MSG

Chop and sauté bacon, onion and celery. Add seasonings, milk, and corn. When this comes to a boil, add instant potatoes and stir until it is desired thickness.

Mrs. Buster Young (Fane)

GAZPACHO
8 servings

1½ cups peeled, chopped
   tomatoes
½ cup finely chopped green
   pepper
½ cup finely chopped celery
½ cup finely chopped
   cucumber
⅛ cup finely chopped onion
2 teaspoons chopped parsley
1 small clove garlic, minced

2 to 3 Tablespoons red wine
   vinegar
2 Tablespoons olive oil
1 teaspoon salt
¼ teaspoon freshly ground
   pepper
½ teaspoon Worcestershire
   sauce
2 cups tomato juice

Place tomatoes, green pepper, celery, cucumber, onion, parsley, garlic, vinegar, olive oil, salt, pepper, Worcestershire sauce, and tomato juice in food processor and turn on and off many times until finely chopped. Do not purée. Cover and chill thoroughly.

Mrs. Bill Parker (Jo)

CREAM OF MUSHROOM SOUP   8 servings

1½ pounds fresh mushrooms
9 Tablespoons butter
2 shallots or scallions, finely
    chopped or 1 small onion
    with 1 clove pressed garlic
6 Tablespoons all-purpose flour

6 cups chicken stock, fresh or
    canned
2 egg yolks
¾ cup heavy cream
Salt
White pepper

Separate mushroom caps and stems; slice ½ of caps about ⅛-inch thick and coarsely chop rest of caps and all stems; in an 8-inch to 10-inch skillet, melt 2 tablespoons butter over medium heat. When foam goes away, add sliced mushrooms; cook and toss constantly with wooden spoon; strain and set aside in a bowl. Add 2 tablespoons butter into same skillet, cook chopped mushrooms and onions 2 minutes. Set aside. In a heavy 4 to 6 quart saucepan, melt remaining butter (5 tablespoons) over moderate heat; remove from heat, add 6 tablespoons flour and mix until smooth on low heat for 2 minutes. Do not brown roux. Remove from heat and allow it to cook a few seconds. Pour chicken broth or stock, beating constantly with a wire whisk to blend stock and roux. Return to heat and stir until cream base comes to a boil, thickens and is perfectly smooth. Add chopped mushrooms and scallions and simmer, stirring occasionally, for 15 minutes. Purée soup in a food mill sieve or in a blender; put back in pan. In a separate bowl, with a whisk, blend egg yolks and cream. Whisk hot soup, 2 tablespoons at a time until ½ cup has been added too yolk-cream mixture; reverse process and slowly whisk mixture into soup. Bring to a boil 30 seconds. Add sliced buttons; season to taste, and serve.

Note: Don't let the long directions scare you! This is truly worth the effort, and doesn't take a long time to prepare.

Mrs. James M. Long, III
Spartanburg, S. C.

TOP OF THE CELLAR OYSTER MUSHROOM SOUP   4-6 servings

2 cups chopped oyster
   mushrooms
¾ cup chopped green onions
¼ cup butter
2 Tablespoons flour
2 cups chicken broth or
   bouillon

1 cup milk
Garlic salt
Celery salt
Pepper

Sauté onions and mushrooms in butter until tender. Stir in flour. Gradually add broth and milk. Season to taste. Simmer for 10 minutes or until thoroughly heated.

Mrs. Sam Rushing (Diane)

COLD TOMATO SOUP

1 (48-ounce) can tomato juice
   cocktail
1 quart buttermilk
1 (10-ounce) can hot and spicy
   tomato juice

½ (0.8-ounce) package
   buttermilk dressing mix

Mix ingredients and refrigerate. Serve cold.

Mrs. Buster Young (Fane)

TOMATO CHEESE SOUP   8 servings

½ cup finely chopped onion
¼ cup butter
1 (29-ounce) can tomato purée
2½ cups water

1 (10-ounce) package sharp
   Cheddar cheese, grated
½ teaspoon salt
1 cup sour cream

Sauté the onion in butter in a large saucepan until soft. Stir in purée, water, cheese, and salt. Heat and stir constantly until cheese melts, but do not allow to boil. Remove from heat and let cool 10 minutes. Stir 1 cup warm soup into the sour cream in a small bowl. Gradually stir back into remaining soup. Serve warm.

Mrs. Doug Wheeler (Lynn)

POTATO SOUP WITH BUTTER DUMPLINGS   10 servings

¼ cup margarine
1 medium onion, chopped
4 cups water
3 pounds potatoes, peeled and
   diced
1 stalk celery, chopped

1 Tablespoon salt
¼ teaspoon pepper
2 Tablespoons chopped parsley
Dumpling Batter
1 (8-ounce) carton sour cream

Melt butter in large soup pot; add onion and sauté until tender. Add water; bring to a boil and add potatoes, celery, salt, pepper, and parsley. Reduce heat and simmer 15 minutes. Drop dumpling batter into soup by teaspoonfuls. Cover and simmer 10 minutes. Remove from heat and gradually stir in sour cream. Heat thoroughly, but do not boil. This is good with or without dumplings.

Dumpling Batter

2 Tablespoons butter, softened
¼ cup plus 2 Tablespoons
   all-purpose flour

2 eggs, beaten
¼ teaspoon salt
Dash of ground nutmeg

Cream butter with flour; beat in eggs. Stir in seasonings, mixing well.

Mrs. Mike Davis (Sheryl)

SAVORY SPINACH SOUP   4-5 servings

½ cup chopped onions
3 Tablespoons butter
1 (12-ounce) package frozen
   chopped spinach
1 cup water
2 chicken bouillon cubes
¼ teaspoon savory

1 Tablespoon all-purpose flour
2 cups milk
¾ teaspoon salt
⅛ teaspoon white pepper
½ cup heavy cream
Croutons

Sauté onion lightly in 2 tablespoons butter. Add spinach, water, bouillon cubes, and savory. Heat to boiling, cover and cook 5 minutes. Turn into blender jar and blend until smooth. Melt remaining tablespoon butter, and stir in flour. Gradually blend in milk. Add salt and pepper and heat but do not boil, stirring constantly. Add blended spinach mixture and cream. Heat to scalding, but do not boil. Serve with croutons.

Mrs. Mike Sanders (Nan)

ZUCCHINI BISQUE

6 servings

1 medium onion, quartered
½ cup butter
1½ pounds zucchini
2½ cups chicken stock
⅛ teaspoon nutmeg

1 teaspoon basil
1 teaspoon salt
Black pepper or Tabasco to
   taste
1 cup heavy cream

Chop onion in food processor. In large pan, melt butter, add onion and sauté until limp. Shred zucchini. Add zucchini and chicken stock to onion. Simmer covered 15 minutes. Purée zucchini in two batches. Add seasonings. Combine batches, add cream and stir until blended. Serve hot or cold. Can be frozen.

Mrs. Karl Horn (Ruth)
Moss Point, Mississippi

ORIENTAL CHICKEN SOUP

6-8 servings

2 to 2½ pound fryer
½ cup uncooked rice
7 cups chicken broth
1 cup sliced celery
2 medium carrots, cut into small
   sticks
1 (14-ounce) can fancy mixed
   Chinese vegetables, drained

½ cup sliced green onion,
   including green tops
1 (8-ounce) can sliced
   mushrooms, drained
3 Tablespoons soy sauce
1½ teaspoons cornstarch

Cook chicken with onion and celery until done. Bone and chop. Combine broth and rice in 4 quart saucepan; cook 10 minutes. Add chicken, celery and carrots. Simmer 10 minutes. Stir in mixed vegetables, mushrooms and green onions and continue to simmer. Stir cornstarch into soy sauce; add to mixture and stir and simmer until soup is thick and clear.

Mrs. Howard Grittman (Ann)

CHICKEN GUMBO

8 servings

3½ pound broiler-fryer
 chicken, cut up
2 cups water
2 teaspoons salt
1 clove garlic, finely chopped
1 large bay leaf, crumbled
2 large stalks celery (with
 leaves), cut diagonally into
 slices (about 1½ cups)
1 medium onion, chopped
 (about ½ cup)

1 (28-ounce) can whole
 tomatoes
1 (10-ounce) package frozen
 sliced okra
1 (7-ounce) can whole kernel
 corn
⅓ cup uncooked regular rice
½ teaspoon Tabasco

Heat chicken pieces, water, salt, garlic and bay leaf to boiling in Dutch oven; reduce heat. Cover and simmer until chicken is done about 45 minutes. Remove chicken and strain broth. Refrigerate chicken and broth. When cool, remove chicken from bones (skin can be removed if desired). Cut chicken into bite-size pieces. Skim excess fat from broth and place broth and chicken in Dutch oven. Stir in celery, onion, tomatoes, frozen okra, corn, rice and Tabasco; break up tomatoes with fork. Heat to boiling; reduce heat. Cover and simmer until okra and rice are tender, 20 to 30 minutes. Garnish with snipped parsley.

Note: If you want to serve at different times, the gumbo will hold covered over low heat for up to 1 hour.

Mrs. Gene McCreary (Susan)

CHICKEN SOUP

6 servings

1 (3 to 4 pound) chicken
2 quarts water
1 teaspoon salt
4 Tablespoons butter

Black pepper to taste
2 Tablespoons corn meal
2 Tablespoons all-purpose flour
1 cup milk

Cook chicken until tender. Skin and bone chicken and return meat to broth. Add butter, salt, pepper to broth. Bring to a boil. In a separate bowl, mix corn meal and flour with milk and stir into broth. Simmer 30 to 45 minutes.

Mrs. Elaine Hewlett

CHICKEN-CORN SOUP
20 servings

1 (5-6 pound) chicken
1 medium onion, chopped
Salt to taste
¼ teaspoon pepper
1 (15-ounce) can whole kernel corn, drained

1 cup all-purpose flour
1 egg, beaten
Celery salt to taste
Onion salt to taste

Boil chicken with onions, salt, and pepper in 3 to 4 quarts of water. Cover and cook over low heat until tender. Remove chicken from broth. Cut into small pieces and return chicken to broth. Add corn. Combine flour, ⅛ teaspoon salt, and a beaten egg in a separate bowl; mix to form crumbs. Bring soup to a boil and add crumbs gradually. Cook for 15 minutes. Add celery salt and onion salt to taste.

Mrs. Terry Russell (Linda)

TURKEY AND WILD RICE SOUP
4 servings

2 Tablespoons butter
1 medium onion, chopped
4 ounces sliced mushrooms
2⅓ cups water
2 cups chicken broth
1 (6-ounce) package long grain and wild rice mix

2 Tablespoons dry Sherry
2 cups diced cooked turkey
1 cup heavy cream
1 egg yolk

Melt butter over medium heat. Add onion and mushrooms. Cook 2 minutes until onion is translucent. Add water and broth. Stir in rice and seasoning packet. Bring to a boil. Reduce heat. Cover and simmer 20 to 25 minutes until rice is tender. Add Sherry and boil 1 minute. Add turkey. Reduce heat to low. Mix cream and egg yolk. Stir in a few spoonfuls of soup. Add to soup in slow steady stream, stirring constantly. Cook only until slightly thickened and hot. Do not boil.

Mrs. Karl Horn (Ruth)
Moss Point, Mississippi

CATFISH GUMBO

2 gallons

1 cup chopped celery
1 cup chopped green pepper
1 cup chopped onion
2 cloves garlic, finely chopped
⅓ cup cooking oil
4 beef bouillon cubes
4 cups boiling water
1 (28-ounce) can tomatoes
2 (10-ounce) packages frozen
    okra, sliced

4 teaspoons salt
½ teaspoon pepper
½ teaspoon thyme
2 to 3 whole bay leaves,
    crushed
1 (6-ounce) can vegetable juice
    cocktail
6 to 9 cups catfish, cut into
    one-inch pieces

Cook celery, green pepper, onion and garlic in oil until tender. Dissolve cubes in water. Add remaining ingredients except catfish. Cover and simmer for 30 minutes. Add catfish and simmer, covered for 15 minutes, or until catfish flakes. Makes two gallons. Serve over rice or alone.

Mrs. Phillip Rizzo (Ramona)

CLAM CHOWDER

4 servings

6-8 slices bacon
1 onion, chopped
2 medium potatoes, cubed
1 Tablespoon all-purpose flour
2 (6½-ounce) can clams,
    reserve juice

Salt to taste
Lots of pepper
2 cups milk

Cut bacon into small pieces and cook until crisp. Drain and reserve fat. Add onion and potatoes to fat. Sauté and cover until potatoes steam done. Stir in flour, juice from clams, a little salt and lots of pepper, milk, clams and bacon. Heat slowly on simmer—it should not boil.

Note: So easy. Serve with crusty bread and a spinach salad.

Mrs. Bill Profilet (Mary)

CRAYFISH GUMBO

8-10 servings

½ cup chopped celery
2 cups chopped onion
½ cup chopped bell pepper
5 cloves garlic
1 Tablespoon tomato paste
1½ cups water
Oregano
1 teaspoon Worcestershire
  sauce

Salt and pepper
Red pepper
½ can cream of mushroom
  soup
3 pounds raw crayfish meat
Rice

Sauté the first 4 ingredients in cooking oil until tender. Add the tomato paste, water, oregano to taste, Worcestershire sauce, salt, pepper, red pepper. Cover and cook slowly for 30 minutes. Add ½ can cream of mushroom soup. Add the raw crayfish. Simmer another 30 minutes. Serve over cooked rice.

Variation: shrimp or chicken may be substituted for crayfish.

Mrs. Ray Travis (Betty)

SUPER SIMPLE CRAB BISQUE

4 servings

1 (10-ounce) package crab
  meat, slightly thawed
or
2 (6-ounce) cans crab meat,
  undrained

1 (10¾-ounce) can tomato soup
1 (10¾-ounce) can cream of
  asparagus soup
1 cup half-and-half

Stir crab meat, soups and cream into lightly buttered crock pot. Cover; cook on low setting 3-5 hours, stirring occasionally. Microwave instructions—combine all ingredients in 2-quart casserole. Microwave on medium for 6-8 minutes, stirring several times.

Mrs. Mark Routman (Terry)

SPICY SEAFOOD GUMBO

8-10 servings

⅔ cup all-purpose flour
4 strips bacon
8 green onions, chopped
1 garlic clove, crushed
2 to 3 pounds shrimp
1 gallon water
4 bay leaves
1 teaspoon salt
1 (28-ounce) can tomatoes, cut up, reserve liquid
2 (10-ounce) boxes frozen okra, cut

1 pint lump crabmeat
1 teaspoon thyme
½ Tablespoon crushed red pepper
2 pints oysters with liquid
1 cup uncooked rice
1 Tablespoon gumbo filé
Salt, pepper, and thyme to taste

Brown only flour in iron skillet. In another skillet cook bacon, crumble, and set aside. Add browned flour to hot bacon grease to make roux. There should be about 4 to 5 tablespoons from bacon. Add chopped green onions and garlic after flour is mixed and cooked. Set aside. Cook shrimp in gallon of water for 3 to 4 minutes with bay leaves and salt. Reserve liquid. Peel shrimp and put back into liquid. Add hot roux to hot stock with bacon, tomatoes and liquid, okra, crab meat, thyme, and red pepper. Cover and simmer 3 hours. Add oysters, liquid and rice. Simmer for 1 hour. Add filé, salt, pepper and thyme. Simmer for 5 minutes. Do not boil after adding filé.

Variation: may add whole catfish fillets instead of crab meat.

Mrs. Don Blackwood (Suzan)

DUCK GUMBO
12-15 servings

4 ducks
Onion, celery leaves, salt and
  pepper
6 Tablespoons shortening
6 Tablespoons flour
2 cups minced onion
3-4 cups diced celery
2 green peppers, chopped
1 bunch green onions, including
  stems, chopped
3 cloves garlic, minced
½ cup chopped parsley
7 cups boiling duck broth

3 cups boiling water
2 Tablespoons salt
2 teaspoons pepper
1 teaspoon MSG
1 (6-ounce) can tomato paste
1 (28-ounce) can tomatoes,
  including juice
1 teaspoon oregano
½ teaspoon red pepper
1 (16-ounce) package frozen
  cut okra
2 teaspoons gumbo filé

To cook ducks, cover with water and season with onion, celery leaves, salt and pepper. Simmer on top of stove until meat falls off bone, about 1½-2 hours. Remove meat from bone. Save the strained broth for gumbo. Melt shortening, add flour and cook over medium heat, stirring constantly until dark brown. Add next 6 ingredients to roux and cook about 5 minutes. Add boiling liquid slowly and stir until roux is dissolved. Add next 7 ingredients. Can be frozen at this point. Cover and simmer 2-2½ hours. Add duck and okra and cook about 1 hour longer. Add filé immediately before serving. Do not boil after adding filé, as this may cause the gumbo to be stringy. May add 2 cups of cooked rice to gumbo or serve over rice. If it needs thickening, add 4 tablespoons cornstarch mixed with ½ cup water.

The Editors

PEACH SOUP
4 servings

1 small plain yogurt
1 (29-ounce) can sliced
  peaches with juice

½ teaspoon almond flavoring,
  more to taste

Put in blender and blend well and chill.

Mrs. Bob Ragan (Marilyn)

FRENCH QUARTER SOUP √   6-8 servings

1 (16-ounce) package
   16 bean mix
1 pound chopped ham
2 teaspoons salt
Water to cover beans
3 stalks celery, chopped
2 bay leaves
½ teaspoon thyme
1 teaspoon parsley
1 (16-ounce) can of tomatoes

1 (10-ounce) can Rotel
   tomatoes
2 medium onions, chopped
2 cloves garlic, crushed
¼ teaspoon red pepper
2 chicken breasts
1 pound smoked sausage
   (sliced thin and grease fried
   out)

Wash and soak dried beans overnight. Drain and add ham, salt, and water to cover beans. Add celery, bay leaves, thyme, and parsley. Simmer 2½ to 3 hours, adding water as needed. Add tomatoes, Rotel, onions, garlic, red pepper, salt and pepper to taste. Cook uncovered 1½ hours. Boil chicken breasts, debone, and save the broth. Add deboned, chopped chicken breasts, sausage, and broth to soup. Continue to simmer until thick.

Mrs. Billy Nowell (Ann)

HAM CHOWDER   6-8 servings

2 to 3 ribs celery
1 small onion
1 hambone
8 cups water
8 cups diced potatoes

3 Tablespoons chopped parsley
3 Tablespoons butter
3 Tablespoons all-purpose flour
8 cups milk
Salt and pepper

Chop celery and onion and add to hambone and water. Bring slowly to a boil. Simmer 1 hour. Remove meat from bone. Add diced potatoes and parsley and boil about 20 minutes. Combine butter, flour, milk; season with salt and pepper and add all to soup.

Mrs. Roger Dicks (Sallie)

KANSAS CITY STEAK SOUP   15-20 servings

½ cup butter, melted
1 cup all-purpose flour
½ gallon water (2 quarts)
1½ pounds ground round or
 chuck or sirloin
1 cup diced onion
1 cup diced celery

1 cup diced carrots
2 cups mixed vegetables
 (canned)
1 (16-ounce) can tomatoes
1 Tablespoon MSG
2 (10-ounce) cans beef broth
1 teaspoon pepper

Melt butter. Stir in flour; stir in water. Cook and stir on low heat until smooth. Brown meat and add to flour/water mixture. Bring to a boil and add celery, onion, carrots, vegetables, tomatoes, MSG, pepper, and bouillon. Bring to a boil. Reduce heat and simmer 4 hours. Salt if needed. This recipe can easily be halved.

Mrs. Mark Koonce (Ann)

HOT ASPARAGUS ROLL-UPS   12 servings

1 (14½-ounce) whole
 asparagus (approximately 12)
12 slices regular sandwich
 bread

½ cup butter
Chives (fresh or frozen) to taste
Seasoned salt

Drain asparagus well. Soften ¼ cup butter and mix with chives to taste. Remove crust from bread and spread butter mixture on each piece. Sprinkle sparingly with seasoned salt. Place well drained asparagus on bread, roll up jelly roll fashion and secure with a toothpick. Melt remaining ¼ cup butter and brush on roll-ups. Bake at 400° watching carefully, until brown and crispy, about 15-20 minutes. These may be frozen after securing with toothpick. Remove from freezer, brush with melted butter and bake.

Mrs. Gertrude Dilworth
Shelby, Mississippi

CUCUMBER-SHRIMP SANDWICHES 1½ cups

Herb Mayonnaise
1 cup mayonnaise
1 Tablespoon vinegar
¼ teaspoon salt
¼ teaspoon paprika
1 teaspoon crushed oregano
1 teaspoon dill
1 Tablespoon onion, grated
⅛ teaspoon garlic salt

1 Tablespoon chopped chives
⅛ teaspoon curry powder
½ teaspoon Worcestershire sauce
Bread
Shrimp, cooked and peeled for garnishing
Cucumbers

Blend all ingredients. Cut bread with a biscuit cutter. Place on a cookie sheet and freeze. When frozen, place bread pieces into a plastic bag and place back into freezer until ready to use. Slice cucumbers the night before and put into a bowl of ice. Spread mayonnaise mixture on thawed bread. Place cucumber slice on each piece of bread. Garnish with a shrimp.

Mrs. J. T. Pannell (Patti)

STUFFED FRENCH BREAD 10-12 servings

1 loaf French bread
¼ cup butter
2 Tablespoons sesame seeds
1 clove garlic, finely chopped
1½ cups sour cream
1 cup Monterey Jack cheese

1 cup Parmesan cheese
1 (14½-ounce) can artichoke hearts, drained and cut-up
1 cup shredded Cheddar cheese

Cut French bread in half lengthwise. Remove center, tearing in chunks. Melt butter, add sesame seeds and chopped garlic. Cook until lightly browned. Add bread chunks and mix. Combine sour cream, Monterey Jack and Parmesan with artichoke pieces. Add to bread mixture. Stuff into bread shells. Sprinkle Cheddar cheese over shells and bake at 350° for 30 minutes. May be made ahead and frozen.

Mrs. Jeff Levingston (Barbara)

SAUSAGE STUFFED FRENCH BREAD

10-12 servings

1 pound sausage, browned
½ cup onion, chopped
1 cup celery, chopped
1 loaf French bread
½ teaspoon sage

Salt to taste
Pepper to taste
2 eggs
¼ cup milk
6 slices American cheese

Brown meat adding onion and celery. Cut top off bread lengthwise and remove center, tearing in chunks. Add pulled bread and seasonings to meat. Mix egg and milk, add to meat mixture and stuff bread. Place top on and bake on a foil covered cookie sheet 20 minutes at 400°. Five minutes before time is up, remove top and add cheese. Replace top, and return to oven for last five minutes.

Mrs. Charles Fioranelli (Vicki)
Mrs. Phillip Gaither (Jane)

HOT HAM SANDWICH

4 servings

4 slices bread, toasted
1 (10-ounce) package broccoli,
cooked
4 slices ham

1 cup sour cream
1 teaspoon mustard
½ cup grated Cheddar cheese

Place toast in layer in casserole, cover with ham, top with broccoli. Blend sour cream and mustard. Spoon over broccoli. Sprinkle with grated cheese. Bake 10 minutes at 400°.

Mrs. Howard Grittman (Ann)

BAKED CRABMEAT SANDWICH

10 servings

20 slices sandwich bread
2 (7½-ounce) cans crab meat
1 small can mushrooms, sliced
⅔ cup mayonnaise

2 (5-ounce) jars Old English
cheese
1 cup butter
2 raw eggs

Trim crusts from bread and fill with mixture of crabmeat, drained mushrooms, and mayonnaise. Cream together cheese, butter and eggs until fluffy. Frost sides and tops of sandwiches generously. Place on cookie sheet (not too close together) and refrigerate for 12 hours. Bake at 400° for 12 to 15 minutes. May be frozen; let thaw 2 hours before baking.

Mrs. Allen Pepper (Ginger)

Sandwiches

HOT CHICKEN SANDWICHES
8 servings

1 cup Cheddar cheese,
  shredded
2 cups cooked chopped
  chicken
2 Tablespoons minced onion
2 Tablespoons stuffed olives
3 hard-boiled eggs, chopped

2 Tablespoons green pepper,
  chopped
2 Tablespoons minced sweet
  pickle
½ cup mayonnaise
8 hamburger buns

Combine Cheddar cheese, chicken, onion, olives, eggs, green pepper, sweet pickle, mayonnaise and mix well. Fill buns and wrap each in foil. They may be prepared ahead and refrigerated until ready to use. Bake in 300° oven about 20 minutes or until the filling is hot and cheese melted.

Note: Crabmeat may be substituted for the chicken, adding the juice of 1 lemon for taste to the mixture.

Mrs. W. P. Skelton (Louise)

GWYN'S HAMBURGERS GALORE

Basic Ingredients

2 pounds lean ground beef
6 whole wheat buns
Head of lettuce

Tomatoes, sliced
Condiments

Method:
Add a little pizazz to your burgers. Whip up any of these delicious toppings and brighten up that plain old patty. Or, for a nice change of pace, serve these toppings on a boneless chicken breast.

Mushroom Sauce Ingredients

⅓ cup butter
¾ cup onion, chopped
1 pound mushrooms, sliced
1 (12-ounce) carton sour cream
2 Tablespoons Sherry
2 teaspoons dill weed

½ teaspoon salt
¼ teaspoon pepper
1 Tablespoon cornstarch
¼ cup butter
¼ cup all-purpose flour
¼ pound Swiss cheese, sliced

Method:
In a medium saucepan, sauté onions and mushrooms in the butter, until tender. Blend in the sour cream, sherry, seasonings, and cornstarch. In a separate large saucepan, melt the butter and stir in the flour. Cook, stirring constantly, for 5 minutes. Slowly blend in sour cream mixture, stirring and cooking until thickened. Top burgers with slices of Swiss and a ladle of sauce for "Stroganoff" burgers. Makes 2 cups.

Blue Cheese Ingredients

½ pound blue cheese
1 teaspoon lemon juice
⅓ cup mayonnaise
2 cloves garlic, pressed

½ teaspoon Worcestershire
⅛ teaspoon salt
⅛ teaspoon pepper
Dash Tabasco

Method:
In a blender or food processor, whip together all ingredients. Do not over purée. Mixture should retain a lumpy quality. Ladle sauce over burgers. Makes 1 cup.

Mexican Salsa Ingredients

1 Tablespoon butter
¼ cup green onions
1 cup stewed tomatoes
4-ounces green chiles, chopped

½ teaspoon chili powder
¼ teaspoon cumin
Dash of Tabasco

Method:
In a medium saucepan, sauté the green onions in the butter, until tender. Add tomatoes, green chiles, chili powder, cumin, and Tabasco. Simmer for 10 minutes over medium heat. Top burgers with slices of Cheddar and a ladle of salsa for "South of the Border" burgers. Makes 1 cup.

Gorgeous George Ingredients

1 pineapple
12 lean bacon slices

¼ pound Swiss, sliced

Method:
Peel and core pineapple. Slice and grill. Grill bacon and pat dry. Top burgers with slices of Swiss, 2 slices of bacon, and a pineapple ring. Serves 6.

The Editors

VEGETABLE SPREAD

36 servings

3 fresh tomatoes, chopped
1 cup chopped celery
1 small onion, chopped
1 bell pepper, chopped
1 cucumber, chopped

1 envelope gelatin
¼ cup cold water
¼ cup hot water
2 cups mayonnaise
1 teaspoon salt

Drain and salt tomatoes, celery, onion, bell pepper, cucumber. Set aside. To 1 envelope plain gelatin dissolved in ¼ cup cold water, add ¼ cup hot water and cool. Add vegetables, then fold in 2 cups mayonnaise and 1 teaspoon salt. Let set in refrigerator.

Mrs. Buster Young (Fane)

AUGUSTINE BREAD

2½ cups spread

1 cup margarine—room
   temperature
½ teaspoon powdered oregano
2 teaspoons dried parsley
½ teaspoon garlic powder
½ cup grated Cheddar cheese

1 teaspoon paprika
1 teaspoon MSG
½ cup grated Mozzarella
2 Tablespoons Parmesan
   cheese

Mix these ingredients together and refrigerate until ready to use. Spread on bread and bake at 350°-400° for 10-15 minutes.

Note: Recommended bread is Earth Grains® San Francisco Style Extra Sourdough or Wheat Rolls. Recipe may be doubled or tripled. Will keep 2 weeks or longer in the refrigerator—tastes like pizza.

Mrs. Jimmy Ervin (Elsie Lynn)

Cheese,
Eggs, Pasta

EGGS SARDOU
2 servings

1 medium onion, chopped
3 cups blanched spinach,
  chopped
Butter
2 or 3 Tablespoons all-purpose
  flour

½ cup heavy cream
1 teaspoon ground nutmeg
4 artichoke bottoms (canned)
4 eggs, poached
Hollandaise sauce (see index)
Paprika

Melt enough butter to cover bottom of skillet. Sauté onions and spinach. Add flour and stir until smooth. Slowly blend in cream until thickened. Add nutmeg. Prepare in this order: two artichoke bottoms, spinach sauce, 2 poached eggs, Hollandaise sauce and sprinkle with paprika.

Mrs. Mike Sanders (Nan)

POACHED EGGS

2 pints water

1 pint white vinegar

Combine water and vinegar. Drop egg in barely simmering water for 2½ minutes. Remove and hold in pan of cool water until ready to use.

Mrs. Mike Sanders (Nan)

EGGS HUSSARD
4½ cups sauce

¼ cup butter
1 clove garlic, pressed
½ cup chopped white onion
3 slices Canadian bacon,
  chopped
1 cup chopped mushrooms
4 to 5 green onions, chopped,
  tops only
3 Tablespoons chopped fresh
  parsley

1 bay leaf, crumbled
1 Tablespoon tomato paste
3 Tablespoons all-purpose flour
1 cup burgandy or red wine
2 cups beef stock or bouillon
Holland rusks
Poached eggs
Hollandaise sauce (see index)

In skillet, melt butter and sauté first 8 ingredients. Add flour and stir until smooth. Add wine and beef stock and blend well. Simmer sauce for 15 minutes. Prepare Hussard in this order. One Holland rusk, one slice Canadian bacon, hussard sauce, one poached egg and Hollandaise.

Mrs. Mike Sanders (Nan)

SUNDAY SOUFFLET   4 to 6 servings

6 Tablespoons butter, melted   1 cup sifted all-purpose flour
6 eggs   1 cup milk
1 teaspoon salt

Preheat oven to 450°. Melt butter in 8-inch heavy skillet, coating the bottom and sides. Beat eggs at medium speed. Gradually add salt and flour, blending well. Add milk and blend thoroughly. Pour batter into skillet and bake until crust is brown, about 20 minutes. To serve, cut into wedges, sprinkle with powdered sugar and top with syrup. It will rise, then fall when served.

Note: This is a cross betwen an omelette and a soufflé. This may be doubled in a 12-inch skillet.

The Editors

FRENCH OMELETTE PICNIC LOAF   4 to 6 servings

1 large loaf French bread   2 cloves garlic, mashed
2 Tablespoons olive oil   1 bell pepper, chopped
5 Tablespoons butter   9 eggs
10-ounces ham, chopped   1 teaspoon salt
1 large potato, diced   ½ teaspoon pepper
12-ounces mushrooms,   Milk
   chopped   1 to 2 cups Swiss cheese,
1 onion, chopped   grated

Slice off top ¼ of loaf and save. Hollow out loaf, leaving ½ inch on sides and bottom for stability. Brush cut surfaces with 1 tablespoon olive oil. Replace top, wrap loaf in foil, and warm in a 300° oven while preparing filling. Sauté ham, potato, mushrooms, onion, and garlic in remaining olive oil and 2 tablespoons butter until tender and slightly brown. Remove garlic. Add bell pepper and cook until eggs are set but not dry. Add vegetable mixture and fold into eggs. Sprinkle grated cheese into egg mixture and cook until eggs are firm. Spoon filling into loaf and cover with "lid". (Depending upon size of loaf, you may have filling left over. It may be reheated for breakfast the next day.) Wrap loaf in several thicknesses of aluminum foil and then in several sheets newspaper. Thus insulated, it may be tucked into a backpack and will stay warm up to 4 hours. Feeds 4 to 6 hungry hikers amply.

Mrs. Jim Tims (Frances)

TEXAS EGGS

10 to 12 servings

10 eggs
3 Tablespoons sour cream

Salt and pepper to taste

Mix above ingredients in blender and pour in 9x13-inch casserole dish. Bake 7 minutes at 400°.

1 pound sausage (½ pound hot
*   and ½ pound mild)*
1 bell pepper, chopped
1 medium onion, chopped

1 cup sliced mushrooms (fresh)
1 (10-ounce) can Rotel
*   tomatoes, drained*

Cook sausage. Add vegetables except Rotel tomatoes and sauté until tender. Drain well. Add tomatoes and pour over egg mixture.

8-ounces American processed
*   cheese*

8-ounces Cheddar cheese
8-ounces Mozzarella cheese

Melt cheeses and spread on top of egg and sausage mixture. Refrigerate overnight or longer. Bake uncovered at 350° until hot and bubbly.

Note: Great for brunch with cheese grits and a hot fruit casserole.

Mrs. William Foshee (Charlene)
Jackson, Mississippi

SCRAMBLED EGGS WITH CREAM CHEESE

4 servings

1 (3-ounce) package cream
*   cheese*
6 Tablespoons heavy cream
1 Tablespoon butter or
*   margarine*
6 eggs

1 teaspoon salt
Dash of freshly cracked black
*   pepper*
Dash cayenne pepper
1 teaspoon chives or parsley,
*   finely chopped*

Work cheese with two tablespoons cream until soft and creamy. Melt butter or margarine in double boiler. Beat eggs, remaining cream, salt, both kinds of pepper and chopped chives or parsley until well mixed. Pour into melted fat, cook over boiling water, stirring frequently, until eggs are set. Now stir in cream cheese mixture and cook a minute or so longer, just enough to heat mixture. Spoon over hot toast.

Mrs. Karl Horn (Ruth)

BREAKFAST STRATA

12 to 14 servings

1 pound hot spicy sausage
1 pound bacon
12 slices bread, trimmed
2½ to 3 cups shredded sharp
  Cheddar cheese

8 eggs
1 quart of milk
1 teaspoon salt
1 teaspoon dry mustard
Worcestershire sauce to taste

Fry sausage and bacon. Drain, dry, crumble and mix together. Butter a lasagna casserole dish. Place ½ bread cubes, ½ cheese and all sausage and bacon mixture in casserole. Top with remaining bread cubes and cheese. Beat eggs and a little Worcestershire, salt, dry mustard and milk. Pour over casserole and refrigerate overnight. Bake 1 hour at 325°.

Optional topping: 1 can mushroom soup diluted with ½ cup milk spread over casserole. Bake 300° for 1½ hours.

Mrs. Nott Wheeler, Sr. (Cherry)

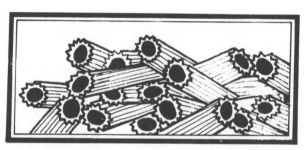

CHEESE-HAM PUFF

4 to 6 servings

2 cups milk
⅓ cup yellow cornmeal
3 eggs, separated
1 cup ground cooked ham
2 Tablespoons butter or
  margarine

1 cup shredded Cheddar
  cheese
¼ teaspoon salt
¼ teaspoon paprika

Heat milk with butter until scalding; stir in cornmeal gradually. Cook for 5 minutes or until thickened, stirring constantly; remove from heat. Stir in cheese. Beat egg yolks; stir into hot mixture. Add salt and paprika, stir until cheese is melted; mix in ham. Beat egg whites until stiff; fold in. Turn mixture into greased 2 quart baking dish. Bake at 325° for 1 hour or until knife inserted in center comes out clean.

Mrs. Inez McCain

CHEESE PUDDING
8 servings

9 thin slices of bread
½ cup margarine, melted
¾ pound mild Cheddar cheese,
  shredded
2 cups milk

1 teaspoon salt
1 teaspoon mustard
¼ teaspoon red pepper
3 egg yolks, beaten slightly
3 egg whites

Remove bread crusts and cut bread into cubes. Pour melted margarine over bread in baking dish. Sprinkle cheese over margarine. Pour milk over ingredients. Add remaining ingredients and combine thoroughly. Beat egg whites until stiff and fold into above mixture. Must be refrigerated overnight. Bake at 350° about 20 minutes or until brown. Good with beef or pork.

Mrs. J. T. Pannell (Patti)

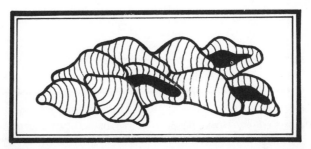

SAUSAGE GRITS
8 to 10 servings

1 pound bulk pork sausage
3 cups hot cooked grits
2½ cups Cheddar cheese,
  grated
3 Tablespoons butter or
  margarine

3 eggs, beaten
1½ cups milk
Paprika

Cook sausage and drain well. Put sausage in 13x9-inch baking dish. Combine grits, cheese and butter, mixing well. Combine beaten eggs and milk and add to grits. Pour mixture over sausage and sprinkle with paprika. Bake 350° for 1 hour.

Note: This may be assembled the day before and refrigerated. Let casserole reach room temperature before baking.

Mrs. W. C. Cox (Mary Elizabeth)
Jackson, Mississippi

CHEESE GRITS SOUFFLÉ   12 servings

2 teaspoons salt
7 cups water
2 cups uncooked grits
1 (6-ounce) roll nippy cheese
1 (6-ounce) roll garlic cheese

1 cup butter, melted
4 eggs, well beaten
½ cup milk
Salt and pepper to taste

Add salt to boiling water and cook grits covered on low heat until done (about 25 minutes). Stir in cheese which has been cut into small pieces. Add butter, eggs, milk, salt and pepper. Spoon into a 3 quart casserole and bake at 350° for 1 hour. For even fluffier soufflé, separate eggs. Add beaten yolks to grits mixture and fold in stiffly beaten egg whites last.

The Editors

CHEESEY HAM AND ARTICHOKES   6 servings

4 Tablespoons butter
4 Tablespoons all-purpose flour
2 cups warm milk
Dash seasoned salt
Dash cayenne pepper
¼ teaspoon ground nutmeg
Paprika
Dash of white pepper
⅔ cup shredded Swiss and
  Parmesan cheese, mixed for
  sauce

4 Tablespoons sherry
2 (1-pound) cans artichoke
  hearts, drained
12 slices boiled or baked ham,
  thinly sliced
⅔ cup shredded Swiss and
  Parmesan cheese, mixed for
  topping
⅔ cup bread crumbs, for
  topping

Melt butter in saucepan; blend in flour. Remove from heat, stirring until thickened. Add seasonings, cheese; stir over low heat until melted. Remove from heat, stir in sherry. Cut artichokes in half and wrap two halves in a slice of ham. Arrange in buttered casserole with sides touching; pour sauce over all. Sprinkle cheesey bread crumbs topping over casserole. Bake 350° for 25 to 30 minutes.

Note: Good for lunch or brunch with eggs, and fresh fruit.

Mrs. Howard Grittman (Ann)
Drew, Mississippi

SHRIMP QUICHE   6 servings

2 Tablespoons green onions,
   minced
3 Tablespoons butter
1 cup shrimp
¼ teaspoon salt
Pinch of pepper
2 Tablespoons dry vermouth

3 eggs
1 cup whipping cream
1 Tablespoon tomato paste
¼ teaspoon salt
Pinch of pepper
8 or 9-inch pie shell, unbaked
¼ cup grated Swiss cheese

Cook onion and butter for 2 minutes; not brown. Add shrimp, and cook 2 minutes. Sprinkle salt and pepper. Add wine and raise heat to boil for a minute. Beat eggs, cream, tomato paste, salt and pepper. Add to shrimp mix and pour into shell; top with cheese. Cook at 375° for 25 to 30 minutes in upper ⅓ of oven. Test with knife for doneness.

Mrs. Ben Mitchell (Margaret Ann)

QUICHE   6 servings

¾ cup all-purpose flour
¼ cup margarine, melted
1 cup shredded Cheddar
   cheese

½ teaspoon salt
½ teaspoon dry mustard

Mix all ingredients listed above and press into a pie pan.

1 (10-ounce) package frozen
   chopped spinach
½ cup chopped green onions
4-ounces mushrooms, sliced
   (optional)

½ cup grated Swiss cheese
6 or 7 strips bacon, cooked and
   crumbled
Beef bouillon cube

Cook spinach with bouillon cube. Mix vegetables, cheese, and bacon with spinach. Pour on top of crust.

1 to 1½ cups of milk
4 eggs, beaten

¾ teaspoon salt
½ teaspoon mustard

Mix ingredients listed above and pour over filling. Bake at 400° for 15 minutes. Reduce heat to 325° and bake 20 to 25 minutes.

Mrs. John Thornell (Nita)

Cheese, Eggs, Pasta

HANK'S VERSION QUICHE

6 servings

1 (9-inch) deep dish pie shell,
cooked 5 to 6 minutes
8 to 10 slices bacon, cooked
and crumbled
1 (14½-ounce) can asparagus,
drained
1 (4-ounce) can of mushrooms,
drained

1 cup grated Swiss cheese
⅓ cup grated Parmesan cheese
1 cup whipping cream
3 eggs
1 teaspoon salt
3 dashes cayenne pepper
½ teaspoon cream of tartar

Cover bottom of pie shell with bacon followed by asparagus, mushrooms, and cheeses. Blend cream, eggs, salt, pepper and cream of tartar. Pour over ingredients in pie shell. Bake 375° for 30 to 50 minutes until center is firm.

Mrs. Billy Tabb (Myrtis)

BROCCOLI-CHEESE PIE

6 servings

6 cups water
2 teaspoons salt
3 ounces uncooked macaroni
(about ¾ cup)
1 egg yolk
2 Tablespoons snipped chives
1 cup shredded Cheddar
cheese (about 4-ounces)

1 (10-ounce) package frozen
chopped broccoli
½ teaspoon salt
4 eggs
1 egg white
1 cup creamed cottage cheese
Paprika

Heat oven to 375°. Heat water and 1 teaspoon salt to boiling; stir in macaroni. Boil until tender, 5 to 8 minutes. Drain; rinse in cold water. Beat egg yolk; stir in macaroni and 1 tablespoon chives. Press mixture against bottom and sides of a greased 9-inch pie plate with back of spoon. Bake 10 minutes; remove from oven. Cool 10 minutes. Increase oven temperature to 425°. Sprinkle Cheddar cheese over crust. Prepare broccoli as directed on package, using ½ teaspoon salt; drain. Arrange broccoli on cheese. Beat eggs, egg white, cottage cheese, 1 tablespoon chives and 1 teaspoon salt; pour on broccoli. Sprinkle with paprika. Bake uncovered 15 minutes. Reduce oven temperature to 300°. Bake until knife inserted 1 inch from edge comes out clean, about 30 minutes. Cool 10 minutes before serving.

Mrs. Gene McCreary (Susan)

FETTUCCINE ALFREDO

6 to 8 servings

*1 pound fettuccine, or any
 pasta or noodles
1 cup butter
1 (4-ounce) can sliced
 mushrooms
½ teaspoon salt
Pepper to taste*

*¼ teaspoon oregano
½ teaspoon garlic powder
¼ cup grated Romano or
 Parmesan cheese
¼ cup shredded Mozzarella
 cheese*

Cook fettuccine in boiling water. Do not overcook. Melt butter in skillet and add all but cheeses. Drain fettuccine. Toss with Romano cheese, then stir in butter mixture. Top with Mozzarella cheese. Serve hot.

Mrs. Charles Fioranelli (Vickie)
Mrs. Gene McCreary (Susan Sims)

SNOW PEAS AND PASTA SALAD

6 servings

*1¾ cups uncooked corkscrew
 macaroni
Oregano dressing (recipe
 follows)
2½ ounces fresh snow peas
 (1 cup)*

*2 cups fresh spinach, torn
1 cup chopped fresh tomato
1 Tablespoon grated Parmesan
 cheese*

Cook macaroni according to package directions; drain well. Pour Oregano dressing over hot macaroni, stirring gently. Let macaroni cool. Place snow peas in wire basket; dip in boiling water about 10 seconds. Drain and add snow peas, spinach, and tomato to macaroni, tossing gently. Sprinkle with cheese. Cover and chill at least 2 hours.

Oregano Dressing   ½ cup
*¼ cup red wine vinegar
¼ cup olive oil
¾ teaspoon dried whole
 oregano*

*⅛ teaspoon garlic powder
⅛ teaspoon freshly ground
 pepper*

Combine all ingredients in a jar. Cover and shake well.

Mrs. Tom Sullivan (Teri)
Denham Springs, Louisiana

ANGEL HAIR WITH BROCCOLI   6 to 8 servings

1 bunch fresh broccoli
Salt to taste
¼ cup light olive oil
4 Tablespoons unsalted butter
1 onion, chopped

1 clove garlic
2 Tablespoons white wine
1 pound angel hair pasta or
*   other small noodles*
Grated Parmesan cheese

Cook, drain and cool broccoli. In a saucepan heat oil and 3 tablespoons of butter. In a skillet, melt 1 tablespoon butter and sauté onions and garlic for 2 minutes. Add wine and cook for 5 minutes. Add melted butter and oil, then broccoli. Heat thoroughly. Cook pasta and drain well. Place pasta in a dish and then broccoli over the pasta. Serve at once with Parmesan cheese sprinkled on top.

Mrs. Billy Tabb (Myrtis)

PRIMAVERA   15 servings

1 pound fettuccine or linguine
1 pound asparagus
2 cups cauliflower florets
1 medium zucchini, sliced
1 carrot, thinly sliced
½ pound mushrooms, sliced
*   (optional)*

1 (10-ounce) package frozen
*   miniature peas, defrosted*
*   uncooked*
1 medium onion, chopped
1 clove garlic, crushed

Cook the noodles and cool. Sauté the vegetables lightly in butter, oil or margarine (unsalted). Mix the vegetables with the pasta and add one of the following dressings:

Cheese Dressing
8-ounces cream cheese, diluted with **milk** to desired consistency. Sprinkle with **Parmesan cheese** and toss with Primavera.

Oil and Garlic Dressing
½ cup mayonnaise   *¾ cup Italian dressing*

Final seasoning: basil, chopped parsley, salt and pepper to taste.

Mrs. Marvin Kravitz (Sylvia)

MACARONI AND CHEESE CASSEROLE   8 servings

*1 (8-ounce) package elbow
  macaroni*
½ cup margarine
*1 pound Cheddar cheese,
  shredded*
2 eggs

1 Tablespoon sugar
Salt and pepper to taste
2 cups milk
¼ cup buttermilk, optional
Paprika

Preheat oven to 325°. Cook macaroni according to package directions. Drain. Allow margarine to melt over macaroni before sprinkling on most of the grated cheese. Stir well. Add salt and pepper to taste, then add sugar and stir again. In a bowl, beat two eggs; add milk, mix and pour into macaroni mixture. If desired, add buttermilk and stir. Pour mixture into a casserole dish and sprinkle with rest of cheese; then with a dash of paprika. Bake for 1 hour and 30 minutes.

Mrs. James Walker (Elizabeth)

STRAW AND HAY   4 servings

4-ounces white linguine
4-ounces green linguine
Boiling salted water
½ cup butter or margarine
*8-ounces cooked ham, cut in
  thin strips*
¾ cup cooked green peas

*1 (2½-ounce) jar sliced
  mushrooms, drained*
2 egg yolks, well beaten
1 cup whipping cream
*1 cup Parmesan cheese,
  (4-ounces), freshly grated*

Cook white and green linguine in boiling salted water until tender. Drain and return linguine to pot. Add butter, ham, peas and mushrooms. In a small bowl, beat egg yolks and cream with a fork or whisk until foamy. Slowly add cream mixture to linguine, mixing well. Stir in ½ cup Parmesan cheese. Stir gently over medium heat, until mixture is thickened. Serve on individual plates. Sprinkle with remaining Parmesan cheese.

Note: Makes 6 appetizer servings, or 4 dinner size portions.

Mrs. John Nolen Canon (Toni)
Tunica, Mississippi

MANICOTTA   8 to 10 servings

Sauce

¼ cup olive oil
1 cup onion, finely chopped
1 clove garlic, crushed
1 (14½-ounce) can Italian
   tomatoes, undrained
1 (6-ounce) can tomato paste

2 sprigs parsley
1 Tablespoon salt
2 teaspoons sugar
1 teaspoon oregano
1 teaspoon dried basil leaves
¼ teaspoon pepper

In hot oil in 6-quart kettle, sauté onion and garlic until golden brown, about 5 minutes. Add tomatoes, tomato paste, 1½ cups water, parsley sprigs, salt, sugar, oregano, basil and pepper; mix well, mashing tomatoes with fork. Bring to a boil. Reduce heat. Simmer covered, stirring occasionally for 1 hour. Preheat oven to 350°.

Filling

2 pound ricotta cheese
1 (8-ounce) package Mozzarella
   cheese, diced
⅓ cup grated Parmesan cheese

2 eggs
1 Tablespoon chopped parsley
1 teaspoon salt
¼ teaspoon pepper

Combine all of the above ingredients and beat with a wooden spoon until well blended.

Shells

Use 1 box of commercially made manicotta shells. Place about ¼ cup filling in the center of each uncooked shell. Spoon some of the sauce in bottom of two 13x9x2-inch baking dishes. Place shells, seam side down, in a single layer in dishes. Cover with remaining sauce. Sprinkle with 2 tablespoons Parmesan. Bake uncovered 30 to 45 minutes or until bubbly. Make sure shells are covered with sauce.

Note: Better if sauce is made ahead of time. Cover shells with sauce and refrigerate several hours before cooking to soften shells.

Mrs. Jim Meyers (Karen)

PASTA WITH CLAM SAUCE   6 servings

3 (10-ounce) cans baby
   clams
Olive oil
2 Tablespoons butter

6 cloves garlic, minced
4 Tablespoons chopped parsley
1½ pounds semolina pasta
   (linguine)

Strain clam juice into saucepan and heat until liquid is reduced by half. Into medium skillet, pour enough olive oil to cover the bottom of pan. Add butter, garlic and 2 tablespoons parsley. Cook over a low flame until garlic is transparent. Add the reduced clam juice, increase heat and let mixture come to a boil. Add clams and the remaining parsley and cook until clams are just heated through. Do not overcook or clams will become tough. Pour over hot drained linguine.

Mrs. Ben Mitchell (Margaret Ann)

GOURMET MUSHROOMS AND NOODLES   4 to 6 servings

½ cup butter
½ pound fresh mushrooms, sliced
¼ cup chopped onion
¼ cup sliced almonds

1 clove garlic, minced
1 (10½-ounce) can beef consommé
1 Tablespoon lemon juice
4 ounces medium noodles

Melt butter. Add mushrooms, onion, almonds, and garlic. Cook 10 minutes over low heat. Add remaining ingredients and cook until noodles are tender, about 10 minutes. Great with roast and steak.

Mrs. Glenn Cox (Janice)
Bogalusa, Louisiana

PASTA SALAD   4 servings

¼ cup sliced zucchini
5 broccoli florets
5 cauliflower florets
¼ cup bell pepper, sliced
1 cup pasta (sea shells, spiral, etc.)
2 Tablespoons sliced black olives

1 clove garlic, minced
¼ cup olive oil
1 Tablespoon red wine vinegar
Salt and freshly ground black pepper
Parmesan cheese

Blanch vegetables for 1 minute in 2 quarts boiling water. Drain and set aside. Bring water in saucepan to boil again and cook pasta. Drain well and place in a mixing bowl. Add vegetables, olives, and garlic. Toss with olive oil until well coated. Sprinkle with vinegar, salt and pepper; toss again. Sprinkle with Parmesan cheese. Serve at room temperature or chilled.

Mrs. Jack Gunn (Margaret)

Cheese, Eggs, Pasta

SISTERHOOD NOODLE PUDDING
16 to 20 servings

1 pound wide noodles
1 cup margarine

3 or 4 Tablespoons raisins

Cook noodles according to package instructions. Drain and toss well with margarine. Grease a large deep rectangular baking dish and scatter the noodles in it. Sprinkle raisins over noodles.

8-ounces cream cheese
1 cup sugar

1 teaspoon vanilla
6 large eggs

Cream above ingredients, adding the eggs one at a time.

2 cups milk

2 cups apricot nectar

Mix milk and nectar and add to cream cheese mixture. Slowly pour over noodles, allowing sauce to seep between noodles.

1 cup cornflake crumbs
2 teaspoons sugar

1 teaspoon cinnamon

Make a topping of above ingredients. Sprinkle over noodles. Dot with margarine. Bake at 350° for 45 to 60 minutes. Let set ½ hour before serving.

Mrs. Moses Landau (Frances)
Mrs. Leonard Rubenstein (Bettie)

CREAMY SPINACH PASTA
8 servings

1 cup small curd cottage cheese
1 cup spinach, raw fresh or frozen
1 teaspoon grated lemon peel
¼ cup chicken broth or milk

¼ cup grated Parmesan cheese
½ teaspoon garlic salt
¼ cup butter, melted
Salt and pepper to taste
1 (7-ounce) package vermicelli

Combine all ingredients except vermicelli in food processor. Pour over hot cooked, drained vermicelli. Toss and serve immediately. A good side dish or main dish with salad and bread.

Mrs. Charles Fioranelli (Vicki)

Salads

ARTICHOKE SALAD
6 servings

2 (14-ounce) cans
  water-packed artichoke
  hearts, drained
1 (8-ounce) can water
  chestnuts, thinly sliced

8 large mushrooms, sliced, or 1
  small can sliced mushrooms,
  drained
6 green onions with tops, sliced

Wash the artichoke hearts and place in a salad bowl with the remaining ingredients. Add the dressing.

Dressing
6 Tablespoons oil
2 Tablespoons wine vinegar

Salt and pepper
1 Tablespoon mayonnaise

Beat well and pour over salad. Keeps in refrigerator for several days.

Mrs. Jeff Levingston (Barbara)

TOMATO-ARTICHOKE ASPIC
24 servings

6 cups V-8® tomato juice
2 teaspoons sugar
2 teaspoons salt
2 teaspoons lemon juice
2 teaspoons Worcestershire
  sauce

1 Tablespoon grated onion
Dash of Tabasco sauce
4 packages gelatin
1 (14-ounce) can artichoke
  hearts, cut into pieces

Boil tomato juice and seasonings five minutes. Add gelatin. Stir until dissolved. Spray a 3-quart casserole with non-stick aerosol. Place artichokes in casserole. Pour hot mixture over artichokes. Chill. Cut in 24 squares. Top with mayonnaise and serve on a lettuce leaf.

Mrs. J. C. Darby (Dorothy Lynn)
Mrs. Charles Fioranelli (Vicki)

ASPARAGUS SALAD
8-10 servings

1 cup boiling water
1 (3-ounce) package lime
  gelatin
¼ teaspoon salt
1 (14½-ounce) can asparagus,
  drained
⅓ cup cold water

½ cup shredded Cheddar
  cheese
1 cup mayonnaise
½ cup milk
1 Tablespoon onion juice
1 Tablespoon vinegar

Dissolve gelatin in boiling water. Add cold water and salt. Layer asparagus and grated cheese in oblong dish. Mix mayonnaise, milk, onion juice and vinegar. Stir into gelatin and pour over asparagus and cheese. Chill until set.

Mrs. H. T. Miller, Jr. (Dotty)
Drew, Mississippi

CORN SALAD
6 servings

1 (12-ounce) can white shoe
  peg corn, drained
½ cup chopped bell pepper
½ medium onion, chopped

1 large tomato, chopped
½ teaspoon salt
½ teaspoon pepper
½ cup mayonnaise

Mix all ingredients and chill for 2 hours before serving.

Mrs. Curtis Lofton (Janis)

AVOCADO MOUSSE
8-10 servings

1 (3-ounce) package lime
  gelatin
1 cup hot water
2 cups avocado purée
Juice of one lemon
3 Tablespoons grated onion
½ cup mayonnaise

1 scant teaspoon salt
Dash of Tabasco sauce
¼ teaspoon Worcestershire
  sauce
¾ cup sour cream
1 teaspoon finely chopped
  parsley

Dissolve gelatin in hot water, then cool. Add remaining ingredients to the avocado purée. Add avocado mixture to the gelatin. Pour into an oiled 1½-quart mold and refrigerate. Unmold on lettuce. The center of this mold may be filled with fresh citrus fruits (grapefruit, orange and mandarin orange sections) and served with Piquant French Dressing (see Index).

Mrs. H. L. Dilworth (Anne)

CONGEALED GAZPACHO   1 six-cup mold

2 packages gelatin
3 cups tomato juice
¼ cup wine vinegar
1 clove garlic, crushed
2 teaspoons salt
¼ teaspoon pepper
Dash of cayenne pepper
2 large tomatoes, chopped and
    drained

¼ cup finely chopped onion
¾ cup finely chopped bell
    pepper
¾ cup seeded and finely
    chopped cucumber, drained
¼ cup chopped pimiento

Soak gelatin in one cup tomato juice and heat to simmer. Add the rest of the tomato juice, vinegar, garlic, salt and pepper. Chill to set. Fold in remaining ingredients and pour into a six-cup mold.

DRESSING   Approximately 1 cup

½ cup sour cream
¼ teaspoon salt

⅔ cup mayonnaise

Mix together and chill at least one hour. Serve dressing with gazpacho.

Mrs. J. M. Denton, Jr. (Trich)
Clarksdale, Mississippi

CUCUMBER SALAD   8 servings

1 (3-ounce) package lime
    gelatin
¼ teaspoon salt
1 cup cottage cheese

1 cup mayonnaise
1 cucumber, peeled and
    shredded
1 small onion, grated

Dissolve gelatin in ¾ cup boiling water. Add remaining ingredients. Pour into mold and chill.

Mrs. Thomas H. Showers (Frances)
Drew, Mississippi

LUNCHEON SALAD

8 servings

First layer

1 Tablespoon gelatin
¼ cup mayonnaise
½ cup water
3 Tablespoons lemon juice
¾ teaspoon salt

2 cups chicken breast, boiled
  and diced
½ cup celery, diced
1 Tablespoon onion, finely
  chopped

Second layer

1 envelope gelatin
¼ cup cold water
1 (16-ounce) can whole
  cranberry sauce

1 (9-ounce) can crushed
  pineapple
½ cup chopped pecans
1 Tablespoon lemon juice

For the first layer, soften the gelatin in cold water and then dissolve this mixture over hot water. Blend in the mayonnaise, water, lemon juice and salt. Add the remaining ingredients to the first layer. Pour into a 10x6x1½ or 8x8 pan and chill until set. For the second layer, dissolve the gelatin as in the first layer and then add the remaining ingredients. Mix well and pour over the first layer. Chill until firm.

Mrs. Jimmy Sanders (Hazel)

MOLDED CHICKEN SALAD

12 servings

2 envelopes gelatin
4 cups chicken broth
3 cups diced cooked chicken
1 cup finely chopped celery
2 hard-cooked eggs, chopped
½ cup mayonnaise

¼ cup chopped sweet pickle
2 Tablespoons lemon juice
2 Tablespoons chopped
  pimiento
½ teaspoon salt
¼ teaspoon pepper

Soften gelatin in 1 cup cool broth; dissolve by stirring over low heat. Add remaining broth. Mix remaining ingredients. Taste; add more salt and pepper, if needed. Chill until partially set. Turn into individual molds or an oblong glass dish. Serve on lettuce leaves with stuffed olives and tomato wedges.

Mrs. Emily Lucas
Lexington, Mississippi

CELESTIAL CHICKEN SALAD ✓   8 servings

4 cups cooked chicken,
   chopped
2 cups celery, chopped
1 (4-ounce) can mushrooms,
   sliced
1 (8-ounce) carton sour cream
1 cup mayonnaise

1 Tablespoon lemon juice
Cayenne pepper to taste
½ cup pecans, toasted and
   chopped
4 slices bacon, fried and
   crumbled

Combine first seven ingredients and mix well. Sprinkle with pecans and bacon just before serving.

Mrs. Buster Young (Fane)
Drew, Mississippi

CHICKEN SALAD   4 servings

4 chicken breasts, cooked
   and diced
1 (7¾-ounce) can ripe olives,
   sliced and drained
1 or 2 medium avocados, diced
Lemon juice

Chopped celery to taste
Chopped onion to taste
Salt
Pepper
Mayonnaise

Combine diced chicken, olives, avocados (which have been sprinkled with lemon juice), celery and onion. Mix with enough mayonnaise to moisten. Salt and pepper to taste.

Mrs. Jimmy Yeager (Neysa)

SPICY CHICKEN SALAD   4-6 servings

4 chicken breasts, cooked,
   skinned, boned and torn into
   pieces
1 medium bell pepper,
   chopped
2 large stalks celery, chopped
½ cup mayonnaise

¼ cup red wine vinegar,
   sprinkled over meat
Lemon pepper seasoning,
   sprinkled generously
4 to 6 slices of jalapeño
   pepper, finely chopped
Salt to taste

Mix all ingredients and refrigerate for a couple of hours before serving.

Mrs. Bill Parker (Jo)

CORNED BEEF SALAD   12 servings

1 (10¾-ounce) can beef
   bouillon
1 (10¾-ounce) can water
1 (3-ounce) package lemon
   gelatin
1 envelope gelatin
1 cup chopped celery

1 small onion, grated
3 boiled eggs, sliced
½ green pepper, chopped
1 (12-ounce) can corned beef,
   chopped
¾ cup mayonnaise

Heat bouillon and water; dissolve lemon gelatin and gelatin in the heated mixture. Add other ingredients. Mold in 13½x9-inch dish and cut into squares.

Mrs. W. C. Cox, Jr. (Mary Elizabeth)
Jackson, Mississippi

HAM CHEESETTES   6 servings

1 envelope gelatin
¼ cup cold water
½ (10¾-ounce) can condensed
   tomato soup
½ cup water
1 (3-ounce) package cream
   cheese, softened

1 teaspoon prepared mustard
1 Tablespoon lemon juice
½ cup mayonnaise
1 cup finely chopped ham

Mix and soften gelatin in ¼ cup water. Heat ½ can condensed tomato soup and ½ cup water; mix together cream cheese, mustard and lemon juice. Combine soup and cream cheese mixtures with gelatin and cool until it begins to thicken. Add mayonnaise and chopped ham. Congeal and serve on a lettuce leaf.

Note: This salad is delicious surrounded by petite English peas that have been marinated overnight in Wishbone® Italian Salad Dressing. Drain before serving. It makes a very good luncheon dish.

Mrs. Frank Alley
Jackson, Mississippi

HORSERADISH MOLD
8 servings

1 envelope plain gelatin
3 to 4 Tablespoons cold water
1 package lemon gelatin
1 cup boiling water
1 (5-ounce) jar plus 2
  Tablespoons horseradish

1 cup mayonnaise
1 cup sour cream
¼ teaspoon dry mustard
2 dashes Worcestershire sauce

Dissolve plain gelatin in cold water. Dissolve lemon gelatin in boiling water and blend together. Let cool. Fold in remaining ingredients and pour into greased mold. Chill until firm. Excellent with cold roast beef.

Mrs. Tom P. Miller (Sandra)
Drew, Mississippi

CRABMEAT LOUIS
4 servings

½ cup mayonnaise
¼ cup chili sauce
1 Tablespoon lemon juice
3 Tablespoons chopped shallots
Dash of Worcestershire sauce
2 Tablespoons chopped sweet
  pickle

3 Tablespoons finely chopped
  bell pepper
¼ teaspoon celery salt
Pepper to taste
1 Tablespoon horseradish
¼ teaspoon salt
1 pound crabmeat

Mix well all of the ingredients except the crabmeat. Serve the mixture over the crabmeat or boiled shrimp. Serve in an avocado half, scooped out tomato or on lettuce. Garnish with sliced hard-boiled eggs.

Miss Rosie Hall

CRAB RAVIGOTTE
2 servings

½ cup mayonnaise
1 Tablespoon parsley
1 Tablespoon capers, chopped
1½ teaspoons horseradish
1½ teaspoons dry mustard

1 Tablespoon pimiento,
  chopped
1 hard-boiled egg, chopped
¼ teaspoon lemon juice
1 cup crab meat

Mix first eight ingredients. Add crabmeat and toss lightly. Refrigerate. Serve with tomato wedges and garnish with pimiento.

Mrs. Richard Findley (Phylis)

WEST INDIES CRABMEAT SALAD
4-6 servings

*1 medium onion, finely
  chopped*
1 pound fresh lump crabmeat
¼ teaspoon salt

¼ teaspoon pepper
4 ounces oil
3 ounces cider vinegar
4 ounces ice water

Spread half of chopped onion on bottom of large bowl. Cover with separated crabmeat lumps. Spread remaining chopped onion on top. Sprinkle with salt and pepper. Pour remaining ingredients in the order listed. Cover and marinate for 12 hours at least. Drain and toss lightly before serving.

Mrs. Warren Williamson (Sally)
Greenville, Alabama

SALMON STUFFED AVOCADO
4 servings

*1 (7¾-ounce) can boned and
  skinned salmon, drained and
  flaked*
½ cup chopped celery
*½ cup frozen petite green peas
  (thawed, not cooked)*
2 or 3 green onions, chopped

*1 hard-boiled egg, mashed with
  fork with mayonnaise added
  to bind*
*2 large avocados, peeled,
  halved and brushed all over
  with lemon juice*
Paprika to taste

Combine first 6 ingredients; mix well and chill. Prepare avocados just before serving. Fill halves with salmon mixture, sprinkle with paprika and serve on Bibb lettuce leaves.

Mrs. Robert Tibbs (Pat)

GOURMET CHINESE SALAD

10 to 12 servings

1 (10½-ounce) package
   frozen small green peas
1 (5-ounce) package yellow rice
2½ pounds shrimp, cooked and
   peeled
1½ cups diced celery

½ cup chopped onion
⅓ pound fresh mushrooms,
   sliced
1 (14-ounce) can artichoke
   hearts, drained and sliced

Steam the green peas. Cook the yellow rice according to package directions. Combine all of the ingredients and cover with soy-almond dressing.

Soy-Almond Dressing
½ cup oil
3 Tablespoons vinegar
2 Tablespoons soy sauce
2 Tablespoons curry powder
¼ cup sliced almonds

1 Tablespoon sugar
½ Tablespoon celery seed
½ Tablespoon salt
½ Tablespoon MSG

Mix well. Add dressing to salad. Chill 5 hours or overnight.

Mrs. Jimmy Sanders (Hazel)

SHRIMP MOLD

8-10 servings

1 (10¾-ounce) can tomato
   soup
2 packages gelatin, softened in
   1 Tablespoon water
1 (8-ounce) package cream
   cheese, softened
1 cup mayonnaise
½ cup chopped celery

½ cup chopped onion
½ cup chopped green pepper
2 (4-ounce) cans shrimp,
   soaked in ice water for 20
   minutes, drained and mashed
Worcestershire sauce to taste
Tabasco sauce to taste
Garlic powder to taste

Heat soup with gelatin until dissolved. Add cheese slowly and stir until smooth. Cool. Add rest of ingredients and pour into oiled mold. Chill until set.

Martha L. Norman
Jackson, Mississippi

Miss Julia McGee

LITE TUNA SALAD
2-3 servings

1 (11½-ounce) can tuna,
  drained
½ cup chopped celery
½ cup chopped bell pepper
¼ cup real mayonnaise

1 Tablespoon freshly squeezed
  lemon juice
1½ Tablespoons soy sauce
⅛ teaspoon garlic powder
1 cup chow mein noodles

Combine first 7 ingredients and chill. Before serving, add noodles to tuna mixture and serve on a bed of lettuce.

Mrs. Bill Parker (Jo)

TUNA SALAD
4-6 servings

1 (3-ounce) package lemon
  gelatin
1 Tablespoon lemon juice
½ cup mayonnaise
¼ teaspoon salt

¾ cup chopped cucumber
¾ cup chopped celery
¼ cup salad olives, chopped
2 teaspoons grated onion
1 (6½-ounce) can tuna

Make gelatin according to package directions, reducing cold water to ½ cup. Add the next 3 ingredients. Chill and whip, then add remaining ingredients. Mix well and chill until well set. Serve with assorted crackers.

Mrs. Ken Strong (Pat)
Mrs. Joe Garrison (Joyce)

MONTEAGLE MANDARIN-RICE SALAD
8 servings

3 cups cooked rice
½ cup sour cream
½ cup homemade mayonnaise
1 cup chopped green onion
1 cup chopped bell pepper
¾ cup chopped celery

Season salt and pepper to
  taste
Dash of Worcestershire sauce
1 (11-ounce) can mandarin
  orange sections, drained

Combine all ingredients, adding oranges last. Refrigerate.

Note: 1 cup sour cream may be used instead of ½ cup sour cream and ½ cup mayonnaise.

Mrs. James Y. Dale (Dabney)
Greenwood, Mississippi

BROWN RICE CHEF SALAD
10 to 12 servings

2⅔ cups water
1 cup brown rice
2 teaspoons salt
1 cup frozen green peas
1 cup ham strips
1 cup Swiss cheese strips
1 (8-ounce) can sliced
  mushrooms

½ cup mayonnaise
1 Tablespoon Dijon mustard (no
  substitutes)
¼ Tablespoon pepper
2 Tablespoons vinegar
½ teaspoon sugar
Cherry tomatoes and avocado

Bring water to boil in medium sauce pan. Add rice and 1 teaspoon salt. Reduce heat, cover tightly and cook over low heat until all water is absorbed. This takes about 45 to 50 minutes. Cook peas and add to rice. Let cool thoroughly. Place mixture in large bowl and add ham, cheese and mushrooms. Blend mayonnaise, vinegar, mustard, sugar and pepper in blender until well mixed. Pour over salad and refrigerate for at least 2 hours. This keeps well for several days. Garnish with avocado and tomatoes just before serving.

Mrs. Nott Wheeler, Sr. (Cherry)

FU SALAD
10 to 12 servings

1⅓ cups white vinegar
1⅓ cups oil
6 teaspoons Italian salad
  dressing mix
2 teaspoons garlic salt
2 teaspoons MSG
3 teaspoons seasoned salt
2 teaspoons pepper
1 large cauliflower

1 (14-ounce) can black olives
1 (7-ounce) jar green olives
2 large white onions, sliced
1 bell pepper, cut into
  bite-sized pieces
2 (14-ounce) cans artichoke
  hearts
3 (4-ounce) cans mushrooms
4 to 5 large carrots

Mix vinegar, oil, and seasonings in a gallon jar. Add vegetables (slice and boil carrots for 5 minutes and cool). Turn and coat often. Marinate 24 hours.

Mrs. Jimmy Sanders (Hazel)

SALAD NICOISE   12 servings

French Vinaigrette Dressing

1 cup olive oil
2 Tablespoons lemon juice
4 Tablespoons wine vinegar
2 Tablespoons Dijon mustard
1 clove garlic, finely minced

Salt and pepper to taste
1 Tablespoon each chopped
   fresh basil, tarragon, and
   oregano, or 1½ teaspoons
   dried of each

Salad

2 large heads of Boston or Bibb
   lettuce, washed, leaves left
   whole
8 new potatoes, steamed until
   tender, peeled (or unpeeled),
   sliced and tossed with one
   Tablespoon minced scallion,
   with salt and pepper to taste
½ pound fresh green beans,
   blanched in boiling salted
   water 3 to 5 minutes,
   refreshed in ice water

2 (7-ounce) cans tuna, drained
   and flaked
3 Tablespoons tiney capers
½ cup olives
1 (2-ounce) can anchovies
   (optional)
3 hard-boiled eggs, peeled and
   halved
4 ripe tomatoes, quartered, or
   12 cherry tomatoes, halved
   and tossed with vinaigrette

Combine vinaigrette ingredients and toss lettuce leaves with 2 Tablespoons of the dressing. Arrange lettuce leaves on a deep round platter. Arrange the potato slices in an outside ring on the lettuce. Make a concentric circle of the green beans. Put the flaked tuna in a mound in the center. Sprinkle the capers and olives around it. Put anchovy fillets on top of eggs and place around the tuna. Dot whole salad with tomato quarters or cherry tomatoes. Spoon the remaining dressing over whole salad and serve at once.

Note: Not as complicated as it looks.

The Editors

Salads

FRESH BROCCOLI SALAD

6-8 servings

2 bunches broccoli, florets only, cut into bite-size pieces
1 (8-ounce) can sliced mushrooms, drained
1 medium red onion, finely chopped
1 jar real bacon bits (not synthetic)

1 cup chopped green olives stuffed with pimiento
1 cup real mayonnaise
½ (1-ounce) package ranch style dressing mix

Mix mayonnaise and dressing mix, then toss all ingredients together.

Note: Can be made a day in advance.

Mrs. Ben Griffith (Kathy)

MARINATED COOKED VEGETABLES

10 to 12 servings

1 small head cauliflower florets, steamed
2 broccoli bunches, florets, steamed
1 (9¾-ounce) can whole baby beets

1 package fresh baby carrots, skinned and steamed until tender

Cook each vegetable individually just enough to be tender (about 5 minutes for cauliflower and broccoli and about 15 minutes for carrots). Drain and set aside until cooled. Pour French Dressing over each in its individual bowl or bag. Refrigerate overnight, occasionally turning vegetables. To serve, drain and arrange on a serving platter.

French Dressing
¼ cup tarragon vinegar
1 teaspoon salt
1 teaspoon sugar
1 teaspoon paprika

½ teaspoon dry mustard
¼ teaspoon garlic powder
Dash of cayenne pepper
1 cup salad oil

Mix all ingredients; refrigerate.

Note: Each vegetable is refrigerated overnight in its own container with marinade. Do not mix them because you will not want the flavors to mingle. This is a very pretty dish.

Mrs. James M. Long, Jr. (Nancy)

ROMAINE SALAD
6 servings

1 large head romaine lettuce,
    torn
2 green onions, chopped
2 large ribs of celery, chopped
1 cup mandarin oranges,
    drained

¼ cup sugar (optional)
½ cup slivered almonds
    (optional)

Combine first four ingredients. Mix well and serve with the following dressing.

Dressing

¼ cup olive oil
2 Tablespoons wine vinegar
½ teaspoon salt

Dash of Tabasco
1 Tablespoon sugar
1 Tablespoon chopped parsely

Heat ¼ cup sugar with almonds until the sugar melts, then add to salad.

Mrs. C. E. Dunlap (Jane)

CAESAR SALAD
6 servings

Salt
1 clove garlic
1 teaspoon dry mustard
1 Tablespoon lemon juice
Tabasco sauce to taste
3 Tablespoons olive oil
3 bunches romaine lettuce

1 Tablespoon grated Parmesan
    cheese
1 (2-ounce) can anchovies,
    drained (optional)
1 egg
½ cup croutons

Sprinkle the bottom of a wooden bowl with salt and rub with garlic. Add mustard, lemon juice and Tabasco and stir with a wooden spoon until salt dissolves. Add olive oil and stir rapidly until liquid blends. Wash the romaine well and dry. Tear leaves into bite-size pieces and add to salad bowl. Sprinkle with Parmesan cheese, add anchovies and break egg over the salad. Sprinkle with croutons and mix gently but thoroughly.

The Editors

HILL COUNTRY SALAD   4 servings

5 slices bacon
5 to 7 cups lettuce, torn
3 green onions, chopped

2 Tablespoons cider vinegar
1 teaspoon sugar
¼ teaspoon salt

Cook bacon until crisp; drain, reserving ¼ cup drippings. Crumble bacon and set aside. Place lettuce in a large bowl; sprinkle with onion, vinegar, sugar and salt. Drizzle reserved hot bacon drippings over greens, tossing gently. Sprinkle with bacon and serve immediately.

Mrs. J. C. Gregory (Donna)

PASTA SALAD   8 to 10 servings

2 cups snow peas, fresh
2 cups broccoli florets
2½ cups cherry tomato halves
2 cups fresh mushrooms, sliced
1 (7¾-ounce) can whole pitted
   ripe olives, drained

1 (8-ounce) package
   cheese-stuffed tortellini,
   uncooked
3 ounces fettuccini, uncooked
1 Tablespoon grated Parmesan
   cheese

Dressing
½ cup sliced green onions
⅓ cup red wine vinegar
⅓ cup vegetable oil
⅓ cup olive oil
2 Tablespoons fresh parsley,
   chopped
2 garlic cloves, minced

2 teaspoons dried basil
1 teaspoon dried dillweed
1 teaspoon salt
½ teaspoon pepper
½ teaspoon sugar
½ teaspoon oregano
1½ teaspoons Dijon mustard

Cook pasta according to package directions. Blanche snow peas and broccoli for about 1 minute. Mix dressing and toss with remaining ingredients.

Mrs. W. C. Cox (Mary Elizabeth)
Jackson, Mississippi

MARINATED PASTA SALAD

10 to 15 servings

1 (12-ounce) package of
   tri-colored corkscrew
   noodles, cooked in salted
   water and drained
2 cups fresh broccoli florets
1 small bell pepper, chopped
1 small purple onion, chopped
1 (3-ounce) can ripe black
   olives, sliced

1 (6-ounce) jar whole
   mushrooms
1 (6-ounce) jar marinated
   artichoke hearts, chopped
1 small zucchini squash, sliced
1 (2-ounce) jar pimiento

After noodles have drained and cooled, add all other ingredients. Mix well in a large bowl and marinate with your favorite oil and vinegar salad dressing. Season to taste with salad seasonings, salt and pepper. Chill several hours before serving.

Mrs. Park Hiter (Becky)

CHICKEN AND PASTA SALAD

6-8 servings

½ pound vermicelli
½ cup lemon garlic dressing*
2 cups cooked chicken, cut into
   chunks
10 fresh mushrooms, sliced
1 cup broccoli florets, blanched
1 zucchini, cut in half lengthwise
   and then cut into slices

1 green pepper, chopped
12 pimento-stuffed green olives,
   sliced
3 Tablespoons red wine vinegar
10 cherry tomatoes, cut into
   fourths
⅛ cup fresh basil (optional)

Cook vermicelli according to package directions until tender; drain. In a large bowl, toss the pasta with the lemon garlic dressing; cover and chill at least 3 hours. In another bowl, toss chicken, mushrooms, broccoli, zucchini, green pepper and olives with red wine vinegar; cover and chill for 3 hours. When ready to serve, add chicken and vegetable mixture to pasta; toss with tomatoes and basil.

*See index for "Jo's Salad Dressing"

Mrs. Bill Parker (Jo)

TORTELLINI ALLA PANNA   4-6 servings

1 (7-ounce) package tortellini
  filled with cheese
1 (4-ounce) wedge Parmesan,
  grated
1 cup whipping cream
¼ cup butter

1 (14-ounce) can artichoke
  hearts, quartered
10 to 12 fresh mushrooms,
  chopped and sautéed in
  garlic butter
2 zucchini, sliced and sautéed

In salted boiling water (at least one palmful of salt added), cook the tortellini by package directions. Drain; add butter and grated Parmesan. Toss until melted. Then add cream, artichokes, mushrooms and zucchini. May be served warm as a vegetable dish or cold as a salad.

Mrs. Allen Pepper (Ginger)
Mrs. W. J. DuBard (Bobbie)
Drew, Mississippi

STUFFED TOMATOES WITH PESTO   25 servings

Pesto: Yields 3 cups
½ cup pignolia nuts (pine) or
  walnuts, chopped
4 cloves garlic, peeled
1 teaspoon salt
½ teaspoon pepper
3 to 4 cups fresh basil leaves

¼ pound freshly grated
  Parmesan cheese
¼ pound freshly grated Romano
  cheese
1½ to 2 cups olive oil

Grind all ingredients except nuts in food processor with ½ cup olive oil. Add the remaining oil and process until smooth and creamy. Add nuts. Store in refrigerator until ready to use.

Tomatoes
25 medium tomatoes
1½ pounds vermicelli

½ to 1 cup Pesto

Hollow tomatoes and drain upside down. Cook vermicelli according to package directions. Drain and mix with Pesto. Fill tomatoes with pasta. Serve cold.

The Editors

Salads

CHERRY ASPIC

1 (16-ounce) can pitted dark
  sweet cherries, cut in half or
  quartered and set aside
2 (3-ounce) packages black
  cherry flavor gelatin
1 cup boiling water

¾ cup port wine
1 cup unsweetened
  applesauce
¼ to ½ cup chopped pecans
  (optional)
Mayonnaise dressing

Drain cherries and save juice. Add enough water to juice to make ¾ cup liquid (if necessary). Dissolve gelatin in 1 cup boiling water. Add cherry liquid and port wine. Stir in applesauce. Chill until partially congealed. Fold in cherries (and pecans, if used). Spoon into a shallow 1½-quart dish or 4-cup oiled mold. Serve with mayonnaise dressing.

Mayonnaise Dressing
1 cup mayonnaise
2 Tablespoons orange juice, or
  more

1 Tablespoon port wine
1 Tablespoon grated orange
  rind

Combine and chill overnight to blend flavors. Spoon liberally over aspic.

Mrs. Robert Tibbs (Pat)

BUFFET APPLES

½ cup sugar
⅓ cup water
¼ cup red hots (cinnamon)
4 large firm apples (Delicious)

Cream cheese
Toasted pecans
Cream

Cook sugar, water, and red hots for 5 minutes. Peel and core apples and drop into hot syrup. Cover and cook gently until tender, but firm, turning while cooking. Remove with slotted spoon and chill. Mix cream cheese with toasted chopped pecans (moisten with cream if necessary). Fill centers of apples. Serve on lettuce and top with mayonnaise.

Mrs. Thomas H. Showers (Frances)
Drew, Mississippi

FROZEN THREE-FRUIT SALAD   16-20 servings

6 ounces cream cheese,
   softened
1 cup mayonnaise
¼ cup lemon juice
¼ teaspoon salt
¼ cup granulated sugar
2 cups pineapple tidbits,
   drained

2 cups mandarin orange
   sections, drained and diced
1 cup chopped maraschino
   cherries
1 cup dark cherries, pitted and
   quartered
1 cup chopped pecans
2 cups heavy cream, whipped

In a large bowl, blend softened cream cheese, mayonnaise, lemon juice, salt and sugar. Gently mix in fruits and nuts; fold in whipped cream. Pour into a 10x4½-inch bundt pan or a 3-quart mold. Cover tightly with foil and freeze overnight. May also be frozen in individual molds or foil muffin liners. Be sure to cover individual mold with foil before freezing. Unmold onto salad greens and garnish with fresh strawberries.

Mrs. C. L. Beckham (Marie)
Shaw, Mississippi

MILLIONAIRE SALAD   12 servings

2 eggs, beaten
5 Tablespoons lemon juice
5 Tablespoons sugar
2 Tablespoons margarine
½ pound marshmallows, cut
1 (20-ounce) can white Queen
   Anne cherries, seeded and
   drained

¼ pound blanched almonds
3 bananas, sliced
1 (20-ounce) can diced
   pineapple, drained
1 cup whipping cream, whipped

Add lemon juice, sugar, margarine and marshmallows to eggs. Cook in double boiler until marshmallows dissolve. Cool. Add almonds, cherries, pineapple and bananas. Fold in whipped cream. Refrigerate at least twelve hours before serving.

Mrs. Mike Davis (Sheryl)

ORANGE SHERBET SALAD

12 servings

1 (6-ounce) package orange
  gelatin
2 cups boiling water

1 (3-ounce) package cream
  cheese

Mix all ingredients together and let set 20 minutes. Use 2-quart dish or 13x9x2-inch pan.

Add

1 pint orange sherbet (stir until
  melted)
1 (11-ounce) can mandarin
  oranges, drained

1 (20-ounce) can crushed
  pineapple, drained

Topping

1 envelope dry whipped topping
  mix
1 (3-ounce) box instant lemon
  pudding

1½ cups milk

Mix 1 envelope whipped topping according to package directions. Mix instant lemon pudding with 1½ cups milk. Stir pudding and whipped topping together and spread over set gelatin.

Mrs. Danny Cooper (Jan)

SPRINGTIME FRUIT SALAD

14-16 servings

1 fresh pineapple, peeled,
  cored and cubed
1 quart strawberries, whole or
  sliced, depending on size
½ cup fresh or frozen
  blueberries, thawed
½ cup fresh or frozen
  raspberries, thawed

1 (11-ounce) can mandarin
  oranges, drained
2 cups orange juice
1 cup sugar
¼ cup cream sherry
½ teaspoon almond extract
½ teaspoon vanilla extract

Combine fruit in a large bowl. Combine remaining ingredients, stirring until sugar dissolves. Pour over fruit mixture, tossing lightly. Chill 2-3 hours.

Mrs. J. C. Gregory (Donna)

SOUTH PACIFIC SALAD   6 servings

3 pineapples
¾ cup sugar
1 pint strawberries
6-inch watermelon wedge

3 bananas, rolled in chopped
*   walnuts or pecans*
1 melon, honeydew or
*   cantaloupe*

Cut the pineapples through the crown into halves using a grapefruit knife; hollow out the fruit to form shells. Remove the core of the pineapple and cut fruit into ½-inch cubes. Sprinkle with ¾ cup of sugar and return to shells. Wash and hull strawberries, reserving 12 unhulled berries for garnish. Cut melon into halves, remove seeds, and scoop out balls with a melon scoop. Using the same method, prepare one cup of watermelon balls. Just before serving, peel bananas, roll in coarsely chopped nuts and slice each banana into sixths with a fluted cutter. Place pineapple halves on a large shiny leaf on a luncheon plate. Then arrange the strawberries, melon balls and banana slices around each shell. Top with the reserved strawberries. Serve with South Pacific Salad Dressing.

South Pacific Salad Dressing
1 Tablespoon cornstarch
2 Tablespoons water
⅓ cup lemon juice
⅔ cup orange juice
1 Tablespoon maraschino
*   cherry liquid (optional)*

1 cup sugar
2 eggs, beaten
1 cup heavy cream, whipped

Mix the cornstarch and water; add the fruit juices, sugar and eggs. Cook in a double boiler, stirring constantly until thick. Cool slightly and refrigerate. Just before serving, fold in the whipped cream.

Note: This dressing is equally delicious on any fruit salad.

Mrs. Keith Griffin (Leslie)

AVOCADO GRAPEFRUIT SALAD

Dressing

¼ cup vinegar
Juice of 1 lemon
¼ cup undiluted frozen orange juice
½ teaspoon salt

2 teaspoons grated orange peel
¼ cup sugar
¼ teaspoon dry mustard
1 cup salad oil

Salad

3 large grapefruits or navel oranges, peeled and sectioned

2 large ripe avocados, peeled and sliced
1 large Bermuda onion, sliced

Note: Especially good with Mexican food.

Mrs. Jack Gunn (Margaret)

CITRUS SURPRISE

6 servings

(Start a day ahead)

¾ cup orange sections
¾ cup grapefruit sections
1 (3-ounce) package any flavor gelatin

⅛ teaspoon salt
1 cup boiling water

Sweeten fruit to taste; set aside. Dissolve gelatin and salt in boiling water. Drain fruit, measuring juice and adding water to make ¾ cup. Add juice to gelatin. Chill 1 cup of the mixture until very thick. Whip until fluffy. (Mixture will be fluffy and thick and double in volume which results in best eating quality and flavor.) Pour into a one-quart mold. Chill until set but not firm. Chill remaining gelatin until very thick, then fold in fruit. Spoon into mold. Chill until firm. Unmold and garnish with mint and sour cream.

Note: To unmold mixture, it will need to chill a long time, at least overnight.

Mrs. Leigh Sanders (Jo Ann)

Sauces,
Salad Dressings

CHILI SAUCE   3½ cups

1 cup chopped onion
1 clove garlic, finely chopped
¼ cup vegetable oil
1 (8-ounce) can tomato sauce
1 cup water
1 to 2 Tablespoons chopped
  jalapeño peppers, seeds
  removed

1 teaspoon ground oregano
½ teaspoon salt
¼ teaspoon ground cumin, if
  desired

Cook and stir onion and garlic in oil until onion is tender, about 5 minutes. Stir in remaining ingredients. Heat to boiling. Reduce heat and simmer uncovered for 20 minutes. Remove from heat; cool 5 minutes. Transfer sauce to blender; cover and blend on medium speed until sauce is smooth. Good on vegetables.

Martha L. Norman
Jackson, Mississippi

CHEESE SAUCE   2 cups

3 Tablespoons butter
3 Tablespoons all-purpose flour
¼ teaspoon salt
⅛ teaspoon pepper

1 cup milk
½ cup sharp Cheddar cheese,
  grated or in small cubes

Melt butter and add flour and seasonings, making a paste. Slowly add milk and stir until thick. Add cheese and stir until melted.

Mrs. Phillip Rizzo (Ramona)

UNIVERSITY SAUCE   4 cups

8-ounces raisins, puréed
2-ounces brandy
½ cup sugar

16-ounces sour cream
1 teaspoon cinnamon
Dash of nutmeg

Combine puréed raisins and brandy in a blender or food processor. Add other ingredients and mix until smooth. Delicious sauce to use with fresh strawberries or other fruit.

The Editors

BEARNAISE SAUCE   1 cup

**3 Tablespoons tarragon
   vinegar
1 teaspoon minced green onion
¼ teaspoon coarsely ground
   black pepper
Dash of dried tarragon
Dash of dried whole chernil or
   parsley flakes**

**1 Tablespoon cold water
4 egg yolks
½ cup butter, softened
1 teaspoon minced fresh
   parsley
⅛ teaspoon salt**

Combine first five ingredients in a small saucepan; bring to a boil over medium heat. Reduce heat to low, and simmer until half of the liquid evaporates. Pour mixture through a strainer, reserving liquid. Discard herb mixture. Combine vinegar mixture and water. Beat egg yolks in top of a double boiler with a wire whisk. Gradually add vinegar mixture in a slow, steady stream. Bring water to a boil (water in bottom of double boiler should not touch top of pan). Reduce heat to low; add butter, 2 tablespoons at a time, beating constantly, until butter melts. Continue beating until smooth and thickened. Remove from heat. Stir in fresh parsley and salt. Serve over beef, poultry or seafood.

Variations:
Sauce Choron (Bearnaise with tomato)
**1 Recipe Bearnaise Sauce   ¼ cup tomato paste
   (omitting tarragon and
   parsley)**

Make Bearnaise sauce omitting tarragon and parsley. Stir in tomato paste until blended. Serve with grilled meats and poultry.

Sauce Valois (Bearnaise with Glaze de Viande)
**1 recipe Bearnaise Sauce
1 Tablespoon glaze de viande
   (meat glaze)**

Stir meat glaze in Bearnaise until blended. Serve with grilled meats.

Sauce Paloise (Mint-Flavored Bearnaise)
**1 recipe Bearnaise (omitting   4 Tablespoons fresh mint
   parsley and tarragon)**

Make Bearnaise Sauce, omitting parsley and tarragon and using 3 tablespoons of mint for boiling. Add remaining tablespoon of mint, chopped fine. Serve with lamb.

The Editors

REMOULADE SAUCE (FRENCH DRESSING BASE)   1 cup

3 Tablespoons wine vinegar
1 to 2 Tablespoons Dijon
   mustard
2 Tablespoons minced green
   onions
2 Tablespoons minced celery

1 teaspoon horseradish
1 Tablespoon minced parsley
½ cup plus 1 Tablespoon olive
   oil
Dash of red pepper
Salt and pepper to taste

Combine vinegar with mustard, green onions, celery, horseradish and parsley. Beat in olive oil, a little at a time and season to taste with red pepper, salt and black pepper. Serve with cold boiled shrimp.

The Editors

TARTAR SAUCE I   1½ cups

1 cup mayonnaise
¼ cup finely chopped dill
   pickle
2 Tablespoons minced parsley
1 teaspoon lemon juice

½ teaspoon grated onion
¼ teaspoon Worcestershire
   sauce
1 Tablespoon capers, optional

Combine all ingredients. Chill and serve.

Mrs. Dan Hammett (Marcia)

TARTAR SAUCE II   1½ cups

1 cup mayonnaise
⅓ cup sweet pickle relish,
   drained
1 Tablespoon lemon juice
1 Tablespoon finely chopped
   fresh parsley

1 Tablespoon finely chopped
   onion
⅛ teaspoon salt

Combine all ingredients; mix well. Refrigerate, covered, until well chilled.

Mrs. Philip Wiggins (Barbie)

BASIC BLENDER MAYONNAISE   1½ cups

2 egg yolks
1 whole egg
1 teaspoon Dijon mustard
½ teaspoon salt
Pinch of white pepper
1 Tablespoon fresh lemon
 pepper

½ cup olive oil mixed with ½
 cup light vegetable oil
1 Tablespoon white wine
 vinegar
1 Tablespoon boiling water

Place egg yolks, whole egg, mustard, salt, pepper and lemon juice in blender. Process until smooth and thick. With machine on, gradually pour in oil in a thin stream. Add the vinegar and boiling water. Adjust the seasonings to your taste.

Variations:
Sauce Montardi (Mustard Mayonnaise)
1 recipe basic mayonnaise   **1½ Tablespoons Dijon mustard**

Add mustard just before serving. Serve with cold poultry or beef.

Sauce Verte (Green Mayonnaise)
1 recipe basic mayonnaise
4 ounces total spinach,
 watercress and parsley

Boil spinach, watercress and parsley for 30 seconds. Immediately drain and rinse under cold running water. Squeeze out as much water as possible. Purée in blender and pass through a sieve. Stir into mayonnaise. Serve with cold fish or shellfish.

Sauce Andalouse (Tomato Mayonnaise with Pimento)
1 recipe basic mayonnaise   **2 Tablespoons pimento cut in**
½ cup tomato paste   **julienne strips**

Whisk tomato paste in mayonnaise until blended. Stir in pimento strips. Serve with cold poultry or beef.

Mayonnaise Collee (Jellied Mayonnaise)
1 recipe basic mayonnaise   *¼ cup chicken stock*
1 package gelatin

Let gelatin soften in small bowl with chicken stock about five minutes in double boiler. Heat, stirring, until gelatin dissolves. Let mixture cool to room temperature. Stir gelatin mixture into mayonnaise and chill just to the point of setting. Pipe out with a pastry bag to garnish cold meats, vegetables or salads.

The Editors

Tip:
First Aid for Broken Mayonnaise
If for any reason your mayonnaise breaks, or separates, it can be brought back. Place one egg yolk in clean bowl and beat until light colored and it begins to thicken. Gradually begin to add separated mayonnaise in droplets, continuing to beat. Once emulsion forms and mixture thickens, add mayonnaise in a thin stream.

CUISINART MAYONNAISE   3 cups

2 egg yolks   *¼ teaspoon paprika*
1 whole egg   *3 Tablespoons fresh lemon juice*
1 teaspoon salt   *1 Tablespoon white vinegar*
¼ teaspoon cayenne pepper   *2 cups corn or safflower oil*

Whiz first five ingredients in the Cuisinart for 1 minute, then add the lemon juice and white vinegar. Turn the Cuisinart back on and slowly pour through the feed tube the two cups of oil. Refrigerate.

Mrs. Jimmy Dale (Dabney)
Greenwood, Mississippi

ROUX

Using a foil pan or any pan that is thin (so it will cook faster), add all-purpose flour to cover bottom of baking pan. You can make a larger quantity at one time. Put in 275° oven and let bake slowly, stirring fairly often. The flour will gradually get brown—let cook until it is a deep, dark brown. When ready to make a roux, add about 1 tablespoon of browned flour to 1 tablespoon of heated oil—it will instantly become brown and roux is ready. Browned flour may be stored in the refrigerator in a covered jar for an indefinite period.

Mrs. Toby Michael (Eleanor)
Rosedale, Mississippi

MUSTARD SAUCE   2 cups

2-ounces dry mustard
⅞ cup sugar
1 teaspoon salt
**2 Tablespoons sifted,
   all-purpose flour (slightly
   more than level)**

**2½ to 3 Tablespoons boiling
   water**
½ cup white vinegar

Scald the first 4 ingredients in the 2½ to 3 tablespoons of boiling water, which has been measured into a cup. Four tablespoons boiling water may be used if needed. Let stand one hour or longer. Place the mixture along with the ½ cup vinegar in a saucepan and cook over medium heat until thick. Cook until mixture coats a spoon. Use a double boiler or stir constantly. Good with sliced ham or ham sandwiches. Keeps well in the refrigerator.

Mrs. Alice Dalton Thurmond
Lexington, Mississippi

SANDRA'S HOMEMADE MUSTARD   4 cups

1 cup vinegar
1 (1.8-ounce) can dry mustard
1 egg

1 cup sugar
¾ cup salad dressing
½ cup prepared mustard

Mix vinegar and dry mustard and let sit overnight. Add egg and sugar and cook over medium heat until thickened. Cool and add salad dressing and mustard. Store in jars and refrigerate.

Mrs. Tom P. Miller (Sandra)
Drew, Mississippi

WHITE SAUCE FOR SHRIMP   2 cups

1 cup mayonnaise
½ cup Durkee's dressing
2 Tablespoons creole mustard
2 teaspoons grated onion
2 Tablespoons horseradish

2 Tablespoons Worcestershire
sauce
Juice of ½ lemon
Hot sauce, salt, pepper to taste

Combine and refrigerate.

Mrs. Murle Parkinson
Drew, Mississippi

"COME BACK" SAUCE   2½ cups

2 cloves garlic, pressed
1 cup mayonnaise
¼ cup chili sauce
¼ cup catsup
1 Tablespoon prepared mustard
½ cup oil

1 Tablespoon Worcestershire
sauce
1 teaspoon black pepper
2 Tablespoons lemon juice
1 small onion, grated

Mix all ingredients together. Keeps well in covered container in refrigerator. Good with shrimp or for salad dressing.

Mrs. Billy Ratliff (Susu)

Variation: Add ½ teaspoon horseradish.

Mrs. J. R. Taylor
Pace, Mississippi

HORSERADISH SAUCE I √

1½ cups

1 cup sour cream
2 Tablespoons tarragon vinegar
½ teaspoon salt
¼ teaspoon pepper

4 Tablespoons horseradish
Dash Tabasco
½ Tablespoon chives

Mix above ingredients and refrigerate. Serve with rare roast beef or use as a party sandwich spread in place of mayonnaise.

Mrs. Will Lewis, Jr. (Patty)
Oxford, Mississippi

HORSERADISH SAUCE II

1¾ cups

1 cup mayonnaise
2 hard-boiled eggs, chopped
1½ Tablespoons horseradish
  sauce
1 teaspoon Worcestershire
  sauce

Salt and pepper to taste
Onion salt to taste
1½ teaspoons parsley flakes
½ teaspoon garlic
1 teaspoon lemon juice

Mix well. Serve over green beans or other vegetables. Also good with roast beef.

Mrs. Joe Garrison (Joyce)

JEZEBEL SAUCE

5 cups

16-ounces apple jelly
16-ounces pineapple preserves
5-ounce jar horseradish

2 teaspoons dry mustard
2 Tablespoons black pepper

Blend in blender or food processor. Keep refrigerated. Good on ham or just with crackers.

Mrs. Steve Clark (Sheila)
Drew, Mississippi

BLENDER HOLLANDAISE   1 cup

1 cup (2 sticks) butter   *Pinch of white pepper*
3 egg yolks   *1 Tablespoon fresh lemon juice*
Pinch of salt

Melt butter over low heat and keep warm. Place egg yolks, salt, pepper and lemon juice in blender and mix at high speed until blended. While blending at high speed, add hot butter in a thin stream. Do not add milky residue at the bottom of the pan. Adjust seasonings.

Variations:

Sauce Maltaice (Orange Hollandaise)
1 recipe Hollandaise   *2 Tablespoons fresh orange*
2 Tablespoons grated orange   *juice*
*   zest*

Stir orange zest and arrange juice into Hollandaise. Serve with asparagus.

Sauce Noisette (Hollandaise with Hazelnut Butter)
1 recipe Hollandaise   *2 Tablespoons softened butter*
2 ounces hazelnuts

Toast hazelnuts in 400° oven about five minutes. Remove skins from nuts by rubbing between your palms. In blender or food processor, grind nuts to a fine powder. Add softened butter and blend thoroughly. Stir into warm hollandaise. Serve with trout or salmon.

Sauce Mousseline (Hollandaise with Whipped Cream)
1 recipe Hollandaise   *⅓ cup heavy cream*

Whip cream until stiff peaks form. Just before serving, fold the whipped cream into Hollandaise sauce. Serve with steamed vegetables, eggs, or poached fish.

The Editors

MARCHAND DE VIN SAUCE
1½ cups

3 Tablespoons butter
2 Tablespoons chopped
scallions or onions
3 Tablespoons all-purpose flour
1 cup beef consommé

1 Tablespoon tomato paste
⅓ cup red wine
Salt and pepper
2 Tablespoons butter
2 Tablespoons chopped parsley

Melt butter and add scallions. Cook until scallions are clear, then add the flour. Cook over medium heat, stirring constantly. When the roux is brown, add the boiling consommé, stirring until sauce thickens. Turn down heat to simmer; add tomato paste and wine. Cook over low heat for 20 minutes or until thick, stirring occasionally. Season with salt and pepper to taste. Take off heat and swirl in butter and parsley. Serve in sauceboat with beef wellington.

The Editors

BORDELAISE SAUCE
1½ cups

2 Tablespoons butter or
margarine
2 Tablespoons all-purpose flour
1 Tablespoon minced green
onion
1 Tablespoon chopped fresh
parsley
1 bay leaf

¼ teaspoon dried whole thyme
⅛ teaspoon salt
⅛ teaspoon coarsely ground
black pepper
1 (10½-ounce) can beef broth,
undiluted
3 Tablespoons dry red wine

Melt butter in a heavy saucepan over low heat; add flour, stirring until smooth. Cook 1 minute, stirring constantly. Stir in next 6 ingredients. Gradually add broth and wine; cook over medium high heat, stirring constantly, until thickened and bubbly. Remove bay leaf. Serve over beef.

The Editors

MORNAY SAUCE
1 cup

1 egg yolk
2 Tablespoons whipping cream
1 cup thin white sauce*
1 Tablespoon minced onion

2 Tablespoons shredded Swiss cheese
¼ teaspoon salt
Dash of white pepper

Beat egg yolk and whipping cream with wire whisk; set aside. Combine warm white sauce and onion in a heavy saucepan. Cook over low heat, stirring constantly, 3 or 4 minutes until onion is tender. Gradually stir about one-fourth of hot mixture into the yolk mixture; add to remaining hot mixture, stirring constantly. Add cheese to sauce; cook, stirring constantly, until cheese melts. Stir in salt and pepper. Serve over poached eggs, seafood, or vegetables.
* check Index for page number.

The Editors

SWEET AND SOUR SAUCE
2 cups

6 to 8 maraschino cherries
1 (8-ounce) can chunk pineapple
1½ Tablespoons cornstarch
1 Tablespoon soy sauce
1 Tablespoon vinegar

1 Tablespoon sugar (brown or white)
2 Tablespoons catsup
2 Tablespoons juice from cherries
½ cup pineapple juice

Place all ingredients in a blender or food processor. May add more pineapple juice to thin. Great with egg rolls.

Mrs. Don Blackwood (Suzan)

LEMON CREAM
4 cups

2 cups mayonnaise
2 cups sour cream
¼ cup fresh lemon juice
2½ teaspoons finely grated
  lemon peel

2 teaspoons white horseradish
2 teaspoons Dijon mustard
1 teaspoon salt

Combine all ingredients in large bowl and blend; refrigerate. Adjust seasoning before serving. Good with any fresh vegetables and cold artichokes.

Note: Can be made 3 days ahead.

Mrs. H. L. Dilworth (Anne)

BAKED BEAN SAUCE
3½ cups

1 (14-ounce) bottle catsup
1 (12-ounce) bottle chili sauce
4 Tablespoons brown sugar
2 large onions, chopped

4 cloves garlic, chopped
2 Tablespoons thyme
2 Tablespoons chili powder

Mix all ingredients together and store in refrigerator. Can be used over leftover meat and heated for a quick sandwich.

Mrs. Buster Young (Fane)

PARSLEY-GARLIC SAUCE
¾ cup

2 egg yolks
1½ Tablespoons lemon juice
1 Tablespoon minced fresh
  parsley
2 cloves garlic, crushed
1 Tablespoon chopped chives

¼ teaspoon dry mustard
⅛ teaspoon ground red pepper
Dash of salt
½ cup butter or margarine,
  softened

Combine first 8 ingredients in top of a double boiler. Place over hot water (not boiling). Beat with a wire whisk until smooth. Add butter, 1 tablespoon at a time, beating constantly, until melted. Continue beating until thickened. Serve over seafood, beef, or vegetables.

The Editors

CURRY SAUCE   1¼ cups

2 Tablespoons butter or
  margarine
3 Tablespoons minced onion
1½ teaspoons curry powder
¾ teaspoon sugar
⅛ teaspoon ground ginger

2 Tablespoons all-purpose flour
1 cup milk
⅛ teaspoon salt
Dash of white pepper
1 teaspoon lemon juice

Melt butter in a heavy saucepan over low heat; add next 4 ingredients, and sauté until onion is tender. Add flour, stirring until smooth. Cook 1 minute, stirring constantly. Gradually add milk; cook over medium heat, stirring constantly, until thickened and bubbly. Stir in salt, pepper, and lemon juice. Serve over poached eggs, poultry, or vegetables.

The Editors

DILL SAUCE FOR LAMB   1½ cups

3 Tablespoons butter
1 Tablespoon all-purpose flour
1 cup chicken broth
¼ cup chopped chives

1¼ teaspoons dill weed
¼ cup finely chopped parsley
1½ teaspoons lemon juice

Heat butter in saucepan, blend in flour and cook until it bubbles. Remove from heat and add chicken broth slowly, stirring constantly. Cook until thickened, about 3 minutes. Stir in remaining ingredients and keep warm to serve. Store leftover sauce in refrigerator.

Mrs. Howard Grittman (Ann)

TERIYAKI SAUCE   1½ cups

1 cup soy sauce
4 cloves garlic
3 Tablespoons sugar
2 Tablespoons lemon juice

2 Tablespoons Worcestershire
  sauce
2 Tablespoons salad oil
Pepper to taste

Mix all ingredients together. Marinade for steaks. Marinate for 5 to 6 hours, turning occasionally. Cook on grill.

Mrs. H. L. Dilworth (Anne)

WHITE SAUCE   1 cup

Thin White Sauce

1 Tablespoon butter or margarine	1 cup milk
1 Tablespoon all-purpose flour	¼ teaspoon salt
	Dash of white pepper

Medium White Sauce

2 Tablespoons butter or margarine	1 cup milk
2 Tablespoons all-purpose flour	¼ teaspoon salt
	Dash of white pepper

Thick White Sauce

3 Tablespoons butter or margarine	1 cup milk
3 Tablespoons all-purpose flour	¼ teaspoon salt
	Dash of white pepper

Melt butter in a heavy saucepan over low heat; add flour, stirring until smooth. Cook 1 minute, stirring constantly. Gradually add milk; cook over medium heat, stirring constantly, until thickened and bubbly. Stir in salt and pepper. Serve over poached eggs, poultry, seafood, or vegetables.

The Editors

CHICKEN MARINADE   3½ cups

1½ cups salad oil
¾ cup soy sauce
¼ cup Worcestershire sauce
2 Tablespoons dry mustard
2¼ teaspoons salt
½ cup wine vinegar
1½ teaspoons dried parsley flakes
2 garlic cloves, crushed
⅓ cup fresh lemon juice
1 Tablespoon pepper

Combine all ingredients and mix well. Use to marinate chicken overnight before cooking over grill.

Note: Marinade can be frozen indefinitely or stored in refrigerator for about 1 week.

Mrs. Bo Ming (Joyce)
Tyler, Texas

AVOCADO-SHRIMP DRESSING 2 cups

1 cup chopped avocado
1 teaspoon lemon juice
½ cup mayonnaise
1 teaspoon horseradish

1 teaspoon grated onion
½ teaspoon salt
2 drops Tabasco
1 cup cooked shrimp (chopped)

Blend all ingredients. Add shrimp. Good on lettuce or as a dip for chips. Keeps well in refrigerator.

Mrs. Bob Buchanan (Sharon)

AUTHENIC DIJON FRENCH DRESSING ½ cup

1 Tablespoon Dijon mustard
2 Tablespoons vinegar

Coarse ground black pepper
¼ cup olive oil or soybean oil

Shake in a small jar or blend with fork.

Mrs. Hite McLean (Keith Dockery)

BERNICE'S FRENCH DRESSING 1⅓ cups

Red wine vinegar and fresh
  lemon juice (equal parts to
  make ⅓ cup)
2 teaspoons salt
1 teaspoon cracked black
  pepper

¾ teaspoon dry mustard
1 teaspoon paprika
⅔ cup olive oil
1 clove garlic

Measure ⅓ cup of wine vinegar and fresh lemon juice combined. Pour over dry ingredients and stir until salt is dissolved. Pour mixture into a jar and add olive oil one tablespoon at a time. Drop garlic clove in bottom of jar. (Take jar out of refrigerator one hour before use.)

Note: This is delicious spooned over grapefruit and avocado sliced on a bed of lettuce. Also is a good green salad dressing.

Mrs. Bill Parker (Jo)

ARTICHOKE SALAD DRESSING   2 cups

*1 (4½-ounce) can marinated
   artichokes, undrained and
   sliced*
*1 (2-ounce) can anchovies,
   chopped, undrained*
½ cup wine vinegar

¼ cup sliced ripe olives
*¼ cup sliced pimento stuffed
   olives*
2 Tablespoons capers
Fresh ground pepper

Combine all ingredients and mix well. Serve over assorted salad greens
with ½ pound sliced fresh mushrooms.

Mrs. Howard Grittman (Anne)
Drew, Mississippi

JACKIE'S SALAD DRESSING   2½ cups

*2-ounce can anchovies,
   drained*
1½ cups vegetable oil
Juice of 1 lemon
½ cup tarragon vinegar
1 small white onion, chopped
¼ teaspoon dry mustard

Dash of tabasco
*Salt and freshly ground pepper
   to taste*
2 or 3 large garlic cloves
*1 Tablespoon Worcestershire
   sauce*

Blend in blender and use on green salad. Good on Romaine.

Mrs. Jeffery Levingston (Barbara)

JO'S SALAD DRESSING   1 cup

2 cloves garlic, pressed
1 Tablespoon salt
1 teaspoon coarse ground
  pepper

½ teaspoon dry mustard
Juice of 3 or 4 lemons
Olive oil
Vegetable oil

Place first four ingredients in shallow bowl. Mash together with a fork until it resembles wet sand. Mix lemon juice and salt mixture, stirring until salt dissolves. Pour into a 16-ounce jar and add oil (½ olive and ½ vegetable oil) to make the lemon mixture equal ⅓ of salad dressing. Keep in refrigerator indefinitely. Remove from refrigerator at least 1 hour before using on tossed salad.

Mrs. Bill Parker (Jo)
Rosedale, Mississippi

HONEY FRENCH DRESSING   3 cups

1 cup vegetable oil
½ cup honey
½ teaspoon salt
½ cup chili sauce

½ cup vinegar
½ cup finely chopped onion
1 Tablespoon Worcestershire
  sauce

Combine all ingredients in a jar with a tight fitting lid. Shake vigorously before serving.

Mrs. Joe Smith III (Suellen)

PIQUATE FRENCH DRESSING   1½ cups

⅓ cup sugar
1 teaspoon salt
1 teaspoon dry mustard
1 teaspoon celery seed
1 teaspoon paprika

1 teaspoon grated onion
4 Tablespoons vinegar
1 cup salad oil
1 clove garlic, optional

Mix the above ingredients. Let dressing stand for an hour; then remove garlic clove and refrigerate. Excellent over fruit, especially a salad of grapefruit and orange sections with slices of avocado.

Mrs. H. L. Dilworth (Anne)

NAN'S SALAD DRESSING   1¾ cups

*2 Tablespoons freshly
squeezed lemon juice*
1 Tablespoon parsley
4 Tablespoons cold water
2 medium cloves garlic, pressed

¼ cup grated Parmesan cheese
½ teaspoon salt
½ teaspoon pepper
¼ teaspoon paprika
8-ounces olive oil

Combine ingredients and stir with a wire whisk. Refrigerate until 1 hour before using. This dressing needs to be room temperature when salad is tossed.

Note: Add ½ cup prepared Ranch dressing for a creamier dressing. It's delicious. As for the salad, I like all salad greens except iceburg lettuce. Usually, the "musts" are fresh mushrooms, cauliflower florets, green onions, julienne carrots, radishes, artichokes, and croutons. It's a delicious and beautiful salad.

Mrs. Mike Sanders (Nan)

FRENCH DRESSING   1 cup

2 teaspoons salt
¼ teaspoon sugar
¼ dry mustard
½ teaspoon lemon juice
*¼ teaspoon Worcestershire
sauce*

3 Tablespoons tarragon vinegar
12 Tablespoons olive oil
*2 Tablespoons blue cheese
(optional)*

Put all ingredients in a jar and shake well.

Note: Better if made the day before.

Mrs. Russell Day (Bobbie)

MISS JULIA'S THOUSAND ISLAND DRESSING   2 cups

To make 2 cups
1 cup real mayonnaise
⅓ cup chili sauce
⅓ cup sour cream
*2 Tablespoons chopped sweet
    pickle*

1 teaspoon celery salt
1 hardboiled egg, chopped

To make 20 cups
10 cups real mayonnaise
3⅓ cups chili sauce
3⅓ cups sour cream

1¼ cups chopped sweet pickle
3 Tablespoons celery salt
10 hardboiled eggs, chopped

To make 72 cups
9 quarts real mayonnaise
12 cups chili sauce
12 cups sour cream
4 cups chopped sweet pickle

¾ cup celery salt
*3 dozen hardboiled eggs,
    chopped*

Combine all ingredients and chill. Keeps for weeks in the refrigerator.

Miss Julia McGee
Rosedale, Mississippi

BLUE CHEESE DRESSING   2 cups

1 cup mayonnaise
1 cup sour cream
Juice of ½ lemon
Juice of 1 small onion

Salt to taste
Worcestershire to taste
**¼ to ½ pound of blue cheese,
    crumbled**

Mix first 6 ingredients and blend well. Add crumbled cheese and mix again.

Mrs. Buster Young (Fane)
Drew, Mississippi

POPPY OR CELERY SEED DRESSING   4 cups

1 cup sugar
2 teaspoons dry mustard
2 teaspoons salt
⅔ cup vinegar

3 teaspoons onion juice
2 cups oil
3 Tablespoons poppy or celery seed

Mix sugar, mustard, salt, and vinegar. Add onion juice. Add oil slowly. Continue to blend til thick. Add seed. Refrigerate. May serve over fruit.

Mrs. M. T. Blackwood (Jauweice)
Drew. Mississippi

FRUIT DRESSING   2 cups

½ cup sugar
1 teaspoon dry mustard
¼ teaspoon salt
1 teaspoon celery seeds

⅓ cup honey
1 Tablespoon lemon juice
4 Tablespoons vinegar
1 cup salad oil

Mix dry ingredients. Add honey, lemon juice and vinegar. Pour oil into mixture slowly, beating constantly. Great on fresh fruit.

Dianne Crews

Meats

FILET OF BEEF IN ASPIC

1 (4-pound) beef tenderloin
Salt

Freshly ground black pepper
Ground allspice

For The Aspic
2 quarts beef stock or broth
½ cup dry white vermouth
3 Tablespoons lemon juice
2 Tablespoons lime juice
1 teaspoon tarragon

1 bay leaf
Crushed shells of 4 eggs
4 egg whites, lightly beaten
3 to 4 envelopes unflavored
  gelatin

For The Garnish
2 very large ripe tomatoes,
  thinly sliced
12 basil leaves
1 lemon, thinly sliced

5 capers
Diced aspic
Springs of parsley

To Cook The Beef:
Preheat oven to 500°. Season beef by rubbing it with salt and pepper and a little allspice. Turn oven down to 225° and roast beef for 1 hour until meat thermometer registers 140°. Let meat stand until cool.

To Make Aspic:
Place beef stock in large saucepan. Add to it any juices that accumulated in pan that beef was roasted in. Add vermouth, lemon juice, lime juice, tarragon, bay leaf, crushed egg shells, and egg whites. Heat mixture slowly until it boils. As soon as egg whites froth up at surface, remove from heat. Strain broth through a lined sieve. You should have about 6½ cups. Remove 1 cup of broth to a clean saucepan and allow to cool completely. Soften 3 envelopes of gelatin in cool stock; then stir over medium heat until dissolved. Stir this into rest of stock. Pour about 2 cups of stock to depth of ¼-inch in a shallow flat-bottomed 13x9-inch pan for diced aspic. Refrigerate until set, then cut into dice. Select a serving platter large enough to hold the sliced beef and tomatoes and pour a layer of aspic into it, to a depth of ¼-inch. Refrigerate to set. Slice beef ⅛-inch to 3/16-inch thick. Arrange, overlapping down the center of the platter over the set aspic. Place sliced tomatoes in 2 overlapping rows on either side of beef. Tuck a basil leaf between each slice of tomato. Place lemon slices on top of the row of sliced beef, with a caper in center of each slice. Stir the aspic over large bowl of ice cubes until it appears soupy and is just about to set. Spoon it carefully over the beef and tomatoes. Refrigerate. Before serving, decorate edges of platter with diced aspic and parsley.

The Editors

Beef

STUFFED FILLET OF BEEF

8 to 10 servings

3 to 4½ pounds beef fillet,
   trimmed and tied with string
Salt and freshly ground black
   pepper

6 Tablespoons oil
2 Tablespoons chopped parsley
   for sprinkling

Stuffing
3 shallots
6½-ounces bacon
2 stalks celery, finely chopped
1½ pounds mushrooms, finely
   chopped

2¾ pounds tomatoes, seeded
   and chopped
Salt and freshly ground black
   pepper

Set the oven at 450°. Sprinkle the beef with salt and pepper. Heat the oil in a roasting pan until very hot and brown the meat well on all sides. Roast the meat in the oven for 11 minutes. Remove the meat and let cool.

For the Stuffing:
In a food processor, chop the shallots and bacon together to a fine paste. In a frying pan, heat the paste for 1 or 2 minutes. Add the chopped celery and mushrooms, mix well and add tomatoes, salt and pepper. Cook over high heat, stirring often, for 25 to 30 minutes until the moisture has evaporated. Taste for seasoning. Cool completely. When the fillet is cool, remove the strings. Slice in ¾ inch slices, leaving each slice attached at the base. Spread 1 to 2 tablespoons filling on each slice and press the fillet back into its original shape.

Wrap the beef in two layers of foil. The beef can be prepared ahead to this point and kept in the refrigerator. Store remaining stuffing in refrigerator. Remove the beef from the refrigerator and allow it to come to room temperature. Set the oven at 425°. Put the beef, still wrapped in foil, in a roasting tin and reheat for 15 minutes or until the stuffing is hot. Leave the beef wrapped in a warm place until ready to serve. Reheat the extra stuffing and spread a layer of it down the center of serving platter. Unwrap the beef, saving juices that escape, and set it on the stuffing on the serving platter. Spoon juices over the beef and sprinkle with chopped parsley before serving.

Mrs. John Tatum (Carol)

RIB EYE ROAST

4 to 8 pound rib eye roast   **Garlic salt**
Seasoned salt   **Worcestershire sauce**
Seasoned pepper   **Butter (not margarine)**

Let roast come to room temperature. Preheat oven to 500°. Rub roast with seasoned salt, seasoned pepper and garlic satl. Drizzle melted butter and Worcestershire sauce over roast. Put roast into shallow baking pan. Do not cover. Put roast in 500° oven. Cook exactly 5 minutes per pound for rare roast. For medium rare, cook 6 minutes per pound. Turn off oven. Do not open door. Leave roast in oven exactly 10 minutes more per pound. Remove from oven. Lightly cover with foil until ready to slice.

Mrs. Albert Simmons (Betty)
Meridian, Ms.

MARINATED ROAST   10-12 servings

4-5 pounds sirloin roast   **1½ Tablespoons Worcestershire**
1 teaspoon MSG   **sauce**
½ cup vinegar   **1 teaspoon prepared mustard**
⅓ cup catsup   **1 teaspoon salt**
2½ Tablespoons vegetable oil   **½ teaspoon pepper**
2½ Tablespoons soy sauce   **½ teaspoon fresh garlic, grated**

Sprinkle roast with MSG. Combine remaining ingredients; pour over meat. Marinate 3 hours turning 3 times. Remove marinade; place on rack in a shallow pan. Broil about 6 inches from heat turning and basting every 10 to 15 minutes. Cooking time about 45 minutes. Works the same on grill.

Mrs. C. E. Dunlap (Jane)

MARINATED ROAST BEEF (FOR SANDWICHES)   12-15 servings

5 pounds boneless beef roast   *Salt and pepper*

Marinade
1 cup red wine vinegar   **¼ teaspoon oregano**
1⅓ cups olive oil   **2 Tablespoons parsley, minced**
1 pod garlic   **1 bay leaf**
**½ teaspoon cracked black
 pepper**

Salt and pepper roast well. Bake uncovered in 350° oven for 2 hours or until done. Refrigerate until cold. Remove fat and slice as thinly as possible, ⅛-inch if you can talk the butcher into doing it for you. Mix all marinade ingredients and pour over roast. Store three days or more in flat covered container. This is great as hors d'oeuvres, for sandwiches, or in a tossed green salad. Marvelous for leftover roast also.

Mrs. James Goodman (Carolyn)

MOVIE ROAST   8 to 10 servings

4 to 6 pound loin roast   **Soy Sauce**
Garlic   **Honey**
Flour

Rub the roast with garlic and flour. Mix soy sauce and honey, totaling about a half a cup. Baste before going to the movie and again upon return. Cook in oven at 350°. With slow cooking, the roast retains its juices and the flavor improves; at 350° it should roast 3 hours for a 6 pound roast.

Note: I don't cut away much of the fat initially, because the combination of the fat and the sauce gives the roast a crispy delicious crust.

Mrs. Stanley Levingston (Sylvia)
Greenville, Mississippi

INDIVIDUAL BEEF WELLINGTONS · 6 servings

1 Tablespoon butter
6 (5-ounce) beef fillets (no fat)
6 Tablespoons red wine
1 cup beef consommé
½ pound mushrooms, minced

2 packages frozen puff patty
 shells, thawed
Salt and pepper
1 egg, well beaten

Melt butter, sear meat on each side. Pour in 2 Tablespoons wine and transfer to another container and chill. Meanwhile, cook the mushrooms in consommé and wine until tender and the liquid has evaporated. Chill this mixture. Separate the patty shells so that there are 2 for each fillet. Press the pastry with fingers until flat. Put 1/6 of the mushroom mixture in the center of a pastry, then a fillet, salt and pepper lightly. Fold pastry over steak, bringing up sides. Top with the matching pastry round, pinching the dough until each fillet is completely covered with pastry. Place on a rimmed sheet pan. Cover and refrigerate as long as overnight. Bake fillets at 400°. 12 minutes for rare, 16 minutes for medium and 20 minutes for well done. After baking them for 5 minutes, brush with egg to make them shiny and pretty. Serve hot with Marchand De Vin Sauce. (See Index)

Mrs. Karl Horn (Ruth)
Moss Point, Ms.

BEEF TENDERLOIN

8 pounds beef tenderloin
1 (5-ounce) bottle
 Worcestershire sauce
2 teaspoons garlic powder
½ cup margarine
Bacon strips

1 teaspoon salt
½ teaspoon pepper
Juice of 3 lemons
1 (6-ounce) can button
 mushrooms

Simmer ingredients to blend flavors. Wrap tenderloin with bacon strips. Baste well and place in 375° oven for 2 hours for medium rare roast. Continue to baste during cooking. Pour some of the basting over the beef when serving and use rest as gravy.

Note: A 4-pound roast will take 45 minutes at 375°.

Mrs. Doug Levingston (Barbara)
Mrs. H. L. Dilworth (Anne)

LOBSTER-STUFFED TENDERLOIN

8-10 servings

1 (3-4 pound) beef tenderloin
3 long lobster tails or 2
(8-ounce) frozen
1 Tablespoon margarine, melted
1½ teaspoons lemon juice

6 slices bacon, partially cooked
½ cup sliced green onion
½ cup margarine
½ cup dry white wine

Butterfly roast; boil lobster tails and remove from shells. Place lobster inside beef. Combine margarine and lemon juice. Drizzle over lobster. Tie the roast together. Place partially cooked bacon over roast. Preheat oven to 500°. Place roast in oven for 5 minutes. Reduce heat to 350°. Cook 10 minutes per pound for rare; 15 minutes for medium. Cook onions in margarine; add wine and garlic salt and serve over meat.

The Editors

LONDON BROIL

4 servings

1 (2-pound) flank steak
1 Tablespoon salad oil
2 teaspoons chopped parsley
1 clove garlic, crushed

1 teaspoon salt
1 teaspoon lemon juice
⅛ teaspoon pepper

Trim fat from steak. Combine remaining ingredients. Brush half of mixture over one side of steak; let stand for 30 minutes to one hour. Place steak, oiled side up, on a pan lined with tin foil and broil 4 inches from heat for 5 minutes. Turn steak and brush with remaining mixture. Broil 4 to 5 minutes longer. Slice thinly on the diagonal across the grain. This steak will be rare—the only way London Broil should be served.

Mrs. Bill Parker (Jo)

HAMBURGER STEAK   4 servings

1½ Tablespoons butter
3 green onions, chopped
2-pounds ground round or
   sirloin

1 teaspoon salt
⅛ teaspoon pepper
2 Tablespoons butter
½ cup dry red (or white) wine

Melt 1½ tablespoons butter in a small skillet and sauté green onions. Place meat in a large bowl and add green onions - butter mixture, salt and pepper. Mix gently. Shape into 4 thick patties. Heat 2 tablespoons butter over moderately high heat and cook patties 4 to 8 minutes, depening on desired doneness. Turn once during cooking and remove to warm plate. Pour off excess fat, add wine and cook stirring constantly until pan juices are reduced to 1½ to 2 tablespoons. Spoon over hot patty when served. Cut mustard butter into four pieces and place one on each patty, so that it melts as eaten.

Mustard Butter
½ cup butter, room
   temperature
2 Tablespoons chopped fresh
   parsley

⅛ teaspoon dried tarragon
1 Tablespoon Dijon mustard

Heat butter, until creamy. Add rest of ingredients and mix well. Place in 10-ounce custard cup or similar mold. chill until firm.

Mrs. Robert Tibbs (Pat)

SHISH KABOB

Any tender beef for grilling,
   cubed
Potatoes, cubed the size of
   meat

Onions
Green peppers
Tomatoes
Mushrooms

Marinate meat for 4 to 8 hours. Cook potatoes almost done. Skewer meat alternating with vegetables. Cook over medium hot coals.

Marinade
1 cup oil
¾ cup soy sauce
½ cup lemon juice
¼ cup Worcestershire sauce

¼ cup prepared mustard
1 to 2 teaspoons pepper
2 cloves garlic, minced

Mr. and Mrs. Jim Walker

CHINESE PEPPER STEAK

1½ pounds sirloin steak
¼ cup oil
1 clove garlic, crushed
½ teaspoon salt
1 teaspoon ground ginger
½ teaspoon pepper
3 medium bell peppers, sliced
2 medium onions, sliced
¼ cup soy sauce

½ teaspoon sugar
1 (10¾-ounce) can beef bouillon
1 (8-ounce) can water chestnuts, sliced
1 Tablespoon cornstarch
1 cup water
4 green onions, chopped

Freeze steak for one hour. Remove steak from freezer and cut in ¼-inch strips. Heat oil in electric skillet to 350°. Add garlic, salt, ginger, and pepper to oil. Sauté until garlic is golden brown. Add steak and brown lightly. Remove steak from skillet. Add bell peppers and onions. Cook 3 to 5 minutes. Return steak to skillet. Add soy sauce, sugar, bouillon, and chestnuts. Dissolve cornstarch in water. Add cornstarch and green onions to skillet. Simmer at 250° for 30 minutes to 1 hour. Serve over hot rice.

Note: Very good served over wild rice.

Mrs. Steve Davis (Debbie)

SHERRIED BEEF
6-8 servings

3 pounds stew beef or round steak, cut in 1½-inch cube
½ of (1-ounce) dry onion soup mix
2 (10¾-ounce) cans cream of mushroom soup

¾ cup sherry
½ cup sautéed canned mushrooms

For Rice Consomme
1 cup rice
1 can water
1 (10¾-ounce) can beef consomme

¼ cup butter

Combine all ingredients in large casserole. Cover and bake at 325° for 3 hours. Serve over consomme rice. For consomme rice: Combine all ingredients and cover and bake 30 to 40 minutes in 350° oven.

Mrs. Paul Warrington (Pat)

STIR-FRIED BEEF

4-6 servings

*1 (8-ounce) flank steak or
tenderloin*

#1 Mixture

1 Tablespoon soy sauce
*1 teaspoon rice wine (scotch or
whiskey)*
5 Tablespoons water
2 teaspoons cornstarch
1 Tablespoon oil

3 cups oil for frying
*6 (1-inch) sections of green
onion*
6 slices of gingeroot
*½ Tablespoon rice wine
(scotch)*

#2 Mixture

*1½ Tablespoons oyster sauce
or soy sauce*
¼ teaspoon MSG
¼ teaspoon sugar

¼ teaspoon black pepper
¼ teaspoon sesame oil
1½ Tablespoons water
1 teaspoon cornstarch

Cut beef across the grain in thin slices; mix with first 4 ingredients and let stand 1 hour, then stir in 1 Tablespoon oil. Heat oil and deep fry meat over medium heat for 20 seconds-remove and drain. Drain oil from skillet all except 2 Tablespoons. Reheat and stir fry green onion and ginger until fragrant. Add beef slice and rice wine and number 2 mixture; toss lightly to mix and remove to serving plate.

Lock and Amy Gore
Merigold, Ms.

INTOXICATED BEEF

4-6 servings

1½ cups water
¼ cup packed brown sugar
3-ounces soy sauce
*¼ cup bourbon or smooth
whiskey*

*2 pounds boneless chuck, cut in
3 pieces*

For marinade, mix together all ingredients except meat. The night before cooking, cut meat in 3 pieces. Sprinkle with tenderizer on both sides. Cover with waxed paper and refrigerate overnight. The next day, soak meat in marinade for 6 hours. Broil medium rare.

Mrs. Buster Young (Fane)
Drew, Mississippi

BARBECUED BRISKET
10 servings

1 5 or 6 pound beef brisket
3 ounces liquid smoke
5 Tablespoons Worcestershire
   sauce
6 ounces barbecue sauce
Celery Salt

Garlic Salt
Onion Salt
2 Tablespoons all-purpose flour
½ cup water
Salt and pepper

Sprinkle liquid smoke and salts over brisket placed in a baking dish sprayed with non-stick cooking spray, and refrigerate overnight. When ready to bake, sprinkle with Worcestershire sauce, salt and pepper—place foil loosely on top. Cook at 250° for 5 hours, uncover and pour barbecue sauce over meat. Cook without foil for another hour—remove to platter and let cool before slicing. Remove fat from sauce remaining in dish. Add flour and water to sauce and stir. Cook until sauce thickens. Serve sauce hot with meat.

Note: Great with rice or on sandwiches with slaw.

Mrs. Bill Parker (Jo)

CORNED BEEF BRISKET IN FOIL
10-12 servings

2 oranges, sliced
2 medium onions, sliced
4 stalks celery, halved
2 cloves garlic, quartered
2 teaspoons dill seed

1 teaspoon rosemary
12 whole cloves
1 stick cinnamon
2 bay leaves
4 pounds beef brisket

Arrange half of seasonings on large sheet of heavy duty metal foil. Place meat on top. Add remaining seasonings. Seal foil package. Leave room for juices to collect. Place in shallow pan. Bake for 3½ to 4 hours at 325°. Slice thin.

Note: May be cooked in a covered casserole dish. It will cook faster and have less juice.

Mrs. F. B. Alyward (Eloise)

SAVORY FLANK STEAK

4 servings

1 (1½ to 2 pounds) flank
  steak
Salt and pepper
2 Tablespoons parsley,
  chopped
1 clove garlic, minced
⅓ cup Parmesan cheese,
  grated

2 Tablespoons shortening
1 (10¾-ounce) can tomato soup
1 can water
1 teaspoon vinegar
1 teaspoon dried oregano,
  crushed

Sprinkle one side of steak with salt, pepper, parsley, garlic and cheese. Roll steak tightly, jelly-roll fashion. Secure with string. In large skillet, add shortening and brown steak on all sides. Dilute soup with water. Combine soup, vinegar, and oregano. Pour over steak. Simmer covered 1½ to 2 hours or until tender. Serve with noodles or spaghetti.

Mrs. F. B. Alyward (Eloise)

BEEF BARBECUE

10-12 servings

4-pound lean beef
1 (1-pound 14-ounce) can
  tomatoes
2 medium onions, chopped
1 quart water
1 Tablespoon chili powder

1 cup catsup
½ cup vinegar
½ cup Worcestershire sauce
Salt and pepper to taste
Garlic powder to taste
Liquid smoke to taste

Cut beef into chunks. Combine all ingredients in heavy pot. Simmer uncovered over low heat for 5 to 6 hours or until beef falls into shreds. The mixture should be thick. Spoon onto hamburger buns.

Note: Do not substitute crockpot for saucepan.

Variation: Country style rolls may be used for hamburger buns. Chuck roast is perfect for lean beef.

Mrs. Billy Latham (Sue)

ANN LANDER'S MEAT LOAF   6 servings

2 pounds ground round steak
2 eggs
1½ cups bread crumbs
¾ cup catsup
1 teaspoon MSG

½ cup warm water
1 (1-ounce) package dry onion
   soup mix
2 strips bacon, optional
1 (8-ounce) can tomato sauce

Mix steak, eggs, bread crumbs, catsup, MSG, water, and soup mix thoroughly. Pour in loaf pan. Cover with 2 strips of bacon if desired. Pour tomato sauce over mixture. Bake 1 hour at 350°.

Mrs. Robert Miller (Barbara)

SWISS MEAT LOAF   6-7 servings

2 pounds ground chuck
1½ cups Swiss cheese,
   shredded
2 eggs, beaten
½ cup chopped onion
½ cup chopped green pepper

1½ teaspoons salt
½ teaspoon pepper
1 teaspoon celery salt
½ teaspoon paprika
2½ cups milk
1 cup dry bread crumbs

Mix all of the ingredients in the order listed. Press into one large greased loaf pan. Bake uncovered for 1½ hours at 350°.

Mrs. Bert Hayes (Cindy)

CARNE GUISADA   6-8 servings

2 round steaks, cubed
Vegetable oil
1 Tablespoon all-purpose flour
4 Tablespoons chopped bell
   pepper
4 Tablespoons chopped onion
1 small tomato, chopped

3 cloves garlic, chopped
¾ to 1 teaspoon cumin seed
⅛ teaspoon pepper
1 (8-ounce) can tomato sauce
1 (16-ounce) can Rotel
   tomatoes
1 Tablespoon salt

Brown round steak in small amount of oil. After it is browned, coat with flour and add other ingredients. Simmer several hours until sauce is thick. Serve rolled up in a warm flour tortilla or over rice. The name of this dish means, simply, stewed meat.

Mrs. Jim Tims (Frances)

BEEF CHOP SUEY

6 to 8 servings

1½ pounds stew beef, cut into bite-sized pieces
1 Tablespoon oil
1 large onion, chopped
4 stems celery, sliced crosswise
1 teaspoon garlic powder
Salt to taste
2 (15-ounce) cans bean sprouts
1 (7-ounce) can bamboo shoots
1 (6-ounce) can mushrooms, stems and pieces
1 (7-ounce) can sliced water chestnuts (optional)
3 large Tablespoons soy sauce
2 large Tablespoons molasses
1 teaspoon MSG
1 Tablespoon cornstarch
1 cup cooked rice

Brown meat in oil. Add onions and celery and sauté. Add garlic powder and salt to taste. Add undrained bean sprouts, bamboo shoots, mushrooms, and water chestnuts. Let come to a boil again. Lower heat to medium and add soy sauce, molasses, and MSG. Let simmer 20 to 30 minutes covered. Add cornstarch in enough water to dissolve. Stir into Chop Suey mixture and serve over crispy Chinese noodles or steamed rice.

Mrs. Vernon Springer (Jimmy Nell)
Drew, Mississippi

15 MINUTE STROGANOFF

5-6 servings

1 pound round steak, ¼ inch thick
⅔ cup water
1 (3-ounce) can broiled mushrooms, sliced
1 (1-ounce) envelope dry onion soup mix
1 cup sour cream
2 Tablespoons all-purpose flour
1 (8-ounce) package egg noodles

Trim fat from meat and reserve. Cut meat diagonally across in very thin strips. Heat fat in skillet until there is 3 Tablespoons melted fat. Remove trimmings. Brown meat. Add ⅔ cup water and mushrooms with liquid. Stir in soup mix. Heat to boiling. Blend sour cream and flour. Add to hot mixture. Cook, stirring continuously, until mixture thickens. Sauce will be thin. Serve over cooked noodles.

Note: Butter may be added to cooking of the trimmings.

Mrs. Paul Warrington (Pat)

BEEF STROGANOFF

1½ pounds sirloin steak
2 Tablespoons all-purpose flour
½ teaspoon salt
½ teaspoon pepper
2 Tablespoons butter
½ cup onions
1 cup mushrooms

1 clove garlic
3 Tablespoons all-purpose flour
1 Tablespoon tomato paste
1 (10¾-ounce) can beef broth
1 cup sour cream
2 Tablespoons cooking sherry
1 (8-ounce) package noodles

Cut meat in 1-inch strips. Roll in flour, salt, and pepper. Brown meat in butter. Add onions, mushrooms, and garlic. Cook until tender. Take meat mixture out of pan. Brown flour. Add tomato paste, broth, and stir until thick. Put meat mixture back in pan. Simmer until tender. Add sour cream and cooking sherry. Simmer for a few minutes. Cook noodles according to directions. Serve meat and gravy over hot noodles.

Note: May need to add more butter when browning flour.

Mrs. John Pressgrove (Jackie)

INSIDE OUT RAVIOLI
8-10 servings

1 pound ground beef
1 medium onion, chopped
1 clove of garlic, minced
1 Tablespoon salad oil
1 (10-ounce) package chopped
  spinach
1 (16-ounce) jar spaghetti
  sauce with mushrooms
1 (8-ounce) can tomato sauce
1 (6-ounce) can tomato paste

½ teaspoon salt
½ teaspoon pepper
1 (8-ounce) package shell
  macaroni, cooked
1 cup shredded sharp Cheddar
  cheese
½ cup soft bread crumbs
2 eggs, well beaten
¼ cup oil

Brown beef, onion and garlic in oil. Cook spinach and drain. Reserve liquid, add water to make 1 cup. Stir together spinach, liquid, spaghetti sauce, tomato sauce, tomato paste, salt and pepper. Simmer 10 minutes. Combine spinach mixture and browned beef mixture. Spread noodles into a 3-quart casserole. Top with sauce. Bake at 350° for 30 minutes. Let stand for 10 minutes before serving.

Mrs. Shep Haaga (Susan)

ROLLADEN   4 servings

*4 large, thin slices flank steak
   (about ¼-inch thick and
   12x6-inches, tenderized)*
*Salt and freshly ground pepper
   to taste*
6 teaspoons prepared mustard
2¼ cups finely chopped onion

4 strips bacon, cooked
*4 dill pickle spears, chopped
   and divided into 4 equal
   portions*
¼ cup margarine or butter
1 Tablespoon paprika
2 cups beef stock

Place the pieces of meat on a flat surface and sprinkle with salt and pepper. Spread each piece with approximately 1½ teaspoons of mustard, then sprinkle each piece with 3 tablespoons of chopped onion. Crumble one piece of bacon on each piece of meat. Sprinkle pickle pieces equally on each portion of meat. Roll the beef top to bottom, enclosing the filling. Tie each roll securely with string or use toothpick. Heat the butter or margarine in a skillet and add the remaining onion. Cook, stirring until golden, then sprinkle with paprika. Cook, stirring about 7 seconds, no longer. Add the beef rolls and turn them in the paprika mixture until well coated on all sides. Add 1 cup of the beef stock and cover. Cook over medium heat about 30 minutes. Make sure that meat does not burn or stick. Turn the meat and add ½ cup of stock. Cover and cook 30 minutes longer. Add the remaining stock, turn the meat, and continue cooking 15 to 30 minutes, or until the meat is fork tender. Serve with rice and use the stock as gravy.

Mrs. Don Aylward (Lee)

TACO CASSEROLE   4-6 servings

*1-pound ground beef (or
   chuck), cooked*
*1 (1¾-ounce) envelope taco
   seasoning*
1 (14½-ounce) can tomatoes

*1 package yellow rice (cooked
   as directed)*
*1 (10¾-ounce) can Cheddar
   cheese soup*

Mix together all ingredients and heat in casserole dish until bubbly.

Top casserole with favorite toppings.
Shredded lettuce
Diced tomatoes
Chopped onion
Chopped olives

Shredded cheese
Crushed corn chips
*Last but not least, add taco
   sauce*

Mrs. Wayne Walley (Kathy)

SOUR CREAM ENCHILADA CASSEROLE

8 servings

Step #1

1 cup water

2 Tablespoons Picante sauce

12 tortillas

Combine water and 2 tablespoons Picante sauce in large shallow dish. Place tortillas in sauce mixture; let stand 5 minutes. Drain.

Step #2

2 pounds ground round

1 onion, chopped

1 teaspoon salt

1/8 teaspoon pepper

2 teaspoons cumin

4 Tablespoons chili pepper

1 teaspoon garlic powder

3/4 cup ripe olives, sliced

1/2 cup Picante sauce

Cook beef and onion until brown; drain. Stir in salt, pepper, cumin, chili powder, garlic powder, olives, and Picante sauce. Simmer 20 minutes.

Step #3

1/4 cup butter

2 Tablespoons all-purpose flour

1 1/2 cups milk

1 (16-ounce) carton sour cream

2 cups Cheddar cheese, shredded

Melt butter in saucepan—add flour and stir until smooth. Cook 1 minute stirring constantly. Gradually add milk; cook over medium heat. Stir often. Cook until thickened. Remove from heat. Add sour cream. Place 1/2 tortillas in 13x9x2-inch baking dish. Pour half of sour cream mixture and then half of meat mixture. Add half of cheese. Repeat layers. Bake at 375° for 25 minutes.

Mrs. Terry Barron (Lynn)

CHALUPA
4-6 servings

1 large bag tortilla chips
1 pound ground beef
1 (1¾-ounce) package taco
  seasoning
1 (10-ounce) can Rotel
  tomatoes, puréed
1 (15-ounce) can refried beans
4 tomatoes, chopped
2 (5¾-ounce) cans black olives,
  chopped

1 large onion, chopped
1 (3-ounce) can chili peppers,
  chopped
Shredded lettuce (½ to ¾
  head)
1½ cups grated Cheddar
  cheese
Sour cream (optional)

Layer ingredients in order given in a 11x9x2-inch pan. Brown ground beef and add dry taco seasoning. Stir to mix well. Heat refried beans in saucepan and add puréed Rotel tomatoes. Heat until bubbly. Pour this combination over ground beef and proceed layering in order. Bake at 350° for 10 to 15 minutes until cheese melts. Serve with extra chips. Also can be served as an appetizer.

Mrs. Bob Buchanan (Sharon)

ZUCCHINI CHILI RELLONAS
6 servings

2 pounds zucchini, sliced and
  steamed until tender
4 eggs, beaten
½ cup milk
1 teaspoon salt
2 teaspoons baking powder
3 Tablespoons all-purpose flour

½ cup chopped parsley
8 ounces canned chili
1 pound Jack cheese,
  shredded
4 slices sandwich bread, cubed
¼ cup margarine, melted

Butter a 9x13-inch dish. Layer half the bread cubes in the dish. Mix zucchini, eggs, milk, salt, baking powder, flour, parsley, chili and cheese. Pour mixture over bread cubes. Place remaining bread cubes over mixture; pour margarine over bread cubes. Bake 30 minutes at 325°. Use as a main dish with a green salad.

Mrs. W. J. DuBard (Bobbie)
Drew, Mississippi

MEXI-MEAT CORNBREAD

6-8 servings

1 (8½-ounce) can
  cream-style corn
2 eggs
1½ cups self-rising corn meal

½ cup bacon drippings
1 cup buttermilk
1 teaspoon soda

Mix corn, eggs, meal, drippings, buttermilk, and soda. Divide mixture into half. Pour half in to a large greased baking dish.

1 pound ground beef
1 medium onion, chopped
½ pound Cheddar cheese,
  shredded

2 hot peppers, chopped

Brown beef and drain. Layer beef, onion, cheese and peppers in baking dish. Cover with remaining half of batter. Bake 45 minutes at 350°.

Mrs. Brady Cole (Rosalie)

VENISON CHILI

6-8 servings

2 Tablespoons butter
1 large onion, chopped
2½ pounds venison or ground
  beef
2 (16-ounce) cans tomatoes
2 (10¾-ounce) cans tomato
  soup
1 teaspoon paprika

½ teaspoon cayenne
1 bay leaf
1 Tablespoons chili powder or
  more
1 clove garlic, mashed
1 teaspoon salt
1 (15½-ounce) can kidney
  beans

Sauté onion, add meat and brown. Add all other ingredients except beans, salt and garlic. Cook about an hour. The last 30 minutes add beans and garlic mashed with salt.

Mrs. Don Blackwood (Suzan)

VENISON STEAK
4 servings

2 medium venison round
  steaks
Salt and pepper
¼ cup all-purpose flour
2 Tablespoons oil
½ green pepper, thinly sliced

1 medium onion, thinly sliced
1 (4-ounce) can mushrooms,
  sliced
1 (10¾-ounce) can beef gravy
¼ cup red wine

Salt and pepper steaks. Cut into serving size pieces. Flour lightly and brown in oil. Drain. Layer meat, green pepper, onion, and mushrooms in skillet or baking dish. Cover with gravy and wine. Bake at 350° for 1½ to 2 hours or until meat is tender.

Mrs. Phillip Rizzo (Ramona)

SCALLOPINI AL LIMONE
4 servings

1½ pounds veal scallops (or
  2½ pounds boneless
  chicken). Cut ⅜-inch thick
  and tenderized until ¼-inch
  thick.
Salt
Pepper
All-purpose flour

2 Tablespoons real butter,
  softened
3 Tablespoons olive oil
¾ cup beef bouillon
6 paper thin lemon slices
1 Tablespoon lemon juice
2 Tablespoons butter

Season the meat with salt and pepper, then dredge in flour. In a heavy 10-inch to 12-inch skillet, melt 2 tablespoons butter with 3 tablespoons olive oil over moderate heat. When foam subsides, add meat, 4 to 5 pieces at a time and sauté for about 2 minutes on each side or until golden brown. Transfer scallops to a heated platter. Pour off almost all fat from skillet, leaving a thin film on bottom. Add ½ cup beef bouillon and boil briskly for 1 to 2 minutes, stirring constantly and scrapping any browned bits in pan. Return meat to skillet and arrange lemon slices on top. Cover and simmer over low heat for 10 to 15 minutes or until tender. To serve, transfer the scallops to a heated platter and surround with lemon slices. Add remaining ¼ cup beef bouillon to skillet juices and boil until reduced to a syrupy glaze. Add 1 tablespoon lemon juice and cook, stirring for 1 minute. Remove from heat, swirl in 2 Tablespoons butter and pour sauce over scallops.

Mrs. C. L. Beckham, Jr. (Marie)

TEXAS RATTLESNAKE CHILI
12 servings

4 Tablespoons oil
1 cup chopped onion
1 cup chopped bell pepper
2 cloves garlic, minced
2 pounds lean ground beef
2 cups cubed rattlesnake meat
  or chicken*
1 to 2 teaspoons cayenne
  pepper

4 Tablespoons chili powder
4 teaspoons salt
4 (16-ounce) cans Rotel
  tomatoes, undrained
2 (6-ounce) cans tomato paste
4 cups water
4 cups (12-ounce) shell
  macaroni

In a large Dutch oven, heat oil and sauté onion, bell pepper, and garlic until tender but not brown. Add ground beef and rattlesnake meat; brown and cook until done, about 10 minutes. Stir in spices, tomatoes, and tomato paste. Bring to a boil, then reduce heat and simmer about 2 hours. Before serving, add water and return chili to a boil. Stir in the uncooked pasta. Continue boiling, stirring frequently for 10 to 15 minutes or until pasta is tender.

*I use chicken.

Mrs. Jim Tims (Frances)

LIVER CREOLE
4 servings

4 slices bacon
1 pound beef liver
3 Tablespoons all-purpose flour
1/3 cup green pepper, chopped

1 (16-ounce) can tomatoes
1½ teaspoons salt
½ teaspoon chili powder
1/8 teaspoon cayenne pepper

Fry bacon until crisp. Remove bacon from skillet and drain all but 3 Tablespoons of fat. Add liver, flour, peppers, tomatoes, salt, chili powder, and cayenne pepper. Cover tightly. Simmer for 20 minutes. Garnish with bacon.

Mrs. Bob Nance (Barbara)

MOUSSAKA

4-6 servings

2 Tablespoons butter
1 cup chopped onion
1½ pounds lamb, ground
1 clove garlic, minced
½ teaspoon oregano
1 teaspoon basil leaves
½ teaspoon cinnamon

2 (8-ounce) cans tomato sauce
2 eggplants, about 1 pound
   4-ounce size
1 teaspoon salt
Pepper to taste
½ cup butter, melted

Cream Sauce
2 Tablespoons butter
2 Tablespoons all-purpose flour
½ teaspoon salt
Dash of pepper
2 cups milk

2 eggs
½ cup grated Cheddar cheese
2 Tablespoons dry bread
   crumbs

Sauté onion, lamb, garlic for 10 minutes. Add herbs, spices, tomato sauce and boil. Simmer ½ hour uncovered. Slice eggplant crosswise ½-inch thick. Place in pan and sprinkle with salt and drizzle with butter. Broil 4 minutes on each side. For the sauce: Melt butter, stir in flour, salt and pepper. Add milk and boil. Beat eggs. Add a little hot cream to eggs and return mixture to saucepan. Mix well and set aside. Grease a 2½ quart baking dish and layer eggplant and cheese. Stir bread crumbs into meat sauce and spoon over eggplant, sprinkle with cheese. Layer rest of eggplant slices. Pour cream sauce over all. Sprinkle with cheese. Bake 35 to 40 minutes at 350°.

Mrs. Vernon Shelton (Pam)
Drew, Mississippi

Lamb

GRILLED LEG OF LAMB
6 servings

1 (5-6 pound) leg of lamb,
  boned and butterflied
3 Tablespoons fresh lemon juice
2 cloves garlic, minced
1 Tablespoon rosemary,
  crushed

½ teaspoon dry mustard
2 Tablespoons Worcestershire
  sauce
2 Tablespoons vegetable oil
1 teaspoon soy sauce
½ teaspoon pepper

Put lamb in large dish. Sprinkle ingredients in order given on both sides of lamb. Cover and refrigerate overnight, turning once. Cook lamb over charcoal, basting with marinade. Cook about 45 minutes over medium hot coals.

Mrs. C. E. Dunlap (Jane)

BROILED LEG OF LAMB
6 to 8 servings

6 to 7 pounds leg of lamb

Marinade
⅔ cup olive oil
3 Tablespoons lemon juice
1 teaspoon salt
½ teaspoon freshly ground
  black pepper

1 teaspoon dried oregano
3 bay leaves, coarsely
  crumbled
1 cup thinly sliced onion
⅓ cup red wine

Cut lamb off bone at thinest point so meat lies flat. Cut away fat and separate thickest clumps of meat with knife to make meat lie even flatter. Marinate lamb for 12 to 24 hours. Turn meat over every few hours. Broil lamb either on a rack in broiler or over charcoal, starting with fat side down and basting from time to time with marinade. Cook approximately 20 minutes on one side and 15 minutes on other. Should be pink in thickest part. Carve and serve hot. HINT: Marinade works best at room temperature, so if you must refrigerate, take out and let it return to room temperature before cooking.

Mrs. Jeffrey Levingston (Barbara)

PORK TENDERLOIN

2 whole pork tenderloins, fat
   removed
¼ cup soy sauce
2½ Tablespoons red wine
1 Tablespoon brown sugar

1 Tablespoon honey
½ teaspoon cinnamon
1 clove garlic, crushed
1 green onion, chopped

Combine soy sauce, wine, sugar, honey, cinnamon, garlic and onion. Coat meat completely. Cover and let stand at room temperature 1 hour or refrigerate overnight, turning to keep coated. Drain and save juice. Bake in preheated 350° oven about 45 minutes. Baste during baking. Cool and slice.

Mrs. Howard Grittman (Ann)

STIR-FRIED PORK   4 servings

½ pound lean pork
2 cups Chinese lettuce
2 green peppers
1 cup onions, diced
1 or 2 slices fresh ginger root

1 Tablespoon soy sauce
1 teaspoon sugar
½ teaspoon salt
2 or 3 Tablespoons oil

Dice pork, lettuce, green peppers, and onions. Mince ginger root, then combine with soy sauce, sugar and salt. Heat oil and stir-fry pork until golden, about 3 or 4 minutes. Add onions and stir-fry ½ minute. Add peppers and stir-fry 1 minute. Add lettuce and stir-fry 1 minute. Add ginger, soy sauce mixture and stir-fry to blend flavors, about 1 to 2 minutes.

Mrs. Stanley Levingston (Sylvia)
Greenville, Mississippi

HONEY GRILLED PORK CHOPS   8 servings

8 (1-inch) pork chops
1 (10-ounce) jar of honey

⅓ cup soy sauce

Mix honey and soy sauce as a marinade. Marinate pork chops for 24 hours. Cook on outside grill.

Mrs. Barry Sullivan (Betty)

SWEET AND SOUR PORK CHOPS

8 servings

2 Tablespoons cooking oil
1 teaspoon salt
1 clove garlic, crushed
1 onion, sliced
1 bell pepper, finely chopped
½ cup frozen pineapple juice
    thawed or ¾ cup canned
    juice

½ cup wine vinegar
½ cup brown sugar
1 teaspoon soy sauce
8 thick center cut pork chops

Sauté in oil the onion, bell pepper, and garlic. Add salt. Add pineapple juice, vinegar, sugar and soy sauce. Cook about 1 minute. Marinate chops in sauce overnight or at least 8 hours before grilling or baking. Baste with sauce while cooking.

Mrs. Roy L. Collins (Linda)

MARINATED PORK TENDERLOIN

4 servings

1½ to 2 pound pork
    tenderloin
½ cup bourbon

½ cup soy sauce
½ cup **Worcestershire sauce**

Mix liquids and pour over meat. Place in refrigerator to marinate for several days, turning occasionally. Cook over medium coals, with foil underneath, for 1 hour, basting regularly.

Mrs. Donald Ensenat (Taylor)
New Orleans, La.

MARINATED GRILLED PORK CHOPS

4-6 servings

¼ cup lemon juice
2 Tablespoons vegetable oil
3 cloves garlic, minced
1 teaspoon salt

¼ teaspoon thyme
¼ teaspoon oregano
¼ teaspoon pepper
6 pork chops, 1-inch thick

Make a marinade out of first seven ingredients. Pour marinade over pork chops. Cover and refrigerate 12 hours. Remove pork chops and save marinade. Grill chops over hot coals 30 minutes on each side. Baste with reserved marinade.

Mrs. C. E. Dunlap (Jane)

PAELLA
12 to 14 servings

2 small fryers (legs, thighs and breasts or 10 breasts)
½ cup vegetable oil
2 thin pork chops, torn into small pieces
3 or 4 slices ham, torn into small pieces
¼ cup minced onion
1 clove garlic, minced
1 tomato, peeled and cubed
Ground red pepper, to taste

1 (16-ounce) can green beans, drained
1 (8½-ounce) can artichoke hearts, drained and cut in half
1 cup frozen lima beans
4 chicken bouillon cubes
1 cup long grain rice
Pinch of saffron
18 to 20 shrimp, peeled and uncooked

Brown chicken pieces in oil, slowly; add pork and ham and cook slowly. Add red pepper. Add green beans, artichoke hearts and lima beans; simmer, covered a few minutes. Add 4 cups water with bouillon cubes. When this boils, add rice and saffron. When rice is tender; add shrimp and cook 6 to 8 minutes. If it seems dry, add a little more water.

Mrs. Fred Baker (Mae)
Greenville, Mississippi

SKILLET SWEET AND SOUR PORK
4 servings

1½ pounds lean pork, cubed
1 (20-ounce) can pineapple chunks
¼ cup brown sugar
2 Tablespoons cornstarch
¼ cup vinegar

2 to 3 Tablespoons soy sauce
½ teaspoon salt
1 small bell pepper, cut into small strips
¼ cup thinly sliced onion

Brown pork in a small amount of hot oil. Add ½ cup water; cover and simmer (do not boil) until tender. Drain pineapple, reserving syrup. Combine sugar and cornstarch. Add pineapple syrup, vinegar, soy sauce and salt. Mix and add to pork. Cook and stir until it thickens. Add pineapple, green pepper, and onions. Cook 2 to 3 minutes. Serve over rice or chow mein noodles.

Mrs. Buster Young (Fane)
Drew, Ms.

SWEET AND SOUR PORK

4 servings

*1 pound boneless pork, cut
into one-inch cubes,
marinated overnight*

Marinade
2 Tablespoons soy sauce   *2 Tablespoons Sherry*
2 teaspoons sugar

Coating
1 beaten egg   *4 Tablespoons water*
½ cup all-purpose flour   *½ teaspoon salt*

Sauce
1 clove garlic or   *½ cup sugar*
2 slices ginger root, finely   *½ cup vinegar*
chopped   *¼ teaspoon salt*
½ to 1 cup sliced vegetables   *2 Tablespoons oil*
(green pepper, carrots,   *1½ Tablespoons cornstarch*
onions, pineapple chunks)   *½ cup water or chicken broth*

Heat oil for sauce in skillet or wok, add garlic and stir-fry. Add vegetables and stir-fry until slightly softened. Add next 6 ingredients. Set aside. Coat pork with coating and deep fry in hot oil until golden brown (2 batches). Place pork in warm oven while you heat sauce. Add pork to hot sauce just long enough to heat, if it is not hot. Serve immediately with cooked rice.

Note: Sweet and sour shrimp may be made in this same way. The above coating recipe may be used for deep fried vegetables out of the garden, even onion rings. Don't allow them to sit in coating too long, however, as it will become watery.

Mrs. Richard Cole (Wendy)

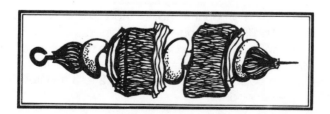

ORIENTAL SPAGHETTI WITH PORK   4-6 servings

1 pound box linguine, cooked and drained
1 pound pork cut into strips, tenderloin if available
½ onion, medium to large, cut into strips
½ stalk celery, sliced into small pieces
1 large green pepper, sliced into strips
½ cup soy sauce
2 pinches MSG
¼ teaspoon garlic powder
1 scallion stalk, chopped

Pre-cook linguine as directed on box, then rinse. Add a little oil to the pasta and refrigerate. In a large frying pan or wok cook the pork strips slowly. When the pork is thoroughly cooked, add celery, onions and green peppers. Toss and cook briefly—the vegetables must stay crisp. Reduce heat a little and add linguine, soy sauce, MSG, and garlic powder, continually tossing until all ingredients are blended well and the cooked linguine is heated through. Garnish with chopped scallions and serve immediately with soy sauce on the side for those who prefer more.

Note: This recipe is a specialty of the house at Salas' Restaurant in Newport, Rhode Island, originating from Guam.

Mrs. Richard Cole (Wendy)

WILD RICE AND SAUSAGE CASSEROLE   6-8 servings

⅔ cup wild rice
1½ pounds sausage (mild or hot)
1 (10¾-ounce) can chicken and rice soup (undiluted)
1 (3-ounce) can sliced mushrooms
½ cup water
1 teaspoon salt
½ teaspoon pepper
1 small bay leaf, crushed
¼ cup chopped onion
⅛ teaspoon garlic salt
⅛ teaspoon paprika

Cook rice and set aside. Cook sausage and drain off fat. Add remaining ingredients to sausage. Combine sausage mixture and rice. Place in casserole dish. Bake at 325° for one hour.

Mrs. Paul Mullins (Libba)

SPAGHETTI ORIENTAL   6 servings

½ pound ground beef*
½ pound pork bulk sausage*
1 medium green pepper
2 cups hot cooked spaghetti
  (about 4 ounces uncooked)
1 can (16-ounces) Chinese
  vegetables, drained
1 can (10¾-ounces) condensed
  cream of shrimp soup
1 can (8-ounce) water
  chestnuts, drained and sliced

1 can (4½-ounce) mushroom
  stems and pieces, drained
½ cup water
1 small onion, finely chopped
  (about ¼ cup)
1 teaspoon salt
¾ cup shredded sharp
  Cheddar cheese (about 3
  ounces)

Heat oven to 375°. Cook and stir ground beef and pork bulk sausage until light brown, 15 to 20 minutes; drain. Slice 3 rings from green pepper; reserve rings for garnish. Chop remaining green pepper. Stir chopped green pepper and remaining ingredients except cheese into meat. Pour into ungreased 2-quart casserole; sprinkle with cheese. Bake uncovered 30 minutes. Top with green pepper rings; bake 5 minutes.

*1 pound ground beef can be substituted for the mixture of ground beef and pork sausage.

Mrs. Gene McCreary (Susan)

GREENWOOD HAM ROLLS   25 servings

1 (10¾-ounce) can cream of
  mushroom soup
1 cup sour cream
1 cup small curd cottage
  cheese
1 egg, beaten

¼ cup chopped onion
5-ounces frozen spinach,
  cooked and drained
½ teaspoon dry mustard
¼ teaspoon salt
25 slices of cooked party ham

Combine soup and half of sour cream and set aside for sauce. Combine rest of sour cream, cottage cheese, eggs, onion, spinach, mustard and salt. Mix and chill for several hours. Spoon 2 teaspoons of filling on each ham slice and roll up. Put in a shallow dish. Pour sauce over top. Cook 20 to 25 minutes uncovered at 350°. Makes 25 ham rolls.

Mrs. Buster Young (Fane)
Drew, Ms.

GRANNY'S HAM LOAF 6-8 servings

2 pounds ham, ground
½ pound veal, ground
½ pound pork, ground
¾ cup milk

¾ cup bread crumbs
2 eggs, slightly beaten
Salt and pepper to taste

Mix well and shape into loaf. Cook in open roaster 300° to 325° for 1½ hours. Start basting immediately.

Baste
1 cup light brown sugar
¾ cup vinegar

1 Tablespoon dry mustard

Serve with Raisin Sauce
½ cup brown sugar
½ Tablespoon all-purpose flour
¼ cup vinegar

1¾ cups water
¼ cup raisins

Mix dry ingredients—add raisins, vinegar and water. Cook to syrup.

Mrs. Robert Neal (Vail)

WILD RICE AND HAM CASSEROLE 4-6 servings

1 (6-ounce) package of
long-grain and wild rice mix
20-ounces frozen chopped
broccoli
2 cups cubed baked ham
1 cup shredded Cheddar
cheese

1 (10-ounce) can cream of
celery soup
1 cup mayonnaise
2 teaspoons prepared mustard
½ cup grated Parmesan cheese

Cook rice according to directions on package; spread over bottom of greased 13x9x2-inch baking dish. Par-boil broccoli in small amount of water about 3 minutes. Drain. Layer over rice. Sprinkle ham over broccoli, then cover with Cheddar cheese. Combine soup, mayonnaise, mustard and spread over Cheddar cheese. Sprinkle with Parmesan cheese. Bake at 350° for 40 to 50 minutes. This recipe was given to me by Anne Henry and it is one of my favorites.

Mrs. Nott Wheeler, Sr. (Cherry)

GOLDEN HAM CASSEROLE

3 Tablespoons butter
1 small onion, finely chopped
1 cup thinly sliced celery
¼ cup chopped green pepper
2 Tablespoons all-purpose flour
1½ cups low-fat milk
1 teaspoon salt
¼ teaspoon pepper

½ teaspoon thyme
¼ teaspoon basil
2 cups cubed cooked ham
1 cup cooked English peas
*1 cup sliced carrots, partially
   cooked*
½ cup buttered bread crumbs
Paprika

Cook onion, celery, and green pepper in butter for 10 minutes. Stir in flour.
Add skim milk and seasonings. Cook over hot heat until slightly thickened.
In a buttered 1½ quart casserole, alternate layers of ham, peas, carrots
and sauce. Sprinkle buttered bread crumbs and paprika over top. Bake
at 375° for 30 minutes. (Great for leftover holiday hams!)

Mrs. Richard Cole (Wendy)

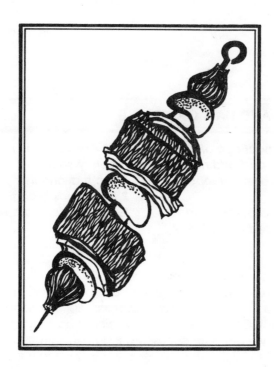

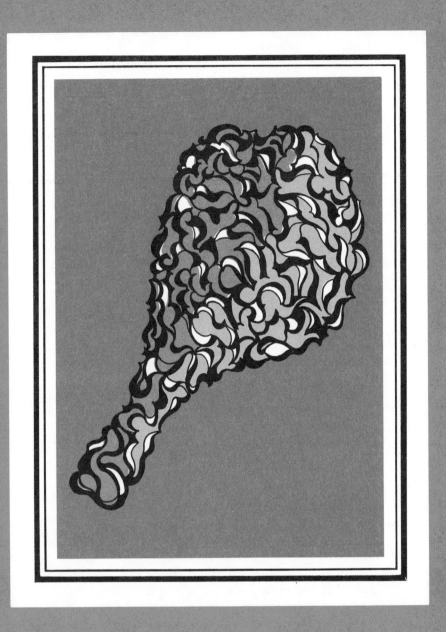

Poultry

CHICKEN-ARTICHOKE CASSEROLE   6 to 8 servings

2 (8½-ounce) cans artichoke
  hearts
2 (4½-ounce) jars sliced
  mushrooms, drained
4 cups cooked chicken breasts,
  cut in large bite sized pieces
1½ cups sharp Cheddar
  cheese, shredded

1 (10¾-ounce) can cream of
  chicken mushroom soup
1 (10¾-ounce) can cream of
  mushroom soup
1 Tablespoon lemon juice
¼ teaspoon curry powder
1½ cups bread crumbs
¼ to ⅓ cup butter, melted

Drain artichokes thoroughly. In a 13x9x2-inch casserole dish, layer the artichokes, mushrooms, chicken and shredded cheese, in that order. Mix soups with lemon juice and curry powder. Pour over first mixture. Top with bread crumbs and melted butter. Bake at 350° until heated through, 30 to 45 minutes.

Mrs. J. J. Stevens (Bea)
Mrs. Leonard Patterson (Tanny)
Drew, Mississippi

BALKAN CHICKEN   4 to 6 servings

4 to 6 chicken breasts,
  seasoned with salt and
  pepper
3 Tablespoons olive oil
2 onions, thinly sliced
2 pods garlic, minced
6 to 8 large fresh mushrooms,
  sliced
2 (1 pound) cans plum
  tomatoes, drained and
  chopped

1 (8½-ounce) can artichoke
  hearts, drained and
  quartered
Crushed red pepper to taste
  (optional)
1 teaspoon paprika
1 teaspoon oregano
1 teaspoon thyme
1 cup uncooked rice
2 cups chicken broth

Brown chicken in oil. Add onions and garlic; sauté about 3 minutes. Add mushrooms and sauté 2 minutes. Add tomatoes, seasonings and artichoke hearts. Cook until liquid is reduced. Add rice and broth to cover chicken. Bake 350° for 40 minutes or until rice is tender. Sprinkle with fresh parsley.

Variation: Substitute 4 to 6 pork chops for chicken.

Mrs. Robert Tibbs (Pat)

COQ SUPREME

6 servings

6 large chicken breast halves
3 (14½-ounce) cans asparagus tips, well drained
1 cup real mayonnaise
2 (10¾-ounce) cans cream of chicken soup

Grated rind of a lemon
1 teaspoon lemon juice
¼ teaspoon curry powder
½ cup grated sharp Cheddar cheese

Cook the chicken breasts gently in a little water with salt, celery and onion. When tender, drain, skin and bone. Mix together other ingredients. In an 9x13-inch casserole, place a layer of well drained asparagus. Cover with chicken breasts. Pour sauce over this. Sprinkle with buttered bread crumbs. Bake at 350° for 25 to 30 minutes until the sauce is bubbly.

Mrs. John Tatum (Carol)

CHICKEN AND ASPARAGUS CASSEROLE

12 servings

6 large whole chicken breasts, cut in half
1 medium onion, chopped
½ cup butter
1 (8-ounce) can sliced mushrooms
1 (10¾-ounce) can cream of chicken soup
1 (10¾-ounce) can cream of mushroom soup
1 (5½-ounce) can evaporated milk

½ pound sharp Cheddar cheese, shredded
¼ teaspoon Tabasco
2 teaspoons soy sauce
1 teaspoon salt
½ teaspoon black pepper
1 teaspoon MSG
1 (2-ounce) jar chopped pimento
2 (14½-ounce) cans whole asparagus
½ cup slivered almonds

Boil chicken breasts in seasoned water until tender. Debone and cut into bite size pieces. Sauté onion in butter and add remaining ingredients except asparagus and almonds. Simmer sauce until cheese melts. To assemble: place a layer of chicken in a large casserole, a layer of asparagus and a layer of sauce. Repeat layers ending with sauce. Sprinkle almonds over the top. Bake at 350° until it bubbles.

Mrs. Howard Grittman (Ann)

CHICKEN LOAF
8 servings

1 (4-pound) chicken, cooked
  and diced
2 cups fresh bread crumbs
1 cup cooked rice
1½ teaspoons salt
¼ cup chopped pimiento
¼ cup grated onion

1 (2-ounce) can chopped
  mushrooms
1 (10¾-ounce) can cream of
  mushroom soup
2½ cups chicken broth
4 eggs, well beaten

Preheat oven to 325°. Mix first 8 ingredients, adding broth and eggs last. Cook in 12x8x2-inch casserole dish until lightly browned, 30 to 45 minutes. Cut into squares and serve mushroom sauce over.

Mushroom Sauce
¼ cup margarine
¼ cup all-purpose flour
1 cup chicken broth
¼ cup cream

1 (2-ounce) can sliced
  mushrooms
1 Tablespoon chopped parsley

In a medium skillet, heat margarine until hot. Add flour and brown slightly. Add chicken broth, cream, mushrooms, and parsley. Spoon sauce over loaf.

Mrs. W. P. Skelton (Louise)
Pace, Mississippi

BAKED CHICKEN NUGGETS
12 to 14 servings

7 to 8 whole chicken breasts,
  boned
2 cups fine, dry bread crumbs
1 cup grated Parmesan cheese
1½ teaspoons salt
1 Tablespoon plus 1 teaspoon
  dried whole thyme

1 Tablespoon plus 1 teaspoon
  dried whole basil
1 cup butter or margarine,
  melted

Cut chicken into 1½-inch pieces. Combine bread crumbs, cheese, salt, and herbs; mix well. Dip chicken pieces in butter, and coat with bread crumb mixture. Place on a greased baking sheet in a single layer. Bake at 400° for 20 minutes or until done.

Mrs. Ben Mitchell (Margaret Ann)

ROLLED HERBED CHICKEN BREAST   8 servings

4 cups fresh bread crumbs,
   toasted
1 teaspoon thyme
½ teaspoon basil
½ teaspoon marjoram
¼ cup parsley, chopped
1 Tablespoon onion, minced
1 clove garlic, minced

6 eggs, beaten
¼ teaspoon salt
4 whole chicken breasts,
   halved, skinned and boned
   (seasoned with red pepper,
   black pepper and white
   pepper)

Preheat oven to 375°. Lightly oil 13x9x2-inch dish. Combine crumbs, seasonings and eggs. Flatten chicken breasts, spread crumb mixture evenly over each. Roll up tucking ends in; arrange seam side down in baking dish. Cut and oil wax paper to fit dish; press paper down on rolls. Bake 20 minutes. Cool. Cover and refrigerate to chill. Slice rolls ¼ inch and arrange on platter. Serve with basil mayonnaise.

Basil Mayonnaise
1 lemon, juiced
½ teaspoon salt
1 egg plus 1 egg yolk
1 clove garlic, minced

¾ cup mazola oil
¼ cup olive oil
¼ cup packed basil leaves

Blend first 4 ingredients in blender, then slowly add oil to thicken. Stir in basil leaves. Chill.

Mrs. Robert Tibbs (Pat)

STUFFED ITALIAN CHICKEN BREASTS   6 servings

6 boned chicken breasts,
   flattened
12 slices pepperoni
3 slices Mozzarella cheese
12 Tablespoons butter

Garlic salt and pepper to taste
1 cup all-purpose flour
1 egg, beaten
¼ cup grated Parmesan cheese
2 cups seasoned bread crumbs

Fold 2 slices of pepperoni, ½ slice Mozzarella, and 2 pats butter into each chicken breast which has been seasoned to taste with the garlic salt and pepper. Fasten with a toothpick. Roll each in flour, dip in egg and roll in mixture of bread crumbs and Parmesan cheese. Place in single layer in a greased 12x8x2-inch baking pan; cover. Bake at 400° for 40 minutes.

Mrs. Leo McGee (Judy)

STUFFED CHICKEN BREASTS

4 servings

4 whole deboned and skinned chicken breasts
1¾ cups cornbread crumbs
¼ cup chopped onion
¼ cup chopped celery
2 Tablespoons margarine

½ Tablespoon Worcestershire sauce
½ cup chicken broth (or enough to moisten)
¾ Tablespoon parsley flakes

Wash chicken breasts. Crumble cornbread into a large mixing bowl. Sauté onion and celery in margarine with Worcestershire sauce. Mix with bread crumbs. Add chicken broth to moisten. Sprinkle parsley flakes over mixture; mix thoroughly. Split each chicken breast on one side and stuff with mixture. Place in 8x8x2-inch greased baking dish and chill.

Gravy
1 (3-ounce) can sliced mushrooms
3 Tablespoons margarine

3 Tablespoons all-purpose flour
1¼ cups chicken broth

Before baking time, make gravy with drained mushrooms browned in margarine. Add flour and chicken broth. When gravy is thick, pour over chicken breasts and bake at 350° for 1 hour.

Mrs. Mike Burchfield (Patsy)

BAKED CHICKEN IN WINE

8 servings

8 chicken breast halves, skinned
1 pound fresh mushrooms, halved
1 cup white wine

½ cup chopped fresh parsley
1 teaspoon dried tarragon
½ teaspoon salt
½ teaspoon pepper

Place chicken breast in 13x9-inch baking dish. Arrange mushrooms around chicken. Pour wine over chicken. Sprinkle parsley, tarragon, salt and pepper. Cover and bake 350° for 1 hour. Good served with wild rice.

Quick and Easy

Mrs. C. E. Dunlap (Jane)

CHICKEN ROLLS WITH VELVET MUSHROOM SAUCE 12 servings

**12 chicken breast halves,
  skinned and boned
12 slices of boiled ham
12 slices of Swiss cheese**

**½ cup butter, melted
2½ cups bread crumbs
½ cup grated Parmesan cheese**

The day before: Flatten chicken breasts with meat mallet. Place 1 slice of ham and 1 slice of cheese on each. Roll up jelly roll fashion, folding in sides to hold ham and cheese. Dip each roll in melted butter, then in combined crumbs and Parmesan cheese. Cover and refrigerate. One hour before serving, arrange chicken in baking pan and bake for 40 minutes at 350°. Meanwhile, make sauce.

Velvet Mushroom Sauce
**1 (10¾-ounce) can cream of
  chicken soup
1 (4-ounce) can of sliced
  mushrooms, undrained
½ cup of milk**

**2 Tablespoons of chives,
  minced
1 cup sour cream
¼ cup chopped parsley**

Combine above and cook over medium heat until it comes to a boil. Stir in sour cream and chopped parsley. Keep warm over low heat. Serve chicken rolls on bed of rice with sauce.

Rice
**6 Tablespoons butter
1 cup sliced green onions
1 cup shredded carrots
½ cup chopped parsley
2½ cups uncooked converted
  rice**

**5 chicken bouillon cubes
4½ cups water
½ bay leaf
1 teaspoon salt
½ teaspoon thyme**

Melt butter in large Dutch oven. Add onions and carrots and sauté. Add rice and stir for 2 or 3 minutes. Add water, bouillon cubes, bay leaf, salt, and thyme. Cover and cook until rice is tender and water absored. Serve with chicken rolls.

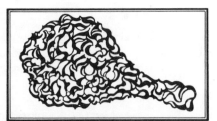

Mrs. Howard Grittman (Ann)

CHICKEN BREASTS AND RICE   6 servings

1 cup raw long grain and wild
   rice mix
2 cups chicken broth
Butter
Salt and pepper to taste
2 (3-ounce) cans sliced
   mushrooms (add mushroom
   liquid to chicken broth to
   make 2 cups)

6 chicken breast halves
½ package dry onion soup mix
1 (10¾-ounce) can cream of
   mushroom soup
½ cup milk
Paprika

Pour chicken broth over raw rice. Dot with butter and add salt and pepper to taste. Drain mushrooms and add to casserole. Put breasts on top of rice. Sprinkle onion soup mix over all. Dilute mushroom soup with ½ cup milk and spoon over each breast. Sprinkle with paprika and cook uncovered at 350° for 1 hour. Cover and cook ½ hour longer.

Quick and Easy

Mrs. Max Dilworth (Gertrude)
Shelby, Mississippi

CHICKEN BREAST ROMANO   6 servings

⅓ cup all-purpose flour
½ teaspoon salt
¼ teaspoon pepper
6 boned chicken breasts,
   skinned
2 Tablespoons melted
   shortening or vegetable oil
¼ cup minced onion
2 cups tomato juice
2 Tablespoons grated Romano
   or Parmesan cheese
1 Tablespoon sugar

½ teaspoon salt
½ teaspoon garlic salt
½ teaspoon whole oregano
¼ teaspoon basil leaves
1 teaspoon vinegar
1 (4-ounce) can sliced
   mushrooms, drained
1 Tablespoon minced parsley
½ cup grated Romano or
   Parmesan cheese
Hot cooked spaghetti (optional)
Parsley sprigs (optional)

Combine flour, salt, and pepper. Dredge chicken in flour mixture, and brown in hot shortening. Drain chicken on paper towels. Pour off all but 1 tablespoon of pan drippings. Sauté onion in reserved drippings until tender. Add next 10 ingredients, stirring well. Return chicken to skillet; cover and simmer 45 minutes or until tender. At serving time, sprinkle chicken with ½ cup Romano cheese. Serve over spaghetti and garnish with parsley sprigs, if desired.

The Editors

CHICKEN PAPRIKASH WITH SPAETZLE
8 servings

12 chicken breast halves
4 Tablespoons butter
16 small white onions (1½ pound)
1 cup chopped onion

1 Tablespoon paprika
8 small carrots (1 pound)
2 (10¾-ounce) cans chicken broth
Salt

Spaetzle
2¾ cups all-purpose flour
3 eggs
1 teaspoon salt

1 cup water
2 Tablespoons butter

Gravy
⅓ cup all-purpose flour
½ cup dry white wine

2 cups sour cream
Parsley

Wash and dry chicken. Brown chicken, half at a time, in 2 tablespoons hot butter. It takes about 20 minutes to brown well. Lift out chicken as it browns. In 2 tablespoons butter in same skillet, sauté whole and chopped onions with 1 tablespoon paprika until lightly browned. Cut carrots diagonally into 1½-inch pieces. Add to onions; sauté 2 minutes. Stir in chicken broth and 2 teaspoons salt. Arrange chicken in skillet in single layer; bring to boiling. Reduce heat; simmer, covered, 45 minutes.

Chicken Paprikash with Spaetzle

Meanwhile, make spaetzle
In large bowl, combine 2¾ cups flour, eggs, salt and water. Beat with spoon until smooth. In large kettle, bring 2 quarts water and 2 teaspoons salt to boil. Spread 2 teaspoons dough on pancake turner, covering surface. With moistened spatula, cut off small pieces of dough, letting them drop into boiling water. Cook ¼ dough at a time. Boil gently, uncovered, until firm and rise to top. Remove with slotted spoon to dish. Add 2 tablespoons butter to dish. Keep warm while cooking rest of dough. When chicken is tender, remove to platter. Cover. Keep warm in 300°oven while cooking spaetzle and making gravy. In small bowl, mix flour with wine until smooth. Stir into liquid (about 3½ cups) left in skillet. Bring to boil, stirring. Reduce heat; simmer 2 minutes. Slowly add sour cream and heat gently. Pour some gravy over chicken. Add parsley before serving.

Mrs. John Tatum (Carol)

ORIENTAL CHICKEN AND RICE
15 servings

*3 cups cooked chicken, torn
into pieces*
*1 (6-ounce) box of long-grain
and wild rice mix*
*1 (10¾-ounce) can cream of
celery soup*
*1 (2-ounce) jar chopped
pimento*

1 medium onion, chopped
1 cup mayonnaise
*2 (16-ounce) cans French style
green beans, drained*
*1 (5-ounce) can sliced water
chestnuts, drained*

Cook rice in chicken broth according to package directions. Mix rice with all other ingredients. Place in 3 quart greased casserole. Top casserole with paprika and chopped parsley. Cook 30 minutes at 350°. Good with garlic bread and a green salad.

Mrs. Mike Sanders (Nan)

VENETIAN CHICKEN
6 to 8 servings

*1 (4-pound) fryer, cut in
serving pieces*
2 Tablespoons margarine
2 Tablespoons olive oil
1 large onion, thinly sliced
1 large carrot, thinly sliced
1 stalk celery, chopped
*1 (1-pound) can Italian tomatoes,
undrained and chopped*
1 Tablespoon dried basil

1 Tablespoon oregano
1½ teaspoons salt
¼ teaspoon cinnamon
⅛ teaspoon black pepper
⅛ teaspoon white pepper
4 whole cloves
½ cup white wine
*¼ pound fresh mushrooms,
sliced*
1 Tablespoon all-purpose flour

Brown chicken pieces in oil in Dutch oven, remove and set aside. Add onions, celery, carrots, and sauté 5 minutes. Add next eight ingredients, bring to a boil and simmer 10 minutes. Add chicken, cover and cook 1 hour. Add mushrooms and cook uncovered 15 minutes. Remove chicken, keep warm. Mix in flour with 2 tablespoons water, stir into sauce to thicken and pour over chicken. Serve with cornbread muffins or over noodles or vermicelli.

Mrs. Robert Tibbs (Pat)

RAYNER'S HUNAN CHICKEN   4 servings

5 to 6 Tablespoons peanut oil
2 whole chicken breasts,
   boned, skinned and cut into
   cubes
½ Tablespoon cornstarch
1 Tablespoon white wine
Pinch of salt
1 Tablespoon shredded fresh
   ginger (matchstick thin—dry
   will do fine)
1 cup sliced celery
1 cup sliced green pepper

1 teaspoon crushed red pepper
   flakes
2 Tablespoons soy sauce
½ cup chicken stock
2 to 3 Tablespoons white
   vinegar
1 Tablespoon minced green
   onions
½ Tablespoon cornstarch
   (blended with ½ Tablespoon
   water)

Toss chicken cubes with the ½ tablespoon cornstarch and wine; set aside. Have a wok in place (or large copper skillet) and all ingredients measured before beginning to stir fry. Heat the wok and add 2 to 3 tablespoons of the peanut oil. When hot, but not smoking, add chicken and cook, tossing and turning cubes occasionlly until they lose their pink color and turn white (they should feel firm to the touch and not springy). Remove from wok and set aside. Reheat wok and add 2 to 3 more tablespoons of the peanut oil; heat. Add salt, ginger, celery, green pepper, red pepper flakes, soy sauce, and chicken stock; stir until mixture boils. Return chicken to wok and add vinegar and green onions. Stir fry for 5 to 10 seconds. Add liquid cornstarch (½ tablespoon cornstarch blended with ½ tablespoon water) to center of wok and stir to thicken the sauce and absorb the excess oil. Serve over hot rice.

Mrs. Bill Parker (Jo)

CHICKEN WITH LEMON MUSTARD SAUCE   6 servings

3 whole chicken breasts,
   skinned and boned
3 Tablespoons butter
1 Tablespoon flour
¾ teaspoon MSG

1 Tablespoon tarragon
¼ teaspoon salt
½ cup chicken broth
1 Tablespoon Dijon mustard
3 thin slices of lemon

Cut chicken in bite-size pieces; sauté in butter. Mix flour, accent, tarragon, and salt. Sprinkle over chicken and cook for 5 minutes, stirring constantly. Add chicken broth, mustard, and lemon slices. Cover and simmer 3 minutes. Sprinkle with fresh chopped parsley.

Quick and Easy   Mrs. Robert Tibbs (Pat)

CHINESE CHICKEN
8 servings

4 whole chicken breasts,
halved and deboned
½ cup cornstarch
½ teaspoon salt

⅛ teaspoon pepper
4 egg yolks, beaten
4 green onions, chopped

Sauce
1½ cups water
½ cup lemon juice
3½ Tablespoons light brown
sugar
3 Tablespoons cornstarch

3 Tablespoons honey
2 teaspoons instant chicken
bouillon
1 teaspoon grated fresh ginger

Pound breasts lightly with mallet. Combine cornstarch, salt, pepper and egg yolks. Dip chicken in batter and fry until golden brown and tender. Cut each breast into three or four pieces. Sprinkle with onion. Combine all sauce ingredients and blend. Cook over medium heat, stirring constantly until sauce thickens. Pour over chicken and serve.

Mrs. Carter Naugher (Leigh)

BAKED CHICKEN ROSÉ
4 servings

4 chicken breasts, deboned
with salt
Seasoned all-purpose flour
6 Tablespoons butter
2 Tablespoons all-purpose flour
¾ cup chicken broth, canned
½ cup rosé wine

¼ cup green onions, thinly
sliced, including tops
⅓ cup water chestnuts, thinly
sliced
1 (4-ounce) can sliced
mushrooms

Dust chicken with seasoned flour; melt butter in baking dish. Place chicken, skin side down. Bake at 350° for 1 hour. Melt another 2 tablespoons butter in sauce pan; stir in flour. Add broth and wine. Cook, stirring constantly, until thickened and smooth. Turn chicken breasts over and sprinkle with onions, mushrooms, and water chestnuts. Pour sauce over all. Reduce heat to 325° and cook 25-30 minutes.

Mrs. Frank Alley (Ivey)
Jackson, Mississippi

SZECHUAN CHICKEN IN GARLIC SAUCE   4 servings

**1 pound boned, skinned
  chicken**

Marinade
1 egg white   **2 teaspoons cornstarch**
1 teaspoon sherry

Seasoning Sauce
2 Tablespoons soy sauce   **2 teaspoons cornstarch,**
2 teaspoons sugar   **dissolved in 2 Tablespoons**
2 teaspoons wine vinegar   **sherry**
1 teaspoon hot sauce

Vegetables
3 Tablespoons peanut oil   **1 teaspoon sesame seed or**
1 Tablespoon garlic, minced   **peanut oil**
1 teaspoon ginger root, minced   **1 cup snow peas**
2 green onions, chopped

Dice chicken into cubes. Place chicken and marinade ingredients in a bowl and stir well. Refrigerate at least 30 minutes or overnight. Combine ingredients for seasoning sauce in bowl. Heat 2 tablespoons peanut oil in skillet or wok until very hot. Add chicken; cook 2 to 3 minutes, or until it turns white. Remove chicken and lower heat. Add remaining tablespoon of peanut oil, garlic, ginger, and green onions; stir-fry for one minute. Turn heat to high; add the teaspoon of sesame seed (or peanut oil), snow peas and chicken. Stir-fry a few seconds; add seasoning sauce and cook for 30 seconds. Serve immediately over hot rice.

Mrs. James Brown (Pat)

DURKEE'S CHICKEN   6 servings

6 chicken breast halves   **½ cup Durkee's Famous Sauce**
½ cup melted butter   **3 cups cooked rice**

Place chicken breasts in single layer in shallow baking dish. Blend butter and Durkee's; pour over chicken. Bake, covered, at 350° for 45 minutes. Uncover, bake 15 minutes more or until brown. Serve chicken atop bed of rice. Pour drippings over all.

Mrs. Warren Williamson (Sallie Sanders)
Greenville, Al.

CHICKEN VERONIQUE   4 servings

4 chicken breasts, halved
**   and boned**
Salt and pepper
½ cup butter, divided
1 teaspoon olive oil

4 cups chicken broth
⅓ cup all-purpose flour
1 cup vermouth
1 cup seedless green grapes
Cayenne pepper to taste

Season chicken and sauté in 2 tablespoons butter and olive oil until golden brown on each side. Add 1 cup chicken broth and simmer covered until tender. Make sauce by melting remaining butter and adding flour in heavy sauce pan. Gradually add 3 cups broth cooking all the time. Add vermouth and season with salt and cayenne. Continue cooking until thick, stirring frequently. Place chicken on serving plate, sprinkle grapes over, then pour sauce over all.

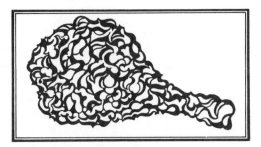

Mrs. H. L. Dilworth (Ann)
Shelby Mississippi

CHICKEN ENCHILADAS   6 to 8 servings

1 package flour tortillas
2 pounds boned, cut-up
**   chicken breasts**
16-ounces sour cream
1 bunch green onions, diced
1 (8-ounce) can tomato sauce
1 (3-ounce) can diced green
**   chiles**

1 (3-ounce) can pitted black
**   olives, chopped, optional**
1 pound jack cheese, shredded
½ pound Cheddar cheese,
**   shredded**
1 Tablespoon cumin
Salt to taste

Brown chicken in Dutch oven and add onions; cook until onions are tender; add chiles, olives, cumin and salt; mix well. Fold in sour cream. Cover the bottom of a Dutch oven with tortillas, put a layer of chicken mixture, cheese and tomato sauce; repeat this twice so you have 3 layers. Cover the last layer with tortillas and sprinkle with cheese. Bake at 350° for 40 to 45 minutes and let stand 10 minutes before serving.

Mrs. Don Blackwood (Suzan)

CHICKEN CHOP SUEY

3 to 4 servings

1 medium onion, finely
  chopped
3 Tablespoons butter
2 to 3 chicken breasts, cut into
  1-inch cubes
2 cups water
2 chicken flavored bouillon
  cubes
1 cup chopped celery
1 (4-ounce) can mushroom bits
  and pieces (or equivalent
  amount sliced fresh
  mushrooms)

1 (8-ounce) can sliced water
  chestnuts
¼ cup bean sprouts
Salt and pepper to taste
½ cup cold water
1 to 2 teaspoons cornstarch
Few dashes of soy sauce

In a large skillet, brown chopped onion in the butter. Add chicken and brown along with onion. Add 2 cups water into which 2 chicken flavored bouillon cubes have been dissolved. Add chopped celery, mushrooms, water chestnuts and bean sprouts. Cook until celery is barely tender; season with salt and pepper. In a small bowl, combine ½ cup cold water, 1 to 2 teaspoons cornstarch and dashes of soy sauce until water is brownish. Add to skillet mixture and stir until slightly thickened. Serve over rice.

Note: May substitute Chinese cabbage, bok choy, asparagus tips, broccoli, brussel sprouts for the celery or use a combination of these as desired.

Mrs. Pete Baughman (Scarlet)

KING RANCH CHICKEN

8 to 10 servings

3 to 4 pound hen
1 onion
1 or 2 ribs celery
Salt and pepper
1 onion, chopped
1 bell pepper, chopped
1 (10¾-ounce) can cream of
  mushroom soup
1 (10¾-ounce) can cream of
  chicken soup

½ pound Cheddar cheese,
  shredded
Chili powder
Garlic salt
1 package frozen flour tortillas
1 (10-ounce) can Rotel
  tomatoes and chilis,
  undrained

Boil hen until tender with onion and celery, salt and pepper. Cut chicken in bite-size pieces and reserve all stock. Combine soups. Just before putting casserole together, soak the frozen tortillas in boiling chicken stock until wilted. Start layering casserole in a 9x13-inch baking dish in this order: tortillas, "dripping with stock," chicken, onion, bell pepper, sprinkling with chili powder and garlic to taste, soup mixture, and cheese. Repeat layers being sure the tortillas are ozzing with stock. Cover casserole with Rotel tomatoes and juice. Juices in this casserole should be about half the depth of the dish. If not, add a little more stock. May be made and frozen several days ahead, but always make at least one day ahead so flavors will blend. Bake casserole uncovered at 375° for 30 minutes. SECRET: a well seasoned stock.

Mrs. James Burris (Ann)
Clarksdale, Mississippi

CHICKEN TETRAZZINI   8 servings

1 (6-pound) hen
1 onion
2 stalks celery
¼ cup margarine
1 medium onion, chopped
1 bell pepper, chopped
5 Tablespoons all-purpose flour
1 pound of soft processed
  cheese, cubed

1 (10¾-ounce) can cream of
  tomato soup
2 (4-ounce) cans whole
  mushrooms, undrained
1 (2-ounce) jar of chopped
  pimiento
1 (12-ounce) package vermicelli

Boil hen in 6 cups of water seasoned with onion and celery until tender. Remove skin from hen and cut into large bite-sized pieces. Reserve the broth and chill. Skim the fat from the broth and reserve. In a dutch oven, over medium heat, combine 5 tablespoons of flour and 3 to 4 tablespoons of chicken fat to make a paste. Reduce to low heat and add 5 cups of broth. Cook and stir until boiling. Turn off heat and add soft cubed cheese, tomato soup, mushrooms, and pimiento. When cheese melts, add chicken and mix well. Cook vermicelli in salted water or leftover broth. Add to chicken mixture and mix well. Put in ovenproof dish and bake at 250° to 300° for 45 to 60 minutes.

Mrs. Elaine Hewlett

CHICKEN SPAGHETTI

6 servings

⅓ cup butter
¼ cup (or more) chopped onion
1 clove garlic, crushed
¼ pound mushrooms, sliced
¼ cup all-purpose flour
2 cups chicken broth
Salt and pepper to taste

2 to 3 cups cooked chicken
1 cup tomatoes, chopped
¼ pound sliced American cheese
½ cup buttered bread crumbs
1 (12-ounce) package vermicelli, cooked according to package directions

In a large skillet, heat butter and add onion, garlic and mushrooms. Cook 10 minutes. Add flour and stir until blended. Slowly add chicken broth and stir over low heat until thick and smooth. Season with salt and pepper to taste. Add chicken, tomatoes, and cheese. Combine the chicken mixture and the cooked spaghetti in a greased 13x9x2-inch casserole dish. Top with bread crumbs. Bake at 375° for 25 minutes.

Mrs. Glenn Hewlett (Elaine)

CHICKEN ROTEL

8 servings

2 large fryers, cooked and chopped
1 clove garlic, crushed
2 large onions, chopped
2 large bell peppers, chopped
½ cup margarine
2½ cups chicken broth
Salt and pepper to taste
1 (10-ounce) can Rotel chili tomatoes

2 Tablespoons Worcestershire sauce
1 pound processed cheese, cubed
2 (6-ounce) cans mushrooms, drained
1 (16-ounce) can English peas
1 (12-ounce) package vermicelli, cooked

Sauté onions, peppers, garlic in oleo until tender. Add chicken, tomatoes, chicken broth and cheese. Cook and stir until cheese melts. Add salt, pepper, Worcesterhire, mushrooms, and peas. Mix well and fold in vermicelli. Make 2 (9x13-inch) casseroles. Bake 30 minutes at 350°.

Mrs. M. T. Blackwood (Jauweice)
Drew, Mississippi

CELESTIAL CHICKEN

4 servings

**4 whole chicken breasts,
  deboned and cubed (large)**
1 cup all-purpose flour
2 teaspoons salt
2 teaspoons paprika

2 teaspoons MSG
1 box sesame seeds, optional
¼ teaspoon pepper
8-ounces whipping cream

Supreme Sauce
¼ cup butter
¼ cup all-purpose flour
2 chicken bouillon cubes
1½ cups water

12-ounces whipping cream
1 teaspoon salt
¼ teaspoon red pepper

Marinate chicken in whipping cream several hours or overnight. Mix dry ingredients. Dip chicken in mix of dry ingredients. Fry at 380° til brown. Dip in prepared sauce. To make sauce, melt butter, blend in flour, salt, red pepper and bouillon cubes. Gradually add water and cook, stirring until mixture thickens. Add cream and heat until serving time. (If too thick, add water or cream.) May be doubled. This can also be served as an appetizer.

Mrs. Roy L. Collins (Linda)

FRANK ANN STEEN'S CHICKEN

6 servings

**4 chicken breasts (or 2 cups
  cooked, chopped chicken)**
¾ cup butter
1 large onion, chopped
3 stalks celery, chopped

4 Tablespoons all-purpose flour
2 cups chicken stock
1 cup milk
Salt and pepper

Cook chicken in well-seasoned stock until done; save stock and cut chicken into bite-size pieces; set aside. In a skillet, sauté onions and celery until done, not brown; add flour and stir until smooth, continuing to stir, slowly, adding chicken stock and milk until mixture is thickened. Add chicken, salt and pepper to taste. Simmer 10-15 minutes. Serve over hot sliced, buttered cornbread.

Mrs. Jim Steen (Ann)

FRIED CHICKEN PIE

6 to 8 servings

1 large recipe of pastry, see index

1 large hen, seasoned, cooked, and chopped

Sauce

2 cups chicken broth
2 cups cream
4 egg yolks, beaten
1 Tablespoon all-purpose flour (heaping)
1 large green pepper, chopped
1 (8-ounce) can sliced mushrooms

3 pieces pimento, chopped
1 (17-ounce) can English peas, drained
Salt to taste
Red pepper to taste
Worcestershire sauce to taste

Mix cream and broth. Add beaten yolks and flour. Cook over medium heat until it thickens. Add enough sauce to chicken to bind together. Roll pastry thin and cut circles the size of a saucer. Place large spoon of chicken mixture on each circle, fold over half and seal edges with a fork. Fry in a large skillet until brown on both sides. Drain and set aside; keep warm. Sauté green pepper and mushrooms. Mix with remaining sauce. Add pimento and English peas. Reheat. Serve sauce over each fried pie.

Mrs. Frank Farrish (Stell)

EASY CHICKEN PIE

6 to 8 servings

1 chicken
1½ cups chicken broth

1 (10¾-ounce) can cream of chicken soup

Simmer chicken in salted water until tender, then debone. Cut up chicken and put in 12x8x2-inch casserole dish. Combine soup and broth and pour over chicken. Variations: add a small (7½-ounce) can of peas and carrots; add two chopped hard-boiled eggs.

Topping

1 cup all-purpose flour
2 teaspoons baking powder
½ teaspoon pepper

1 teaspoon salt
1 cup milk
½ cup margarine, melted

Mix dry ingredients with milk and melted margarine. Pour over chicken. Bake at 450° for 35 to 40 minutes or until brown.

Mrs. Mark Koonce (Anne)

MAMA'S CHICKEN PIE   6 to 8 servings

1 large (2½-3 pound) fryer   **1½ - 2 teaspoons salt**
** chicken**

Boil chicken in salted water in 6-quart Dutch oven until tender; remove, cool, and debone, reserving broth.

Pastry
2 cups sifted all-purpose flour   **6 Tablespoons shortening**
3 teaspoons baking powder   **⅔ to ¾ cup milk**
½ teaspoon salt

Sift flour with baking powder and salt. Cut in shortening until mixture resembles coarse crumbs. Add milk all at once and mix just until dough follows fork around bowl. Knead lightly 2 or 3 times and separate dough into 2 balls. Turn out onto floured waxed paper and roll out very thin (⅛ to ¼-inch). Cut pastry into 1½-inch strips.

Broth Mixture
5 to 6 cups chicken broth   **1½ to 2 cups milk**
2 Tablespoons butter or   **Salt and pepper to taste**
** margarine**
3 to 4 Tablespoons all-purpose
** flour**

Add margarine to reserved broth. In a cup, mix flour and ½ cup milk to a smooth consistency. Slowly add to broth, stirring constantly. Add remainder of milk and simmer over low heat until thickened. Salt and pepper to taste. To assemble pie, put layer of chicken in 9x13-inch dish, cover with strips of pastry and pour some broth over. Then add another layer of chicken and top with strips of pastry. Pour broth over until it rises to top of layers. Bake in 450° oven until bubbly and light brown on top (approximately 40 minutes). Allow to "rest" 15 minutes after removing from oven before serving.

Note: In broth mixture, flour and milk amounts may have to be adjusted for the amount of broth you have.

                                        Mrs. Keith Griffin (Leslie)

SMOKED TURKEY

3½ cups

1½ cups salad oil
½ cup soy sauce
¼ cup Worcestershire sauce
2½ teaspoons salt
1 Tablespoon ground black
  pepper

½ cup vinegar
1 Tablespoon dried parsley
2 large garlic pods, chopped
½ cup lemon juice

Mix above ingredients well in medium mixing bowl. Use as baste for turkey prior to smoking. Baste turkey and place in oven at 300°. Baste every 10 minutes for 50 minutes, then cook turkey in smoker.

Note: Turkey Breast

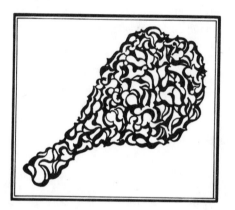

Mrs. DeLoach Cope
Hollandale, Mississippi

CORNISH HENS FOR TWO

2 servings

½ cup orange liqueur
1 cup white wine
½ cup soy sauce
1 (6-ounce) can undiluted
  orange juice, thawed

2 cornish hens, thawed and
  drained

In large bowl, make a marinade of the liqueur, wine, soy sauce and orange juice. Place hens in mixture the day before you wish to serve. Turn hens every 6 hours. Heat grill to medium heat and cook hens until well done. Baste with leftover marinade. These can be baked on rack in the oven at 350° for 1 hour if desired; however, grill is preferable. Serve with salad and wild rice.

Mrs. Bert Hayes (Cindy)

MARTHA'S DOVE POT PIE
4 to 6 servings

12 dove breasts
3 carrots
3 medium potatoes
1 (16-ounce) can string beans
6 green onions
1 small green pepper

1 Tablespoon Worcestershire
½ teaspoon sweet basil
Dash of oregano
Salt and pepper
Cooking oil
1 can of 10 biscuits

Cut vegetables into bite-sized pieces. Salt and pepper doves generously, sprinkle with oregano and dredge in flour. Sear on all sides in heavy skillet over a medium fire, cooking for about 15 minutes. Add Worcestershire sauce and onions. Before the onions are brown, pour in enough water to cover the meat and add basil and green pepper. Cover and simmer 45 minutes. Cook vegetables for 15 minutes. When doves have finished simmering, add remaining vegetables. Place the biscuits on top, moistening them with gravy from doves. Place skillet in 375° oven until biscuits are brown. This is one of the best recipes for dove I have ever tried and was given to me by Martha Hiter.

Mrs. Nott Wheeler (Cherry)

SKILLET DOVES WITH WINE SAUCE
6 servings

15 - 17 doves
½ cup all-purpose flour
1 teaspoon salt
⅛ teaspoon pepper
1 teaspoon paprika
¼ cup butter

1 clove garlic, crushed
¼ cup chopped ripe olives
½ cup water
½ teaspoon Worcestershire
 sauce
¼ to ½ cup white wine

Coat doves with flour seasoned with salt, pepper and paprika. Brown on all sides in butter in 10-inch skillet. Add garlic, olives, water, and Worcestershire sauce; cover tightly. Simmer 45 minutes. Turn doves; add wine. Cover; simmer 45 minutes longer. Serve over rice with sauce.

Mrs. Richard Findley (Phylis)

FANNIE LOU'S DOVES

6 to 8 servings

16 doves
⅓ cup olive oil
2 teaspoons celery salt
2 teaspoons curry powder
2 teaspoons garlic salt
2 teaspoons salt
2 teaspoons pepper

½ teaspoon dry mustard
1 (8-ounce) can sliced
  mushrooms
Water
Juice of 1 lemon
3 teaspoons Worcestershire
  sauce

Dip each dove in olive oil. Place breast down in a Dutch oven or un-covered roaster. Sprinkle generously with celery salt, curry powder, garlic salt, salt and pepper, and dry mustard. Pour mushrooms and juice over doves. Add enough water to have ½-inch liquid on bottom of roaster. Cover and bake at 250° for 5 hours. Add lemon juice and Worcestershire sauce. Bake for 30 minutes more. Serve with wild rice and sausage casserole.

Mrs. Paul Mullins (Liba)
Mrs. James Walker (Elizabeth)

SMOTHERED QUAIL

6 servings

12 quail, seasoned with salt
  and pepper
12 Tablespoons butter
6 Tablespoons all-purpose flour

4 cups chicken broth
1 cup sherry or Madeira wine
Salt and pepper

Season quail with salt and pepper. Brown in heavy skillet in butter. Remove quail to baking dish. Add flour and stir well, being sure that the flour is mixed with the browned residue in the skillet. Cook until golden brown. Stirring constantly, slowly add broth, sherry, salt and pepper to taste. After gravy has thickened and is smooth, pour it over quail in baking dish and bake, covered, at least 1 hour at 350°.

Note: This gravy is excellent for any use. A small can of evaporated milk added to it makes it creamier and have a slightly richer flavor.

Mrs. Mike Sanders (Nan)

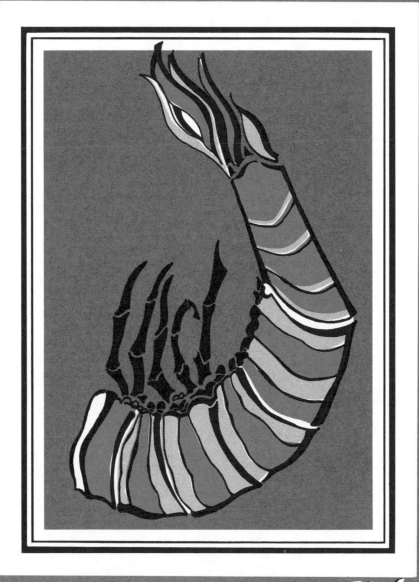

Fish,
Seafood

FETTUCCINI WITH CRAB MEAT   6 to 8 servings

1 (8-ounce) package
  fettuccini
1 Tablespoon butter
1 cup heavy cream
2 Tablespoons chopped parsley

1 teaspoon Italian seasoning
8-ounces crab meat
¼ cup Parmesan cheese,
  grated

Cook fettuccini according to package directions and drain. Melt butter in shallow pan. Add cream, parsley and Italian seasoning and reduce to ⅓. Add drained fettucini and crab meat. Place in ovenproof serving dish. Sprinkle with Parmesan cheese. Place under broiler until golden brown.

Note: Crab meat may be substituted with ham, fresh mushrooms or tomatoes.

Mrs. H. L. Dilworth (Anne)

CRAB MEAT AND MUSHROOMS IN WINE SAUCE   4 servings

1 pound fresh crab meat
¼ pound fresh mushrooms or 1
  large can of mushrooms
2 Tablespoons butter
2 Tablespoons all-purpose flour
½ cup milk

½ cup white wine
½ teaspoon dry mustard
Salt and pepper to taste
Hot sauce to taste
¾ cup breadcrumbs

Pull crab meat apart and remove stiff membranes. Sauté mushrooms in butter. Make a cream sauce, blending melted butter, flour, milk, wine, mustard, salt, pepper and hot sauce. Cook sauce 2 to 3 minutes. Add crab meat and mushrooms. Place in casserole dish, sprinkle top with breadcrumbs and dot with butter. Bake uncovered at 350° for 30 minutes. Take out of oven and cover for about 10 minutes before serving. This can be made with shrimp or crab meat or a combination.

Mrs. Judy Harbin
Gautier, Mississippi

DEVILED CRAB
4 servings

4 Tablespoons butter
2 Tablespoons all-purpose flour
1 cup milk
1 Tablespoon chopped parsley
2 teaspoons lemon juice
1 teaspoon prepared mustard

½ teaspoon horseradish
1 teaspoon salt
2 cups crab meat
2 hard-cooked eggs, chopped
½ cup buttered bread crumbs

Melt butter in heavy saucepan, add flour, and stir until smooth. Add milk and other ingredients except crab meat, eggs, and crumbs. Cook until thick. Fold in crab meat and eggs. Place in 2-quart casserole or ramekins. Top with bread crumbs. Bake at 400° for 10 minutes. Nice as first course or may be served as a casserole over rice. May substitute and use half crab meat and half shrimp pieces.

Mrs. Will Lewis, Sr.
Oxford, Mississippi

CRAB CUSTARD
4 servings

1 pound crab meat
¾ cup milk
¾ cup cream
4 eggs

1 teaspoon dry mustard
Pinch of cayenne pepper
Butter
Lemon slices for garnish

Preheat oven to 350°. Butter a heavy casserole and spread the crab meat evenly over the bottom. Place the milk, cream, eggs, seasoned salt, mustard and cayenne pepper in a blender and blend at medium speed for 1 minute. Pour the mixture over the crab and dot with butter. Bake uncovered for 25 to 30 minutes, or until the custard is set. Garnish with lemon slices and serve immediately.

Daisey Redman
Four Great Southern Cooks

CRAB BAKE

10 servings

1/4 cup margarine
1 small bell pepper, chopped
1 small onion, chopped
1/2 cup celery, minced
1 pound crab meat
1 cup breadcrumbs

1 Tablespoon mustard
1 Tablespoon mayonnaise
2 eggs, beaten
1/4 teaspoon garlic salt
Salt and pepper to taste

Sauté bell pepper, onion and celery in margarine. Set aside. Mix crab meat with 3/4 cup breadcrumbs. Add mustard, mayonnaise, eggs, garlic salt and salt and pepper to taste. Add sautéed vegetables. Put in casserole dish or a buttered crab shell and top with remaining breadcrumbs. Bake 30 to 35 minutes in 400° oven until lightly browned. This may be prepared in advance and frozen.

Mrs. Judy Harbin
Gautier, Mississippi

BAKED AVOCADO WITH CRAB MEAT

8 servings

4 avocados
Lemon juice

8 small cloves garlic

Cut avocados in half lengthwise, remove seed and peel. Brush with lemon juice. Place garlic and 1 tablespoon lemon juice in cavity of each half. Set aside.

2 Tablespoons butter
2 Tablespoons all-purpose flour
1 cup half-and-half cream
1 to 2 pounds of crab meat
1/2 cup fresh mushrooms,
   chopped

2 Tablespoons dry sherry (not
   cooking sherry)
1/2 teaspoon salt
1/4 teapsoon white pepper
1/2 cup shredded sharp
   Cheddar cheese or more

Melt butter in heavy saucepan, add flour, stirring constantly. Add half-and-half. Cook until thick and bubbly. Add everything except crab meat. Cook, stirring until cheese melts. Adjust seasonings. Gently stir in lump crab meat. Remove garlic and lemon juice from avocado halves and fill with crab meat mixture. Place in buttered 13x9x2-inch dish. Bake 350° for 10 minutes. Sprinkle with additional cheese and bake another 5 minutes.

Mrs. Robert Tibbs (Pat)

SHRIMP AND ARTICHOKES IN SCALLOP SHELLS   6 servings

1 pound shrimp, cooked and peeled
1 (14-ounce) can artichoke hearts, rinsed and quartered
½ pound fresh mushrooms, sliced
4 Tablespoons butter, divided
2 Tablespoons all-purpose flour
1 cup milk
½ Tablespoon Worcestershire sauce

¼ cup sherry
Salt to taste
¼ teaspoon dried thyme
½ teaspoon oregano
¼ to ½ cup Parmesan cheese, grated
Paprika
Fresh parsley, chopped

Arrange artichokes in six scallop shells or ramekins; add shrimp evenly divided over artichokes. Sauté mushrooms in 2 tablespoons butter, arrange over shrimp and artichokes. Make the sauce by melting 2 tablespoons butter, add flour and cook until well blended. Stir in milk, seasonings, and sherry. Cook and stir until mixture thickens. Spoon over shrimp mixture. Sprinkle cheese over sauce and dust each with paprika. Bake 375° for 20 minutes. Garnish with chopped parsley.

Note: May be baked in 13x9-inch baking dish.

Mrs. Howard Grittman (Ann)
Drew, Mississippi

SHRIMP MOSEA   4 servings

2 pounds shrimp, deheaded, unpeeled
½ cup margarine
6 cloves garlic, sliced
Pinch rosemary
Pinch oregano

¼ teaspoon salt, or to taste
¼ teaspoon ground black pepper
½ cup white wine
2 bay leaves

Heat margarine until very hot. Add all ingredients except wine. Heat until shrimp are pink or until peels begin to slightly loosen (about 5 to 10 minutes). Add wine and simmer until shrimp are done. Serve with hot crisp French bread.

Mrs. Johnny Brackin (Linda)

BROILED SHRIMP

6 servings

3 pounds fresh shrimp,
  cleaned, in the shells
1 Tablespoon seasoned salt
½ cup melted margarine
4 Tablepoons lemon juice
½ cup Italian dressing
2 cloves garlic, pressed

6 Tablespoons Worcestershire
  sauce
½ teaspoon Tabasco
3 Tablespoons soy sauce
3 Tablespoons cracked black
  pepper

Rub seasoned salt into shrimp. Combine other ingredients and marinate shrimp in sauce several hours. Cook in shallow pan under broiler for about 8 minutes. Turn and continue cooking until shrimp are done (5 to 8 minutes more). Serve with lots of bread.

Mrs. Leo McGee (Judy)

CREAMY SHRIMP SHELLS

6 servings

1½ pounds shrimp, cooked,
  peeled, and deveined
¼ cup chopped green onion
1 clove garlic, pressed
2 Tablespoons melted butter or
  margarine
¼ cup all-purpose flour
½ teaspoon salt
1½ cups half-and-half cream

½ cup dry white wine
¼ cup soft breadcrumbs
2 Tablespoons grated Parmesan
  cheese
2 teaspoons chopped parsley
¼ teaspoon paprika
1½ Tablespoons melted butter
  or margarine

Reserve 6 whole shrimp; cut remainder in half lengthwise, and set aside. Sauté onion and garlic in 2 tablespoons butter until tender. Stir in flour and salt; remove from heat, and gradually add half-and-half, stirring constantly. Bring to a boil, and cook 1 minute, stirring constantly, until very thick. Stir in wine and shrimp. Spoon shrimp mixture evenly into 6 buttered (5-inch) baking seashells. Set aside. Combine breadcrumbs, cheese, parsley, paprika, and 1½ tablespoons butter; stir until crumbly. Sprinkle over shrimp mixture; bake at 350° for 15 to 20 minutes or until heated thoroughly. Garnish with whole shrimp.

The Editors

SHRIMP CURRY
6 servings

⅓ cup butter
½ cup chopped onion
¼ to ½ cup chopped green
   pepper
2 cloves garlic, minced
2 cups sour cream
2 teaspoons lemon juice

2 teaspoons curry powder
¾ teaspoon salt
Dash chili powder
½ teaspoon ginger
Dash white pepper
3 cups shrimp, cleaned, cooked
   and split lengthwise

Melt butter in skillet; add onion, green pepper and garlic. Cook until tender. Stir in sour cream, lemon juice and seasoning; add shrimp. Stir until heated through. Serve over cooked rice or in patty shells.

Mrs. Bill Simmons (Evelyn)
Starkville, Mississippi

OEUFS-CREVETTES
1 serving

For each serving
1 teaspoon butter
3 or 4 shrimp, cooked and
   peeled
1 egg

1 Tablespoon cream
1 Tablespoon Swiss cheese,
   grated
Salt and pepper

Melt butter in ramekin or custard cup. Add shrimp. Break egg over shrimp. Season. Pour on cream and top with cheese. Bake at 400° for 8-10 minutes.

Mrs. Ben Mitchell (Margaret Ann)

SHRIMP FILLED AVOCADOS
6 servings

½ cup vegetable oil
½ cup lime juice
2 Tablespoons vinegar
2 teaspoons capers
1½ teaspoons salt

½ teaspoon dill weed
½ teaspoon dry mustard
Dash cayenne
1 pound small shrimp
3 avocados

Combine first 8 ingredients. Cook shrimp; peel and clean. Pour marinade over shrimp and chill, covered for several hours. Stir occasionally. Peel and half the avocados. Brush with marinade. Arrange on lettuce and fill with shrimp.

Mrs. John Tatum (Carol)

SHRIMP BAKED IN AVOCADO   2 servings

1 avocado
1 (10-ounce) package of frozen
   shrimp
1 Tablespoon lemon juice
Celery leaves
4 Tablespoons butter

2 Tablespoons all-purpose flour
½ cup heavy cream
1 (4-ounce) can sliced
   mushrooms
2 Tablespoons sweet wine
½ cup stuffing mix

Peel, split, and slightly salt avocado. Boil shrimp for 1 minute in salted water with lemon juice and celery leaves. Drain. Melt butter, then add flour and cream to make a white sauce. Cook a minute, then remove from heat. Add mushrooms, wine and shrimp to the sauce. Pour over each avocado half and top each half with stuffing mix and heat thoroughly in 300° oven.

Mrs. Allen Pepper (Ginger)

SHRIMP KABOBS   4 servings

2 pounds fresh jumbo shrimp,
   peeled and deveined
½ pound sliced bacon, cut
   each piece into 3 pieces
1 (10½-ounce) can pineapple
   chunks
¼ cup dry sherry
⅛ cup brown sugar, firmly
   packed

2 teaspoons Worcestershire
   sauce
4 teaspoons soy sauce
2 Tablespoons oil
Dash of garlic salt, or to taste
2 large bell peppers
1 large red or white onion

Wrap shrimp in bacon and secure with toothpicks. Place in single layer in a shallow pan. Drain pineapple, reserving liquid. Save pineapple chunks for skewering. Add sherry, brown sugar, Worcestershire sauce, soy sauce, oil, and garlic salt to pineapple juice. Shake well and pour over shrimp and bacon. Marinate overnight or 8 hours, turning once. Drain and save marinade. Parboil peppers for 2 to 4 minutes. They must still be firm. Cut into large pieces for skewering. Also, cut the onion into large pieces. Spray skewers with a non-stick coating. Skewer shrimp with bacon, alternating with pineapple chunks, bell pepper pieces and onion. Grill over medium hot coals or a gas grill, turning frequently while basting with reserved marinade. Can also be served as an appetizer.

Mrs. Roy Cole (Gail)

MICROWAVE SHRIMP IN GARLIC BUTTER   2 servings

**1 pound shelled, raw,
    deveined shrimp**
½ cup butter
2 Tablespoons Sauterne wine
**2 teaspoons dried or frozen
    chives**

**⅛ teaspoon minced garlic or
    1 clove garlic, crushed**
1 to 2 drops of Tabasco

Place shrimp in a 2-quart casserole dish. Stir together remaining ingredients. Pour over shrimp and stir to coat. Cover with plastic wrap. Microwave on high 5 to 6 minutes.

Mrs. Wayne Blansett (Diane)

SCAMPI   4 servings

**1½ pounds medium to large
    fresh shrimp**
1 cup all-purpose flour
Dash of salt
½ cup of butter

**3 Tablespoons fresh or freeze
    dried parsley**
2 cloves garlic, crushed
1 teaspoon Dijon mustard
2 teaspoons lemon juice

Shell and devein fresh shrimp. Mix the flour and salt together and dust shrimp with flour mixture. Arrange a single, non-overlapping layer of shrimp in flour ramekins or small individual casseroles. At this point you may refrigerate shrimp several hours or until ready to cook. When ready to serve, heat butter, lemon juice, parsley, garlic and mustard until hot and well mixed. Pour half of sauce over shrimp and broil for five minutes in oven. Turn shrimp and baste with remaining sauce and broil another 5 minutes or until shrimp are firm. Remove from oven and serve immediately.

Mrs. Nott Wheeler, Sr. (Cherry)

BAKED STUFFED SHRIMP WITH SCALLOPS

4 servings

Jumbo shrimp, 16 to 20
1 cup cracker crumbs, finely
  crushed
1 cup potato chips, finely
  crushed
½ cup butter or margarine,
  melted

1 pint raw scallops, finely
  chopped
Garlic salt
Onion salt
Celery salt
Parmesan cheese, grated

Flatten shrimp in a buttered shallow baking pan. Mix cracker crumbs, potato chips, butter and scallops. Season shrimp with salts and generous amounts of scallops mixture on each flattened shrimp. Sprinkle with Parmesan cheese. Bake at 350° for 20 minutes or until shrimp meat has turned white.

Joseph Bremon
Governor - Maine

MARGURITE'S SHRIMP AND PASTA

6 to 8 servings

2 pounds shrimp
1 cup butter
3 cloves garlic, chopped fine
1 cup fresh mushrooms (or 1
  (4-ounce) can)

½ cup dry white wine
1 (7-ounce) package vermicelli
½ cup chopped parsley
Parmesan cheese
Salt and pepper

In heavy pan, melt butter and add shrimp, mushrooms, and garlic. Cook over low heat, stirring until shrimp are pink. Add wine and cook 5 more minutes. Boil vermicelli until tender and drain. Pour shrimp sauce and parsley over pasta. Add salt and pepper and toss again. Top with Parmesan cheese.

Mrs. Chuck Weiss (Patti)
Moss Point, Mississippi

SHRIMP IN BEER I

6-8 servings

5 pounds fresh shrimp,
  deheaded
3-4 cans beer
1 pint white vinegar
⅛ cup red pepper

⅛ cup black pepper
¼ cup salt
2 Tablespoons celery seed, tied
  in cheesecloth

Bring ingredients to a boil. Add shrimp. Cook until done, approximately 10 minutes. Do not overcook. Peel and eat, using a parsley, lemon-butter sauce to dip shrimp in.

Note: This has a very strong pungent aroma, so you would be wise to be sure that you cook under a very effective ventahood—or even better, an outdoor fish cooker is ideal. This is a super roll-up-your sleeves, casual, and delicious experience.

Parsley Lemon-Butter Sauce:
½ cup butter
3 Tablespoons fresh lemon juice

½ Tablespoon parsley

Heat and serve with shrimp.

Mrs. Warren Williamson (Sallie Sanders)
Greenville, Alabama

SHRIMP IN BEER II

4 servings

3 cups beer
1 cup water
1 teaspoon salt
2 pounds fresh shrimp, shelled
  and deveined
2 onions, very thinly sliced
2 lemons, very thinly sliced

2 Tablespoons capers (optional)
⅔ cup oil
½ cup white tarragon vinegar
¼ cup finely chopped parsley
1½ teaspoons salt
½ teaspoon ground pepper
Dash hot sauce

Day before serving: In a large saucepan, bring beer and water to boil, add 1 teaspoon salt. Add shrimp and cook 3 to 5 minutes until they turn pink; remove from liquid with slotted spoon, and drain on paper towels. In a large bowl, make alternate layers of shrimp, onion slices, lemon slices, and capers. Put oil, vinegar, parsley, salt, pepper, and hot sauce in small jar with a cover; cap tightly and shake until well-blended. Pour over shrimp. Cover and chill at least 8 hours. At serving time, drain the shrimp and serve or use with a dip. It is very good with a large salad and fresh French bread.

Mrs. Jim Brown (Pat)

SHRIMP STEPHAN   4 to 6 servings

¼ pound butter
Juice of 1 lemon
3 garlic cloves, pressed
2 teaspoons chives
4 drops Worcestershire sauce

1 pound fresh shrimp, peeled
¼ cup croutons
6 teaspoons grated Parmesan
   cheese
½ glass dry white wine

Place butter, lemon juice, garlic and Worcestershire sauce in skillet and cook 2 minutes. Add shrimp and cook 4 minutes; stir. Add croutons, cheese and wine; cook 1 minute. Serve over a hot bed of rice.

Mrs. Marvin Kravitz (Sylvia)
Cleveland, Ohio

SHRIMP WITH WILD RICE   4 servings

White Sauce
½ cup all-purpose flour
½ cup butter, melted

4 cups chicken broth
¼ teaspoon white pepper

Gradually add flour to ½ cup melted butter. Cook over low heat; stir constantly until bubbly. Add broth slowly, cook until smooth and thick. Stir constantly. Add white pepper and simmer 2 to 3 minutes.

½ cup butter, melted
½ cup green pepper, thinly
   sliced
1 cup onion, thinly sliced
1 cup fresh mushrooms, thinly
   sliced

4 cups cooked wild rice
2 pounds shrimp, cooked
2 Tablespoons Worcestershire
   sauce
Few drops Tabasco

Sauté green pepper, onion, and mushrooms in butter. Drain. Combine white sauce, sautéed vegetables, rice, and shrimp. Add Worcestershire and Tabasco. Spoon into greased casserole. Bake for 45 minutes at 300°.

Variation: Add 12-ounces frozen crab meat, thawed, or 2 (7¾-ounce) cans crab meat.

Mrs. Sid Blackstone (Delia)
Lithonia, Georgia

SHRIMP CASSEROLE   10 to 12 servings

2½ pounds shrimp (boiled in salt water)
1 (10¾-ounce) can cream of mushroom soup
2 Tablespoons onion, chopped
2 Tablespoons celery, chopped
2 Tablespoons melted butter
2 Tablespoons lemon juice
1 teaspoon Worcestershire sauce
1 teaspoon Dijon mustard
¼ teaspoon pepper
½ pound Cheddar cheese, shredded
1 (6-ounce) box long grain and wild rice mix—cook according to directions
3 Tablespoons pimento (small jar)
¼ cup slivered almonds
3 Tablespoons fresh parsley (snipped)

Combine all of the above. Cover and bake at 350° for 30 minutes or until bubbly. Remove foil the last 10 minutes. Sprinkle extra cheese on top.

Mrs. Johnny Grafe (Nita)
Moss Point, Mississippi

SHRIMP MARINARA   4 servings

1 medium onion, chopped
¼ cup olive oil
1 medium green pepper, chopped
1 carrot, scraped and finely chopped
1 cup fresh mushrooms, sliced
2 cloves garlic, pressed
⅓ cup frozen petite English peas (thawed)
½ cup chicken broth or dry white wine
1 (6-ounce) can tomato paste
1½ teaspoons dried whole basil
1 teaspoon dried whole oregano
Pinch of sugar
¼ teaspoon white pepper
¼ teaspoon black pepper
½ to 1 cup water
1½ pounds shrimp, peeled and deveined
1 (12-ounce) package vermicelli

Sauté onions in hot oil in large skillet—stir 1 to 2 minutes. Add next 4 ingredients and sauté until tender. Add peas, broth (or wine), tomato paste, seasonings and stir well; thin to desired consistency with ½ to 1 cup water. Bring to a boil, reduce heat and simmer 5 minutes. Add shrimp; cook 3 to 5 minutes until shrimp is done. Serve over hot vermicelli.

Note: May use well drained oysters instead of shrimp. Cook until oysters curl and excess liquid is cooked down. Sauce should be thick.

Mrs. Robert Tibbs (Pat)

ORIENTAL FRIED SHRIMP   4 servings

2 pounds jumbo fresh shrimp,   **½ cup all-purpose flour**
   peeled and deveined   **4 eggs**
½ cup freshly squeezed lemon   **2 teaspoons salt**
   juice

Pour lemon juice over shrimp and let stand for 10 minutes. Drain. Split shrimp to resemble a butterfly. Place flour in a small bag, add shrimp (a few at a time), and shake. Beat eggs, add salt and dip each shrimp. Fry in moderately hot oil turning carefully until each side is properly brown. Drain and serve with cocktail sauce or sweet and sour sauce. This fried shrimp is very light and crispy.

Mrs. Bill Winstead (Betty)
Moss Point, Mississippi

SHRIMP CREOLE I   18 servings

½ cup butter   **3 bay leaves**
1⅓ cups diced green pepper   **8 whole cloves**
1⅓ cups chopped onions   **5 pounds raw shrimp, shelled**
2½ cups diced celery   **and deveined**
½ cup all-purpose flour   **2 teaspoons Worcestershire**
3 (1 pound and 13-ounce) cans   **sauce**
   tomatoes (10 cups in all)   **⅛ teaspoon hot sauce**
1½ Tablespoons salt   **1 Tablespoon lemon juice**
½ teaspoon pepper   **⅔ cup white wine**
2 Tablespoons brown sugar,   **3½ quarts cooked rice**
   firmly packed

Melt butter in a 8-quart heavy kettle. Add green pepper, onions, and celery. Sauté about 10 minutes, or until vegetables are tender. Remove from heat. Add flour and blend thoroughly. Add tomatoes gradually, stirring constantly. Add salt, pepper, sugar, bay leaves, and cloves. Bring to a boil. Reduce heat and simmer, uncovered, over low heat about 45 minutes, stirring occasionally. Meanwhile, clean shrimp and rinse thoroughly. Add shrimp to the thickened tomato sauce and cook about 5 minutes. Stir in Worcestershire sauce, hot sauce, lemon juice, and white wine. Serve over hot rice.

Mrs. Kirkham Povall (Hilda)

SHRIMP CREOLE II   6 to 8 servings

¼ cup oil
2 large onions, chopped
4 ribs celery, chopped
1 medium bell pepper,
  chopped
2 Tablespoons all-purpose flour
1½ cups water
5 (8-ounce) cans of tomato
  sauce
2 teaspoons vinegar
1 teaspoon sugar

1 Tablespoon horseradish
1 (8-ounce) can mushrooms
1 (8-ounce) can of English peas,
  drained
1 teaspoon Worcestershire
  sauce
1½ teaspoons salt
1 teaspoon black pepper
4 pounds raw shrimp, peeled
2 cups cooked rice

Combine first 4 ingredients in oil and sauté until color changes. Add 2 tablespoons flour and stir. Add water and mix well. Add 5 cans of tomato sauce. Stir until hot. Turn to low heat and simmer about 2 hours until sauce is cooked to medium thickness. Add vinegar, sugar, horseradish, English peas, mushrooms and seasonings. Finally add raw shrimp and let simmer for 5 to 10 minutes. Let sauce and shrimp sit awhile before serving. This improves flavor; then reheat before serving over rice.

Mrs. M. T. Blackwood (Jauweice)
Drew, Mississippi

SHRIMP CREOLE III   6 servings

¼ to ⅓ cup shortening
1 medium onion, chopped
2 stalks celery, chopped
1 large clove garlic, chopped
2 Tablespoons parsley
2 teaspoons salt
½ teaspoon cayenne pepper or
  hot sauce
1 (2-ounce) can tomato paste

½ cup chopped green pepper
  (optional)
2 bay leaves
1 (15-ounce) can tomato herb
  sauce
1 (6-ounce) can vegetable juice
  (tomato)
2 pounds raw shrimp, peeled
  and deveined

Melt shortening in a large heavy skillet over low heat. Sauté vegetables until clear and limp. Add ¾ of the can of tomato paste and mix thoroughly. Cook about 5 to 10 minutes, then add the tomato sauce. Stir and mix thoroughly. Add vegetable juice as needed. (Do not make too thin.) Add seasonings and allow mixture to cook 20 to 25 minutes. Add shrimp and cool 10 to 15 minutes longer. Serve over rice with hot French bread.

Mrs. John Abide (Marcia)

SHRIMP AND SCALLOP PILAF
4 servings

2 Tablespoons butter or
  margarine
¼ teaspoon turmeric or saffron
1 cup long-grain white rice
1 medium onion, chopped
1 clove garlic, minced
1 (13¾-ounce) can chicken
  broth plus enough water to
  measure 2½ cups

8-ounces sea scallops, halved if
  necessary
8-ounces shrimp, peeled and
  deveined
½ teaspoon salt (optional)
Pepper to taste

In large skillet, melt butter over medium heat; stir in tumeric. Add rice, onion and garlic. Cook about 3 minutes until onion is translucent, stirring often. Pour in broth mixture; bring to a boil. Reduce heat; cover and simmer 15 minutes longer or until scallops are opaque and shrimp turn pink. Taste and season.

Mrs. James Beard (Patty)

LOUISIANA PASTA
4 servings

4 Tablespoons butter
4 Tablespoons green onion,
  chopped
4 Tablespoons garlic, minced
1 pound raw shrimp
2 (10-ounce) containers oysters

Salt, red and black pepper to
  taste
Lemon pepper to taste
Garlic powder to taste
Cooked pasta to serve 4

Peel and devein shrimp. Melt butter (or half butter and half olive oil). Stir in onion, garlic and shrimp. Cook until shrimp turns pink, stirring often. Add drained oysters and continue cooking until edges curl. Pour over hot pasta and serve immediately.

Variation: Scallops can be substituted for oysters

Mrs. Mark Routman (Terri)

SEAFOOD LASAGNE
12 servings

8-ounces lasagne noodles
1 pound ricotta cheese
¾ cup chopped parsley
Salt and pepper to taste
Dash hot sauce
Pinch nutmeg
2 cloves garlic, minced
4 eggs, beaten
4 Tablespoons all-purpose flour

4 Tablespoons butter (not oleo)
1 cup hot milk
2 cups half-and-half milk
⅓ pound Mozzarella cheese, shredded
1 pound shrimp, peeled and chopped
10-ounces oysters or clams
8-ounces crab meat

Cook lasagne according to directions on package. Drain and place in ice water. Mix ricotta cheese, parsley, salt, pepper, hot sauce, nutmeg, garlic, and eggs. Set aside. Make a light colored roux with the flour and butter. Add hot milk and half-and-half. Cook over low heat for 5 minutes, stirring constantly. Grease a 9x13x2-inch casserole dish. Cover bottom with noodles. Spread ½ of ricotta cheese mixture onto noodles. Mix Parmesan cheese and mozzarella cheese, spread ⅓ of this mixture onto ricotta cheese mixture. Sprinkle ⅓ of shrimp, oysters, and crabmeat on top. Repeat process. Cover with ⅓ of sauce. Top with a layer of noodles, a layer of sauce, layer of cheeses, then the seafood. Cover with foil. Bake at 350° for 45 minutes. Serve bubbly hot.

Mrs. Billy Nowell (Ann)
Mrs. Bill Braden (Billie Jo)
Spring, Texas

SEAFOOD IN CREAM SAUCE
6 to 8 servings

3 Tablespoons butter, melted
2 Tablespoons all-purpose flour
2½ cups half-and-half cream
1 teaspoon salt
2 Tablespoons chopped parsley
¼ teaspoon black pepper
½ teaspoon MSG
1 teaspoon dry mustard

1 teaspoon Worcestershire sauce
4 hard-boiled eggs
1 pound shrimp, boiled and shelled
2 or 3 lobster tails, cooked and cubed
1 (6½-ounce) can crab meat

Make a white sauce with the butter, flour, and half-and-half. Add all the seasonings. Cool. Add sieved egg yolks and slivered egg whites. Add seafood. Heat thoroughly and serve over rice.

Mrs. Brady Cole (Rosalie)

TONI'S GARLICY SHRIMP AND LINGUINI
4 servings

1 cup margarine or butter
4 cloves garlic
¼ cup olive oil
3 cloves garlic
1 teaspoon red pepper

¼ cup fresh parsley
1 pound linguini noodles
1 Tablespoon salt
1 pound peeled raw shrimp
1 teaspoon salt

Peel shrimp and set aside. Sauté 4 cloves of garlic in butter for 10 minutes in small skillet. Set garlic butter aside. Put ¼ cup olive oil, 3 cloves of garlic, 1 teaspoon red pepper, and ¼ cup fresh parsley in blender and blend for 10 seconds. Pour olive oil mixture into a large heavy skillet and set aside. Boil linguine in large pot of boiling water with 1 tablespoon of salt according to directions. Drain linguini in colander and then put back in large pot. Pour garlic butter over noodles and toss gently. Place over high heat skillet with olive oil mixture. Place shrimp and 1 teaspoon salt in skillet with olive oil mixture and cook over high heat 3 to 5 minutes, depending on size of the shrimp. Serve shrimp over garlic buttered noodles. ABSOLUTELY SCRUMPTIOUS. This can be sprinkled with Parmesan cheese.

Mrs. John Nolen Canon (Toni)
Tunica, Mississippi

INDIVIDUAL SEAFOOD IMPERIALS
4 servings

2 Tablespoons green onions, finely chopped
1 Tablespoon green pepper, finely chopped
3 Tablespoons butter, melted
1 Tablespoon chopped pimento
1 Tablespoon dry mustard
⅛ teapsoon dried thyme leaf (not powdered)

3 Tablespoons all-purpose flour
1 cup milk
1 teaspoon Worcestershire sauce
¼ teaspoon salt
1½ pounds fresh lump crabmeat, picked over and drained
3 Tablespoons mayonnaise

Sauté onions and green pepper in butter until tender. Stir in pimento, mustard, and thyme. Lower heat, add flour, stirring until smooth. Add milk, stir and cook until thickened. Add Worcestershire sauce and salt. Remove from heat and gently stir in crabmeat and mayonnaise. Bake at 375° for 20 minutes. Broil 1 to 2 minutes to lightly brown top.

Note: 1½ pounds crabmeat fills 4 large seafood shells

Mrs. Bob Tibbs (Pat)

COMPANY SEAFOOD BAKE   8 to 10 servings

¾ cup margarine
1 pound fresh mushrooms,
   cleaned and sliced
6 Tablespoons all-purpose flour
1 teaspoon salt
½ teaspoon pepper
3 cups half-and-half
½ cup (2-ounces) shredded
   sharp Cheddar cheese

¼ teaspoon Worcestershire
   sauce
2 pounds shrimp, cooked and
   deveined
1 to 2 cups lump crab meat
¼ cup dry sherry
1 cup buttered bread crumbs

Melt margarine in large skillet. Add mushrooms and sauté until tender. Add flour, salt, pepper and cook until mixture bubbles. Remove from heat and add half-and-half and mix thoroughly. Return to heat and cook, stirring until thickened. Add cheese and Worcestershire sauce and stir until cheese melts. Add seafood and sherry, mix and pour into a 9x12-inch baking dish. Cover with crumbs. Bake at 350° for 40 to 45 minutes, or until hot and bubbly. Serve over hot rice.

Mrs. Richard Cole (Wendy)

SEAFOOD CASSEROLE   4 servings

1 medium bell pepper,
   chopped
1 medium onion, finely
   chopped
1 cup finely chopped celery
1 (6½-ounce) can fancy crab
   meat
1 (6½-ounce) can claw crab
   meat
2 (5-ounce) cans shrimp, or 10
   ounces frozen cooked shrimp

½ teaspoon salt
Red and black pepper to taste
1 Tablespoon Worcestershire
   sauce
1 cup mayonnaise
1 cup sour cream
¾ cup rice, cooked
Bread crumbs

Mix all ingredients together and place in a 2-quart casserole dish. Sprinkle top with bread crumbs. Bake at 350 for 30 minutes.

Mrs. Joe Smith, III (Suellen)

BAKED FLOUNDER AND SHRIMP
2 servings

½ cup melted butter
¼ cup dry sherry
Juice of 1 lemon
Dash of garlic salt
Soy sauce and Worcestershire
  sauce to taste
2 fresh flounders, about 1
  pound each

1 dozen fresh shrimp, peeled
  and deveined
1 (6-ounce) can sliced, broiled
  in butter, mushrooms,
  undrained
Whole lemon, sliced

Mix all ingredients, except flounder, shrimp, mushrooms, and lemon slices. Pour in a large baking dish. Add flounder and place sliced lemon on top. Bake at 350° on a gas grill or in over, basting frequently, until flounder begins to flake easily with a fork, about 20 minutes. Place shrimp and mushrooms around flounder and continue cooking and basting until shrimp turn pink and curl, about 5 to 10 minutes.

Mrs. Roy Cole (Gail)

FLOUNDER IN SPINACH
4 servings

2 (10-ounce) packages
  chopped spinach, cooked
  and drained
1 cup sour cream
1 onion, chopped
1½ Tablespoons all-purpose
  flour

2 Tablespoons lemon juice
1 teaspoon salt
1½ pounds flounder fillets
Paprika

Mix all ingredients except flounder and put into shallow baking dish. Arrange flounder on top. Sprinkle with paprika and cook 20 minutes at 350°.

Daral Glick Spencer
Atlanta, Georgia

BLACKENED REDFISH

6 servings

¾ pound unsalted butter,
  melted in a skillet

Seasoning mix

1 Tablespoon sweet paprika	½ teaspoon dried thyme leaves
2½ teaspoons salt	½ teaspoon dried oregano
1 teaspoon onion powder	leaves
1 teaspoon garlic powder	6 (8 to 10-ounce) fish fillets
1 teaspoon ground red pepper	(preferable redfish, pompano
(preferably cayenne)	or red snapper), cut about ½
¾ teaspoon white pepper	inch thick
¾ teaspoon black pepper	

Heat a large cast-iron skillet over very high heat until it is beyond the smoking stage and you see white ash in the skillet bottom (the skillet cannot be too hot for this dish), at least 10 minutes. Meanwhile, pour 2 tablespoons melted butter in each of 6 small ramekins; set aside and keep warm. Reserve the remaining butter in its skillet. Heat the serving plates in a 250° oven. Thoroughly combine the seasoning mix ingredients in a small bowl. Dip each fillet in the reserved melted butter so that both sides are well coated; then sprinkle seasoning mix generously and evenly on both sides of the fillets, patting it in by hand. Place in the hot skillet and pour 1 teaspoon melted butter on top of each fillet (be careful, as the batter may flame). Cook, uncovered, over the same high heat until the underside looks charred, about 2 minutes (the time will vary according to the fillets thickness and the heat of the skillet). Turn the fish over and again pour 1 teaspoon butter on top; cook until fish is done, about 2 minutes more. Repeat with remaining fillets. Serve each fillet while piping hot. To serve, place one fillet and a ramekin of butter on each heated serving plate.

Variation: Substitute catfish for redfish

From: Chef Paul Prudhomme's Louisiana Kitchen

REDFISH EUGENIE
6 servings

2 cups heavy cream	*1 teaspoon salt*
1 Tablespoon dried sweet basil	*1 teaspoon red pepper*
1 Tablespoon dried oregano	*1 teaspoon black pepper*
1 cup onion tops and parsley,	*1 teaspoon white pepper*
mixed	*Dash nutmeg*
2 pounds crayfish tails, peeled	*All-purpose flour*
6 to 8-ounces redfish fillet	*1 cup margarine*

For sauce, pour cream into large skillet on medium-high heat, stirring often. Let cream simmer until it thickens. While simmering, add basil, oregano, chopped onion tops and parsley and let cook together. Cream should become thick. To test, drip cream from spoon; drops should be thick, and the last drop should remain on the spoon. Once consistency has been reached, add crayfish. Continue to stir, bringing cream back to a simmer; continue cooking until thick. Pat fillet dry. Season fish by sprinkling salt and red, black, and white peppers over both sides of fillet. Lightly coat with flour mixed with nutmeg. In large skillet, melt margarine. Once hot, pan-fry fillet over medium-heat, turning just once on each side. Cook until golden brown. Place on serving plate. Pour generous amount of sauce over fish, distributing crayfish tails evenly.

Chef Alex Patout
Patout's Restaurant
New Iberia, Louisiana

BAYOU LAND CRAYFISH PIE

6 servings

1 pound crayfish tails
¾ cup butter
1 bunch green onions, chopped
½ cup chopped parsley
3 Tablespoons all-purpose flour

1 pint half-and-half cream
3 Tablespoons sherry
Salt, red and black pepper to
taste
1 (9-inch) pie shell, baked

In a skillet, sauté crayfish tails in ¼ cup butter for 10 minutes. In another skillet, sauté green onions and parsley in ½ cup butter. Then blend in flour and gradually add cream, stirring constantly to make a thick sauce. Season to taste. Combine tails with sauce and place mixture in pie shell. Bake at 350° for 20 minutes. Freezes well.

Bayou Land Seafood
Breaux Bridge, Louisiana

CRAYFISH ETOUFFEE

8 servings

½ cup margarine
⅔ cup all-purpose flour
2 cups chopped onion
2 cups chopped green pepper
2 cups chopped celery
4 cloves garlic, diced
4 cups chicken broth

½ cup chopped parsley
2 teaspoons salt
¼ teaspoon black pepper
¼ teaspoon red pepper
1 pound crayfish tails (fresh or
frozen)
6 cups hot cooked rice

To make roux, melt butter in large iron pot. Blend in flour slowly and cook on medium to low heat for 10 to 15 minutes, until roux is caramel color. Add onions, green pepper, celery, and garlic. Cook 2 to 3 minutes. Stir in chicken broth, parsley, salt, black pepper, red pepper, and crayfish tails. Simmer 20 minutes, stirring often. Serve over rice.

Mrs. Roger Dicks (Sallie)

FRIED CRAYFISH TAILS

6 servings

**1 pound crayfish tails, fresh
   or frozen
1 cup yellow cornmeal
1 teaspoon salt**

**1 teaspoon black pepper
¼ teaspoon cayenne pepper
Shortening or vegetable oil**

Rinse crayfish under cold water and drain. Mix cornmeal, salt, black pepper, and cayenne pepper thoroughly. Roll damp crayfish in seasoned meal to coat well. Heat oil in deep fryer to 375°. Fry crayfish a few at a time until browned. Drain. Serve with red seafood sauce.

Mrs. Roger Dicks (Sallie)

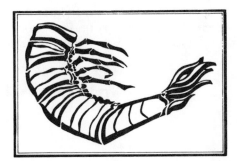

CRAYFISH ELEGANTE

4 servings

**1 pound crayfish tails
¾ cup butter or oleo
1 small bunch green onions,
   chopped
½ cup chopped parsley**

**1 pint half-and-half cream
3 Tablespoons sherry
Salt and red pepper to taste
3 level Tablespoons all-purpose
   flour**

In skillet, sauté crayfish tails in ¼ cup butter for 10 minutes. In another skillet, sauté green onions and parsley in ½ cup butter. Blend in flour and gradually add half-and-half, stirring constantly to make a thick sauce. Add sherry, then crayfish tails, being careful not to include fat in bottom of skillet. Season with salt and red pepper to taste. Serve in patty shells. Freezes well.

Note: Before cooking crayfish tails, lay on paper towels and wipe gently to remove some of the fat.

The Editors

CRAYFISH CREOLE OVER PERCH   6 to 8 servings

1 pound of cooked crayfish
  meats
6 to 8 (white perch) fillets
1 cup chopped onion
1 cup chopped green pepper
1 cup chopped celery
2 Tablespoons bacon drippings
1 Tablespoon Worcestershire
  sauce

Hot sauce to taste
1 teaspoon salt
½ teaspoon pepper
2 (8-ounce) cans tomato sauce
1 cup raw rice, cooked as
  directed

Sauté crayfish, onion, green peppers, celery in bacon drippings. Add other ingredients, except rice and fillets. Simmer until vegetables are tender. Place fillets in a greased 13x9x2-inch baking pan. Pour sauce over fillets. Bake at 400° until fish is tender and flakes with a fork. Serve over a bed of hot rice.

Mrs. Paul Mullins (Libba)

BAYOU LAND CRAYFISH JAMBALAYA   6 servings

2 Tablespoons oil
1 Tablespoon all-purpose flour
1 cup chopped onion
½ cup chopped celery
½ cup chopped bell pepper
1½ cups water
2½ cups crayfish tails

¼ cup fat (if available)
2 cups water
½ cup chopped green onions
1¼ cups raw rice
Parsley
Salt and pepper to taste

Make a golden roux with oil and flour. Add onion, celery, pepper and crayfish fat and simmer. Add 1½ cups water and simmer for one hour. Add crayfish tails and cook for 10 to 15 minutes. Add 2 cups water. Bring to a boil and add green onions, rice, parsley, salt and pepper. Stir to blend and cook covered on low heat for about ½ hour or until rice is tender. Fluff rice before serving.

Bayou Land Seafood
Breaux Bridge, Louisiana

CROWN ROOM'S SHRIMP STUFFED CATFISH　　6 servings

1 small onion, chopped
3 green onions, chopped
¼ pound fresh mushrooms,
　chopped
3 Tablespoons butter, melted
½ cup soft bread crumbs
2 Tablespoons chopped fresh
　parsley

Juice of ½ lemon
6 (7 to 9-ounce) catfish fillets
½ pound medium shrimp,
　cooked and peeled
¾ cup shredded Swiss cheese
Paprika

Sauce
⅓ cup butter
⅓ cup all-purpose flour
2⅔ cups milk
⅓ cup dry white wine

2 egg yolks
½ teaspoon dry mustard
Dash of red pepper

Sauté onions and mushrooms in butter until tender; add bread crumbs, parsley, and lemon juice, mixing well. Spread 2 tablespoons of stuffing mixture down the center of each fillet; top with shrimp. Roll fillets up, securing with a wooden pick. Place each fillet, seam side down, in a lightly greased individual baking dish. Pour about ½ cup of sauce over each fillet. Bake at 350° for 25 minutes; sprinkle with cheese and bake an additional 3 minutes or until cheese melts. Sprinkle with paprika.

Sauce: Melt butter in a heavy saucepan over low heat; add flour, stirring until smooth. Cook 1 minute, stirring constantly. Gradually add milk and wine; cook over medium heat, stirring constantly. Beat egg yolks until thick and lemon colored. Gradually stir about ¼ of hot mixture into yolks; add to remaining hot mixture, stirring constantly. Cook over medium heat, stirring constantly until thickened and bubbly. Stir in mustard and red pepper.

The Crown Room
Indianola, Mississippi

Fish

FISH FILLET'S FLORENTINE

4 (6 to 8-ounce) catfish fillets
½ cup dry white wine
2 (10-ounce) packages frozen chopped spinach, thawed and well drained
Salt and freshly ground pepper

1 (10¾-ounce) can cream of shrimp soup, undiluted
4 Tablespoons butter
Freshly grated Parmesan cheese
Paprika

Preheat oven to 350°. Butter an 8-inch square baking dish. Poach fish in wine 4 to 5 minutes; drain. Spread spinach evenly in dish and season with salt and pepper to taste. Arrange fish over spinach and top with soup. Dot with butter and sprinkle with cheese and paprika. Bake 20 minutes. Serve immediately.

Mrs. Allen Findley (Shirley)

VERSATILE CATFISH
8 servings

8 medium catfish fillets

Mix and pour over fish
1¾ cups mayonnaise
1 Tablespoon creole mustard
1 Tablespoon hot sauce
2 teaspoons garlic powder
1 teaspoon seasoned salt
2 Tablespoons lemon juice

1 Tablespoon Worcestershire sauce
1 Tablespoon curry powder
1 teaspoon lemon pepper
Cracker or bread crumbs

Place fish in a greased pan. Pour sauce over to coat fish. Top with crumbled crackers or seasoned bread crumbs. Bake at 375° about 30 minutes. Fish will flakes easily when done.

Mrs. Jimmy Yeager (Neysa)

SOUFFLÉ-STUFFED CATFISH
6 servings

6 medium catfish fillets
3 Tablespoons butter, melted
1 cup cheese cracker crumbs
½ cup commercial buttermilk
  salad dressing

1 (12-ounce) package frozen
  spinach soufflé
Lemony cheese sauce (recipe
  below)

Brush sides of fish with butter. Dredge in cracker crumbs; set aside. Pour salad dressing into a lightly greased 13x9x2-inch baking dish. Cut frozen souffle into 6 equal parts. Roll each fillet around a piece of souffle, place seam side down in baking dish. Cover and bake 375° for 40 minutes. Uncover and bake another 15 minutes or until fish flakes easily when tested with a fork. Spoon lemony cheese sauce into a shallow serving platter; arrange fillets in sauce. Garnish with lemon slices.

Lemony Cheese Sauce
1 (8-ounce) package cream
  cheese, cut into cubes
1 egg, beaten
2 Tablespoons lemon juice
1 teaspoon sugar
½ teaspoon dry mustard

¼ teaspoon dried whole
  tarragon
½ to ¾ cup commercial
  buttermilk salad dressing
¼ cup grated Parmesan cheese

Combine first 6 ingredients in a medium saucepan; cook over low heat, stirring frequently, until cream cheese melts. Stir in salad dressing and Parmesan cheese. Cook just until thoroughly heated.

Mrs. Allen D. Findley (Shirley)

BAKED CRISPY CATFISH
4 to 6 servings

½ cup Caesar salad dressing
1 cup crushed potato chips
½ cup shredded sharp
  Cheddar cheese

2 pounds catfish fillets

Dip fillets in salad dressing and place in a single layer, skin side down, in a baking dish. Combine crushed chips and cheese and sprinkle over fillets. Bake at 500° for 10 to 15 minutes or until fish flakes when tested with a fork.

Mrs. Phillip Rizzo (Ramona)

CATFISH PARMESAN
6 servings

6 skinned, pan-dressed
    catfish, fresh or frozen
1 cup dry bread crumbs
¾ cup grated Parmesan
    cheese
¼ cup chopped parsley
1 teaspoon paprika
½ teaspoon whole oregano

¼ teaspoon basil
2 teaspoons salt
½ teaspoon pepper
½ cup butter or margarine,
    melted
Lemon wedge
Parsley

Pat fish dry. Combine bread crumbs, Parmesan cheese and seasonings. Mix well. Dip fish in butter and roll each in crumb mixture. Arrange fish in a well greased 13x9x2-inch baking dish. Bake 375° about 25 minutes or until fish flakes easily when tested with a fork. Garnish with lemon wedges and parsley.

Mrs. Jim Adams (Signe)

CONTINENTAL CATFISH
6 servings

6 skinned catfish fillets
1 teaspoon salt
Dash of pepper
⅓ cup margarine, melted
1 cup chopped parsley
1 egg, beaten

¼ cup milk
1 teaspoon salt
1 cup dry bread crumbs or
    cracker crumbs
½ cup Swiss cheese, grated
3 Tablespoons oil

Pat fillets dry and sprinkle with salt and pepper. Combine margarine and parsley to make parsley butter. Combine egg, milk, and salt. Dot fish with half the parsley butter. Dip fish in egg mixture and roll in bread crumbs and cheese which have been combined. Place on a well oiled aluminum lined broiler pan 15½x12-inches. Drizzle remaining parsley butter, crumb mixture and oil over fish. Bake at 500° for 15 to 20 minutes until fish flakes with fork.

Mrs. Emmett Findley

CAJUN CATFISH

4 to 6 servings

8 to 10 fresh catfish fillets
1 (8-ounce) can tomato sauce
1 Tablespoon vinegar
2 Tablespoons vegetable oil
1 teaspoon garlic powder
1 teaspoon onion salt
½ teaspoon celery salt

½ teaspoon paprika
Salt and pepper to taste
3 Tablespoons parsley flakes
1 teaspoon lemon-pepper
  seasoning
1 Tablespoon grated Parmesan
  cheese

Combine ingredients for sauce except Parmesan. Brush fish with sauce, salt and pepper. Sprinkle with Parmesan cheese. Bake at 350° for about 40 minutes. Then broil for 3 minutes to brown top.

Note: These fish can be prepared for baking and frozen until ready to use.

Mrs. Emmett Cox (Martha)

TROUT IN FOIL

1 speckled trout fillet per
  person
Imported olive oil
1 onion, quartered
2 garlic cloves, split
2 celery ribs

3 bay leaves
Juice of 1 lemon
Dash of Worcestershire sauce
Salt and pepper to taste
Dash of Tabasco

Pour olive oil on foil paper, salt and pepper fish and place on foil. Put seasonings on top of fish, cover all with a little olive oil, and fold paper tightly closed. Put in pan and bake at 350° about 30 or 40 minutes. Open foil and brown under the broiler. Remove seasonings and serve on platter with lemon wedges.

Mrs. Schorten Monget

BATTER FOR SHIRMP AND OYSTERS

1 cup all-purpose flour
½ teaspoon sugar
1 egg

1 cup ice water
2 Tablespoons vegetable oil
Salt and pepper to taste

Mix and dip.

Mrs. Paul Warrington (Pat)

Fish

SCALLOPED OYSTERS

4 servings

½ cup dry bread crumbs
½ cup coarse cracker crumbs
5 Tablespoons butter, melted
1 pint oysters
½ teaspoon salt
⅛ teaspoon pepper

Dash of nutmeg
2 Tablespoons parsley,
 chopped (optional)
¼ cup oyster liquor
¼ cup milk

Combine bread crumbs, cracker crumbs, and butter. Alternate layers of oysters and crumb mixture, sprinkling each layer with seasonings. Combine oyster liquor and milk, pour over layers; top with crumbs. Bake in a moderate oven 350° for 1 hour. For unusual flavor, substitute canned cream of mushroom soup for all of liquid.

Mrs. Charles Lawrence (Mary Kathyrn)

OYSTERS MOSKA

8 to 10 servings

6 pints fresh oysters
3 cups bread crumbs, seasoned
1 Tablespoon crushed red
 pepper
2 Tablespoons lemon juice

¾ cup olive oil
1 clove garlic
3 Tablespoons chopped parsley
1 cup grated Parmesan cheese

Broil oysters until they curl. Then mix other ingredients together and pour over oysters. Bake at 350° until mixture is hot.

Mrs. Vernon Shelton (Pam)
Drew, Mississippi

HINTS: HOW TO OPEN OYSTERS IN THE HALF SHELL

Raw oysters that have been opened just before serving are found to be at their best. Shucking should be done by a strong hand with an equally sturdy instrument. But there is a trick and it works. Scrub oysters well under running water with a stiff vegetable brush. Then put them on a cookie sheet in a moderately hot oven 400° for 5 or 6 minutes, depending on their size. Remove from oven and drop into ice water. The heat relaxes the muscle and they can be opened very easily with a table knife. The shell is so heavy, the heat does not affect the oyster at all. Oysters to be eaten raw are left loose in the deeper half of the shell, arranged on a chilled plate and served with a cut lemon and freshly ground pepper.

Mrs. Allen Pepper (Ginger)

Vegetables,
Side Dishes

ARTICHOKES SMOTHERED WITH TOMATOES AND HERBS

Juice of 2 lemons   *1 artichoke*

To prepare artichoke, cut off stem and pointed top. Trim the prickly points off leaves with scissors. Soak trimmed artichokes for 30 minutes in a bowl of water and lemon juice. This softens the artichokes and prevents discoloration. Remove from water and pry apart the center of the artichoke and scoop out the hairy core with a sharp teaspoon. Stand artichokes upright in a deep covered casserole.

Topping
1 shallot, finely minced
1 small onion, thinly sliced
1 Tablespoon olive oil
1 medium tomato, peeled, seeded, and coarsely chopped

1 Tablespoon chopped parsley
¼ teaspoon salt
Freshly ground pepper
½ teaspoon tiny capers (optional)

Combine all topping ingredients. Spoon some of the mixture into center cavity of artichoke, and sprinkle rest over tops and between outer leaves. Add enough water to cover bottom third of artichokes. Bring to boil, and reduce heat so that artichokes simmer. Cover and cook until tender but not mushy, about 30 to 45 minutes. Serve hot, warm or at room temperature. Garnish with fresh basil, oregano, or marjoram. Allow 1 artichoke per person.

Mrs. W. C. Cox (Mary Elizabeth)

ASPARAGUS CROQUETTES   15 servings

2¾ cups fine cracker crumbs, divided
2 (14½-ounce) cans cut asparagus, drained
1 (10¾-ounce) can cream of mushroom soup, undiluted

8-ounces sharp Cheddar cheese, shredded
Vegetable oil

Combine 1¾ cups cracker crumbs and next 3 ingredients, mixing well. Shape mixture, ¼ cup at a time, into oval croquettes. Roll croquettes in the remaining 1 cup cracker crumbs. Deep fry croquettes in hot oil for 2 to 3 minutes or until golden brown. Drain on paper towels. Serve immediately.

Mrs. Charles Fioranelli (Vicki)

ASPARAGUS WITH ORANGE AND CASHEWS 8 servings

2½ pounds fresh asparagus
4 Tablespoons butter
3 Tablespoons all-purpose flour
2 cups heavy cream
Salt to taste

White pepper to taste
1 orange, peeled and sectioned
½ cup chopped cashew nuts
Grated orange rind for garnish

Steam asparagus until tender. Make cream sauce by melting the butter in a small saucepan and stirring in flour. Stir over low heat for two minutes, then gradually add the cream and cook until thick, stirring constantly. Season to taste with salt and white pepper. Section the orange and cut into large pieces. Add to cream sauce. Arrange asparagus on serving dish and salt lightly. Pour the sauce over the asparagus and sprinkle with cashew nuts and grated orange rind. Serve immediately.

Mrs. H. L. Dilworth (Anne)

ASPARAGUS AND PEA CASSEROLE 6 servings

4 Tablespoons butter, melted
4 Tablespoons all-purpose flour
2 cups milk
2 teaspoons onion juice
1 teaspoon Worcestershire
  sauce
Salt and pepper to taste
1 (2-ounce) jar pimiento

½ cup shredded sharp
  Cheddar cheese
1 (17-ounce) can asparagus
  spears
1 (8-ounce) can water
  chestnuts, sliced
1 (17-ounce) can English peas
Buttered bread crumbs

Make a white sauce from butter, flour, and milk. Add onion juice, Worcestershire, salt, pepper, pimiento, and cheese. In buttered 2 quart oblong casserole, place layer of asparagus, white sauce, water chestnuts, peas, and another layer of white sauce. Top with buttered bread crumbs and heat in 350° oven until thoroughly heated, about 20 to 30 minutes.

Mrs. Will Lewis, Jr.
Oxford, Mississippi

PINEAPPLE HARVARD BEETS

6 to 8 servings

½ cup sugar
½ Tablespoon cornstarch
¼ to ½ cup mild vinegar
1 Tablespoon horseradish
    (optional)
¼ cup water or beet stock

1 (16-ounce) can beets or 12
    small cooked beets
1 (16-ounce) can pineapple
    chunks
2 Tablespoons butter

Blend sugar, cornstarch, vinegar, horseradish and water. Boil for 5 minutes. Add sliced beets and pineapple. Let stand for at least 30 minutes. Just before serving, bring to boiling point. Add butter. This is also good cold.

Ms. Nona Watson

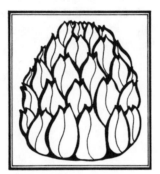

BROCCOLI IN CHEESE CUSTARD

6 servings

1 (10-ounce) package frozen,
    chopped broccoli
¾ cup instant nonfat dry milk
1¼ cups hot water
2 eggs, slightly beaten
½ cup Cheddar cheese,
    shredded

3 Tablespoons butter, melted
2 Tablespoons lemon juice
1 teaspoon salt
⅛ teaspoon pepper

Cook broccoli according to package directions; drain. In large bowl, beat milk and water until smooth. Stir in eggs, cheese, butter, lemon juice, salt and pepper. Place broccoli in 1¼ quart casserole and pour custard over broccoli. Set casserole in shallow pan filled with hot water 1-inch deep. Bake at 350° 35 to 40 minutes or until knife inserted near center comes out clean.

Mrs. Joe Garrison (Joyce)

BROCCOLI STRATA

10 servings

2 pounds fresh broccoli
8-ounces Swiss cheese,
  shredded
4 eggs, beaten
1 cup milk
1 medium onion, chopped

1 teaspoon salt
1 teaspoon prepared mustard
Pepper to taste
6-ounces Mozzarella cheese
  slices

Cut broccoli florets into bite-sized pieces. Peel stems if tough and cut into cubes or slices. Cook broccoli in small amount of water until tender; drain. Sprinkle 1 cup of Swiss cheese on bottom of ungreased baking dish. Layer broccoli over cheese. Blend eggs, milk, onion, salt, mustard, and pepper. Pour over broccoli. Sprinkle remaining cup of Swiss cheese over broccoli; then cover with slices of Mozzarella. Bake uncovered at 325° about 1 hour or until a knife inserted in center comes out clean. Remove from oven. Let stand 10 minutes before serving.

Mrs. Leo McGee (Judy)

FRIED CABBAGE

4 servings

1 head cabbage, chopped
1 cup chopped bell pepper
1 cup chopped celery
1 cup chopped onion
2 Tablespoons cooking oil

1 (12 to 16-ounce) smoked
  sausage, chopped
3 Tablespoons sugar
3 Tablespoons vinegar
1 teaspoon cayenne pepper

Stir fry the cabbage, bell pepper, celery, and onion in oil for 20 minutes. Boil smoked sausage and add to cabbage. Mix together sugar, vinegar, and cayenne pepper and add to cabbage. Simmer about 20 minutes or longer.

Note: Great with hot buttered cornbread.

Mrs. Jody Correro (Glenda)

CARROT AND SQUASH CASSEROLE

4 to 6 servings

1 (6-ounce) corn bread
* stuffing mix*
½ cup butter
1½ cups sliced squash
1 cup chopped onion
2 carrots, sliced

1 (2-ounce) jar pimiento,
* chopped*
1 (8-ounce) carton sour cream
1 (10¾-ounce) can cream of
* mushroom soup*

Melt butter and add stuffing mix. Put ⅓ mixture in bottom of 9x13 baking dish. Mix other ingredients and layer on top of stuffing. Place remaining stuffing mixture on top. Bake at 350° for 30 to 35 minutes.

Mrs. S. R. Blakeman (Mary James)

CARROTS LYONNAISE

4 to 6 servings

1 pound carrots cut into
* julienne strips 3 inches long*
1 chicken bouillon cube
½ cup boiling water
4 Tablespoons margarine
2 cups sliced onion

¾ cup water
1 Tablespoon all-purpose flour
¼ teaspoon salt
Dash of pepper
Dash of sugar

Dissolve bouillon cube in boiling water. Add carrots and cook covered 10 minutes. In a large skillet, melt the margarine and add the onion slices. Cook covered for 15 minutes, stirring occasionally. Mix the water, flour, salt, and pepper. Add to onions and bring to a boil. Add the carrots and chicken stock mixture. Simmer uncovered 10 minutes or until carrots are tender. Serve hot. Add a dash of sugar just before serving.

Judy Jones

CARROT AND ZUCCHINI CASSEROLE
6 servings

1 pound carrots, cut
   diagonally into ½-inch slices
2 to 4 zucchini, cut diagonally
   into ½-inch slices
½ cup mayonnaise
2 Tablespoons grated onion
½ teaspoon salt

½ cup Italian style bread
   crumbs
¾ teaspoon prepared
   horseradish
½ teaspoon pepper
¼ cup butter or margarine,
   melted

Cook carrots and zucchini in a small amount of boiling salted water for 5 minutes or until tender. Drain well. Reserve ¼ cup cooking liquid. Combine reserved liquid, mayonnaise, onion, horseradish, salt and pepper; add to carrots and zucchini, stirring well. Spoon mixture into a lightly greased 8-inch square baking dish. Combine bread crumbs and butter; sprinkle over casserole. Bake at 375° for 15 to 20 minutes.

Mrs. W. P. Skelton (Louise)

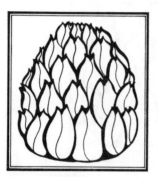

CALIFORNIA CARROTS

1 bunch carrots, sliced ¼-inch
   thick
1 medium onion thinly sliced
   and cut in half
6 pieces bacon fried crisp,
   broken into pieces, reserve
   pan drippings

Dash salt, pepper, Beau Monde
and Cavenders'

Cover carrots with water. Add onion, bacon, 2 tablespoons of bacon drippings, salt, pepper, Beau Monde and Cavenders'. Boil and cook until tender. May be stored in refrigerator overnight so that seasonings can be more effective. Heat when ready to serve.

Mrs. J. T. Davis (Mary Anna)

MAMMY'S FRIED CORN   6 servings

2 cups fresh cut corn
2 Tablespoons bacon drippings
1 Tablespoon sugar
½ teaspoon salt
½ teaspoon pepper

½ cup water
¼ cup margarine
1 Tablespoon all-purpose flour
½ cup milk

Put drippings into a heavy skillet. Have heat moderately high. Add corn, sugar, salt, and pepper. Scrape skillet until corn begins to brown and stick. Continue cooking until corn is golden brown. Reduce heat to low and add enough water to cover corn. Cover the skillet and simmer until corn is tender. Stir occasionally. When corn begins to stick, add more water. When corn becomes tender, add margarine, flour, and milk. Continue to cook until thick.

Mrs. Billy Nowell (Ann)

CORN FRITTERS   2 dozen

1 egg, beaten
3-ounces milk
1½ cups all-purpose flour
1 teaspoon baking powder

½ teaspoon salt
1 Tablespoon melted butter
1 (17-ounce) cream-style corn

Mix all ingredients together and blend well. Drop from a tablesoon into deep fat and fry until golden brown.

Mrs. Troy Odom (Mary Ann)

RATATOUILLE   8 to 10 servings

2 cups pared and sliced
  eggplant
2 cups sliced squash
3 tomatoes, peeled and sliced
3 medium onions, sliced
2 bell peppers, sliced in rings
⅓ cup oil (½ olive oil and ½
  cooking oil)

2 cloves garlic
⅓ teaspoon cumin
½ teaspoon dill
⅓ teaspoon oregano
1 teaspoon salt

Arrange vegetables in a shallow dish. Crush garlic with salt and add to oil. Pour oil mixture over vegetables. Cover and bake 1 hour at 350° or until vegetable are done.

Mrs. Don Aylward (Lee)

EGGPLANT CASSEROLE

6 to 8 servings

1 medium onion, chopped
1 large green pepper, chopped
½ cup butter
1 large eggplant, peeled and
** cubed**
½ cup raw rice
1 (14-ounce) can tomatoes

¼ teaspoon oregano
1 (10¾-ounce) can beef
** bouillon**
½ teaspoon salt
½ teaspoon pepper
2 dashes Tabasco
1 cup grated Cheddar cheese

Sauté onions and green pepper in butter. Add rice and brown. Add all other ingredients except cheese. Bake in greased casserole dish at 350° for 30 minutes. Sprinkle cheese on top and cook another 30 minutes.

Mrs. Billy Tabb (Myrtis)

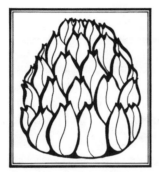

ESCALLOPED EGGPLANT PYRAMIDS

6 to 8 servings

1 eggplant, cut in ½ inch
** slices**
1 large or 2 medium tomatoes,
** sliced**
1 large onion, thinly sliced
¾ cup butter, melted
½ teaspoon salt

½ teaspoon dried basil
½ pound Mozzarella cheese,
** sliced**
½ cup Italian bread crumbs
2 Tablespoons grated Parmesan
** cheese**

On a medium sized heatproof platter, arrange eggplant slices. Stack a tomato slice and onion slice on top of each eggplant slice. Drizzle with ¼ cup butter. Sprinkle with salt and basil. Bake covered in a preheated 450° oven for 20 minutes. Remove from oven and cover with Mozzarella cheese. Stir bread crumbs into remaining butter and sprinkle on top. Sprinkle with Parmesan cheese. Bake uncovered for 10 minutes.

Mrs. Billy Tabb (Myrtis)

EGGPLANT PUFFS

4 to 6 servings

4 to 5 eggplants, peeled and
cut into strips
1 egg, beaten
1 Tablespoon salad oil

½ to ⅔ cup milk
½ cup self-rising flour
Salt and pepper to taste

Boil eggplants until tender; drain and mash. Make batter by combining egg, oil, milk, flour, salt, and pepper. Add to eggplant; drop by spoonfuls into hot oil and fry until brown.

Mrs. Troy Odom (Mary Ann)

SEARCY'S SQUASH

6 servings

3 cups sliced squash
2 Tablespoons chopped onions
2 eggs, beaten
1 (3-ounce) package cream
cheese
¾ cup shredded Cheddar
cheese

½ teaspoon pepper
½ teaspoon Worcestershire
sauce
½ teaspoon salt

Cook squash and onions in salty water; drain. Add the remaining ingredients to squash and onion in the order listed. Put in greased casserole. Cover with bread crumbs and dot with butter. Bake at 350° for 30 minutes.

Mrs. Billy Tabb (Myrtis)

GLAZED ACORN SQUASH

4 to 6 servings

1 large acorn squash
⅓ cup orange juice
½ cup firmly packed brown
sugar

¼ cup light corn syrup
¼ cup butter
2 teaspoons grated lemon rind
⅛ teaspoon salt

Cut squash into ¾ inch slices; remove seeds and membrane. Arrange rings in lightly greased baking dish. Pour orange juice over squash rings. Cover and bake 350° for 30 minutes. Combine next 5 ingredients in saucepan; bring to a boil; reduce heat and simmer 5 minutes. Pour sugar mixture over squash. Bake uncovered for additional 10 to 20 minutes.

Mrs. Mark Routman (Terry)

POSH SQUASH
6 to 8 servings

2 pounds yellow squash,
    sliced
2 eggs
1 cup real mayonnaise

1 small onion, chopped
¼ cup green pepper, chopped
1 cup grated Parmesan cheese
Salt and pepper to taste

Cook squash just until tender, about 6 to 8 minutes. Beat eggs and add all ingredients to eggs. Pour into buttered baking dish. Dot with butter or top with buttered crumbs. Bake 30 to 45 minutes at 350°.

Mrs. Ed Hartsock (Betts)
Jackson, Mississippi

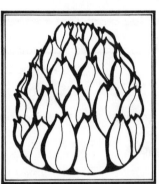

STUFFED SQUASH WITH SHRIMP
8 to 10 servings

6 large yellow squash
4 Tablespoons vegetable oil
1 large onion, chopped
½ cup chopped green pepper
2 (6½-ounce) cans shrimp,
    drained
2 eggs, beaten
Bread crumbs from 2 slices
    bread

2 Tablespoons Worcestershire
    sauce
4 Tablespoons parsley flakes
1 (4-ounce) can mushrooms,
    chopped
Bread crumbs
Salt and pepper to taste

Parboil squash. Halve squash and scoop out centers. Place squash skins on baking sheet. Sauté onion and pepper in vegetable oil. Add shrimp, eggs, bread crumbs, Worcestershire sauce, parsley, 1 cup water and mushrooms. Cook until thickened. Salt and pepper to taste. Stuff mixture into shells. Mix additional bread crumbs and butter; sprinkle over top. Bake 375° for 20 minutes.

Mrs. Winston Hayles (Eunice)

TOMATO PIE
6 servings

1 deep dish pie crust
Parmesan cheese
Swiss cheese
Monterey Jack cheese

Fresh tomatoes
Italian seasonings
Garlic powder
Butter

Bake pie crust as directed and sprinkle with Parmesan cheese while hot. Grate Swiss and Monterey Jack cheeses. Make a layer of sliced tomatoes, sprinkle with Parmesan, Italian seasonings, garlic powder and grated cheeses. Repeat layers topped with seasonings and cheese. Dot with butter. Bake at 350° for 20 to 25 minutes until cheese is melted and starts to brown. Let set 10 minutes before cutting.

Note: A wonderful way to use homegrown tomatoes.

Mrs. Jeff Levingston (Barbara)

CHEESE BROILED TOMATOES

Slice a fresh tomato in half horizontally. Pierce the inside of each half with a fork. Sprinkle each half with sherry, fresh or dried dill and broil 1 minute. Remove from broiler. Mix equal parts of real mayonnaise and sharp Cheddar cheese (a little more cheese than mayonnaise) and a dash of Worcestershire. Spread a generous tablespoon on each half and broil for 2 minutes. The tomato should be still firm, but the mixture should form a crust. These are good hot or cold.

Mrs. Stanley Levingston (Sylvia)

FRESH GREEN BEANS
4 to 6 servings

Peel and season lightly with salt and pepper enough new potatoes for two per person. Toss with oil to coat. Kentucky Wonders green beans are preferred (2 to 3 pounds). Wash well and snap beans. Drain well and pat dry with paper towels. Heat enough oil to cover the bottom of the pan. Add geen beans and cook stirring constantly until they turn dark green and are lightly coated with oil. During this time, season with salt and sugar. If you have 2 pounds, use 2 teaspoons of sugar. Add salt to taste. Lower heat, add potatoes, and a piece of ham to season. Add no water. Cover and cook stirring occasionally until beans are done and liquid is cooked away.

Mrs. Robert Tibbs (Pat)

Vegetables

COMPANY GREEN VEGETABLES

2 (10-ounce) packages of
  frozen broccoli florets or 3
  cups fresh
1 (10-ounce) package small
  green peas
1 large carrot, sliced
1 cup diagonally sliced celery
Dash of MSG
1 (10½-ounce) can of chicken
  broth

3 Tablespoons soy sauce
2 to 3 teaspoons sugar
¼ teaspoon ginger
1 clove garlic, minced
1 (6-ounce) package frozen
  Chinese pea pods, thawed
2 Tablespoons water
1 Tablespoon corn starch

Put broccoli, peas, carrots, and celery into skillet over low heat. Sprinkle with MSG. Mix broth, soy sauce, sugar, ginger, and garlic. Pour over vegetables in skillet. Cover and bring to a boil. Cook 10 minutes and baste. Remove vegetables from skillet. Keep warm over low heat. Stir corn starch mixed with water into sauce. Cook 1 minute. Transfer pea pods to a long heated platter. Sprinkle with MSG. Spoon a portion of sauce over the pods. Cover with hot vegetables. Spoon remaining sauce over all.

Mrs. Jimmy Sanders (Hazel)

HOT GREEN BEANS AND ARTICHOKES

4 servings

1 (0.7-ounce) package dried
  French dressing
1 (16-ounce) can whole green
  beans
¼ cup olive oil
2 Tablespoons wine vinegar

¼ teaspoon pepper
1 Tablespoon salt
1 (6-ounce) can mushrooms
1 (14-ounce) can artichoke
  hearts

Mix dressing according to directions and set aside. Marinate drained beans in mixed oil, vinegar, pepper, salt and mushrooms. Marinate drained artichoke hearts in French dressing. When ready to serve, mix together, bring to a boil and serve hot.

Mrs. Thomas H. Showers (Frances)
Drew, Mississippi

CANNED GREEN BEANS

4 to 6 servings

Drain 2 (16-ounce) cans whole green beans and rinse well. Cover the bottom of a 2 or 3 quart saucepan with bacon grease and heat. Add drained green beans. Season with salt and sugar. For 2 cans, add 1 heaping teaspoon sugar. Stir well. Lower to medium heat. Cook, stirring occasionally, until liquid is cooked away. When time to serve, add 4 to 6 slices of crisply fried bacon that has been well drained and crumbled.

Note: These beans taste like fresh beans. Add no water!

Mrs. Robert Tibbs (Pat)

VEGETABLE PIE

6 servings

3 to 4 Tablespoons butter
½ to 1 pound fresh mushrooms,
** sliced**
½ onion, sliced
2 zucchini or yellow squash,
** sliced**
1 green pepper, sliced
1 tomato, sliced

1 teaspoon salt
¼ teaspoon pepper
Dash garlic salt
1 (10-ounce) pie shell, unbaked
1 cup mayonnaise
1 cup shredded Mozzarella
** cheese**

Sauté first 4 vegetables in butter until crisp, but not soft. Drain well and add seasonings. Place tomato slices in bottom of pie shell. Add other vegetables. Mix mayonnaise and cheese and spread over vegetables. Bake uncovered at 350° for 1 hour.

Mrs. J. J. Stevens (Bea)
Drew, Mississippi

VIDALIA ONION CASSEROLE

4 to 6 servings

5 large Vidalia onions, peeled
** sliced thin**
½ cup butter

24 butter crackers, crumbled
Parmesan cheese

Sauté sliced onions in butter for 15 to 20 minutes. Place half of the onions into a casserole, top with half of crumbs and sprinkle cheese. Repeat layers, ending with cheese. Bake uncovered in a 325° oven for 30 minutes.

Mrs. Sid Blackstone (Delia)
Lithonia, Georgia

SWEET VIDALIA CASSEROLE   8 servings

½ cup uncooked rice
1 teaspoon salt
5 cups boiling water
7 medium Vidalia onions, thinly
   sliced

¼ cup unsalted butter
1 cup Jarlesberg or Swiss
   cheese, slivered
⅔ cup half-and-half cream

Cook rice in boiling salted water for 5 minutes. Drain well. Sauté onions in melted butter until softed. Blend rice with onions, cheese, and half-and-half. Put into greased, shallow baking dish. Bake at 325° for 1 hour.

Mrs. Jimmy Sanders (Hazel)

LUNCHEON MUSHROOMS IN SOUR CREAM   6 servings

2 pounds fresh mushrooms
1 bunch green onions, chopped
½ cup butter
Juice of ½ lemon
2 teaspoons salt
Dash white pepper
Dash ground nutmeg

1 (8-ounce) carton sour cream
3 Tablespoons sherry or white
   wine (optional)
3 English muffins, split, or 6
   frozen puff patty shells
Parsley sprigs

Rinse, pat dry and slice thinly the mushrooms. Sauté onions in butter until wilted. Add mushrooms and sauté over medium heat, about 5 minutes. Add lemon juice, salt, pepper and nutmeg. With a wooden spoon, fold in sour cream. Add sherry. Heat until warmed through. Serve on buttered toasted English muffin halves or in hot patty shells. Garnish with a sprig of parsley. Also makes a good stuffing for crepes.

Mrs. Ben Mitchell (Margaret Ann)

OKRA AND FRESH TOMATOES   8 servings

4 cups okra, sliced
3 cups tomatoes, peeled and
  chopped
3 Tablespoons bacon fat

1 medium onion, sliced
1 green pepper, diced
Salt and pepper to taste
¼ teaspoon sugar

Prepare okra and tomatoes. Sauté onion and green pepper in fat, stirring often until onion is browned. Add remaining ingredients and cook, covered over medium heat for 30 minutes. Uncover and cook another 5 minutes.

Note: This is delicious as a vegetable dish or as a soup base.

Mrs. Buster Young (Fane)

SPINACH MADELEINE   6 servings

2 (10-ounce) packages frozen
  chopped spinach
4 Tablespoons butter
2 Tablespoons all-purpose flour
2 Tablespoons chopped onion
½ cup evaporated milk
½ cup vegetable liquor
½ teaspoon pepper

¾ teaspoon celery salt
¾ teaspoon garlic salt
Salt to taste
1 teaspoon Worcestershire
  sauce
1 (6-ounce) roll jalapeño
  cheese, cubed

Cook spinach according to package directions; drain and reserve liquor. Melt butter in saucepan over low heat. Add flour, stirring until blended and smooth, but not brown. Add onion and cook until soft, but not brown. Add milk and vegetable liquor slowly, stirring constantly to avoid lumps. Cook until smooth and thick. Add pepper, celery salt, garlic salt, salt, Worcestershire, and cheese. Stir until cheese is melted. Combine with spinach. May be served immediately or put into a casserole and refrigerated overnight. Also freezes well.

Mrs. Mark Koonce (Anne)

Vegetables

SPINACH AND ARTICHOKES
8 servings

2 (10-ounce) packages frozen
chopped spinach
1 (8-ounce) package cream
cheese
2 Tablespoons lemon juice

½ cup margarine
1 teaspoon garlic salt
2 (14-ounce) cans artichokes
Cracker or bread crumbs for
topping

Cook spinach according to package directions; drain and set aside. Whip cream cheese, lemon juice, margarine, and garlic salt. Add to spinach. Line a greased casserole with artichokes. Add spinach. Sprinkle with cracker or bread crumbs. Dot with extra margarine and bake at 350° for 25 minutes.

Note: This recipe may be halved.

Mrs. Murle Parkinson
Drew, Mississippi

Mrs. Philip Adams (Mona)

SPINACH AND ARTICHOKE SOUFFLÉ
6 servings

2 (10-ounce) packages of
frozen, chopped spinach
½ pound fresh mushrooms,
sliced
6 Tablespoons butter
1 Tablespoon all-purpose flour
½ cup milk

½ teaspoon salt
⅛ teaspoon garlic powder
1 (14-ounce) can artichoke
hearts, drained
1 cup sour cream
1 cup mayonnaise
¼ cup lemon juice

Cook spinach according to package directions; drain. Sauté mushrooms in 4 tablespoons butter. Melt remaining butter in saucepan; blend in flour, add milk. Cook, stirring until thickened. Add seasonings, mushrooms, and spinach. Arrange artichokes in baking dish, pour spinach mixture over. Blend sour cream, mayonnaise, and lemon juice. Stir over low heat until heated. Pour over spinach mixture over artichokes. Garnish with whole mushrooms if desired. Bake 375° for 15 to 20 minutes.

Mrs. Buster Young (Fane)
Drew, Mississippi

PARMESAN POTATOES

4 to 6 servings

**6 medium potatoes, peeled
and sliced
¼ cup all-purpose flour
¼ cup grated Parmesan cheese**

**¾ teaspoon salt
⅛ teaspoon pepper
¼ cup margarine**

Shake potatoes in bag with flour, cheese, salt and pepper. Pour into a 9x13-inch baking dish sprayed with cooking spray. Pour melted margarine over potatoes. Bake at 350° for 1 hour, turning at least once.

Mrs. Terry Barron (Lynn)

POTATOES MAGNOLIA

4 servings

**4 medium red potatoes, cut
in half
½ cup butter**

**1 package dry Italian salad
dressing mix**

Melt butter in a 9x9-inch casserole. Sprinkle seasoning over butter. Place potatoes, cut side down in dish. Bake at 375° for 45 minutes. Good with steak or any meat dish.

Mrs. Charles Fioranelli (Vicki)

POTATO SOUFFLÉ

4 to 6 servings

**4 to 5 medium red potatoes
¾ cup milk
2 Tablespoons butter**

**Salt and pepper to taste
2 egg whites, stiffly beaten**

Boil and drain potatoes. With an electric mixer, whip potatoes, add milk, butter, salt and pepper to taste. Whip until light, about 10 minutes. Fold in beaten egg whites and place in a well greased casserole. Bake 30 minutes at 350°. Serve immediately.

Mrs. Elaine Hewlett

POTATOES AU GRATIN   4 to 6 servings

3 cups cooked, diced
  potatoes
¼ cup margarine
½ cup all-purpose flour
2 cups light cream
½ cup sour cream

Salt, pepper, and Tabasco to
  taste
Shredded Cheddar cheese
Paprika
Buttered bread crumbs

Place potatoes in a greased casserole. Make a white sauce of the margarine, flour, and cream. This can be done on top of the stove or in the microwave. Cook until it is thick. Add sour cream, salt, pepper and pepper sauce. Pour white sauce over potatoes and top with bread crumbs. cheese and paprika. Bake at 350° for 20 minutes.

Mrs. Michael Davis (Sheryl)
Roswell, Georgia

JALAPEÑO CHEESE POTATOES   6 to 8 servings

4 potatoes, cooked, peeled
  and sliced
2 Tablespoons butter
4 green onions, chopped
1 green pepper, chopped
¼ cup butter

1 Tablespoon all-purpose flour
1 cup milk
1 (2-ounce) jar pimiento,
  drained and chopped
3-ounces jalapeño cheese
3-ounces garlic cheese

In a skillet, sauté the onions and pepper until soft. In a saucepan, melt butter, add flour and then milk. Stir until mixture thickens. Add the onion mixture, pimientos and the cheese. Simmer until cheeses have melted. Place the potatoes in a lightly greased baking dish. Pour in the sauce and bake at 350° for 45 minutes.

The Editors

POTATO HINTS:

Mix butter, garlic salt and parsley to taste. Cool until firm. When filling twice baked potatoes, whip potatoes as usual and fill half full. Put 1½ teaspoons ball of butter mixture on potato. Cover with remaining mashed potatoes and top with grated cheese.

The Editors

CRAB STUFFED POTATOES
6 servings

6 baking potatoes
1 (6½-ounce) can lump crab
 meat
¼ cup chopped bell pepper

¼ cup chopped onion
1¼ cups sour cream
½ cup grated Cheddar cheese
Salt and pepper to taste

Bake potatoes. Cut off top and scoop out potato. Combine potato with crab meat, peppers, onions. Add sour cream to moisten. Spoon mixture into potato jackets. Cover with cheese and bake at 400° for 10 to 15 minutes.

Note: Great with a salad for lunch.

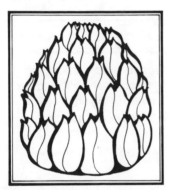

Mrs. Bob Buchanan (Sharon)

SWEET POTATO SOUFFLÉ
6 to 8 servings

3½ cups mashed sweet
 potatoes
1 cup sugar
½ teaspoon salt

2 teaspoons vanilla
½ cup melted butter
½ cup half-and-half
2 eggs

Topping
1 cup brown sugar
1 cup chopped pecans
⅓ cup all-purpose flour

1 cup flaked coconut
¾ cup melted margarine

In a large bowl, beat drained sweet potato pieces with mixer. Add remaining ingredients and beat well. Pour contents into greased soufflé dish and bake 15 minutes at 350°. While this is baking, prepare topping. Put brown sugar, pecans, flour and coconut in bowl and mix well. Drizzle melted margarine over and toss again until well coated. Remove soufflé from oven and sprinkle topping over. Return to oven for 15 minutes more.

Mrs. Mark Routman (Terry)

Vegetables

SWEET POTATO CASSEROLE · 6 servings

8 sweet potatoes, boiled and
  peeled
½ cup butter
1 Tablespoon brown sugar
1 orange rind, grated

Juice of 2 oranges
1½ teaspoons cinnamon
¼ teaspoon ginger
¼ teaspoon cloves
Marshmallows

Combine first 8 ingredients. If the mixture is stiff, add more orange juice. Pour into round deep casserole. Bake at 350° for 20 to 30 minutes. Top with marshmallows and bake until they melt.

Mrs. Terry Barron (Lynn)

LEE'S BAKED BEANS · 8 to 10 servings

1 (32-ounce) can
  pork-n-beans
5 to 6 slices bacon, fried and
  crumbled

1 large onion, chopped
1 (15-ounce) chili, with or
  without beans
½ box brown sugar

Combine pork-n-beans, bacon, onion, chili and brown sugar. Bake at 325° for 1 hour.

Mrs. Don Aylward (Lee)

JUSTIN WILSON'S RED BEANS AND RICE · 4 to 6 servings

1 pound red kidney beans
2 large onions, chopped
2 cloves garlic, minced
1 hot green pepper, chopped
  or 1½ teaspoons hot sauce
Claret wine

Water
Olive oil
¼ pound ham or salt shoulder
  or pickled pork
Salt

Wash beans. Place in bowl and add onions, garlic, and pepper. Pour a mixture of one half wine and one half water over beans to cover by an inch. Soak overnight. You may have to add more wine and water before cooking. Cover bottom of heavy pot with ½ cup olive oil; add meat. Pour in beans and liquid; bring to boil. Turn heat down and cook slowly several hours until done. Add salt last 30 minutes of cooking time. Serve over rice.

Note: May substitute white beans and sautern.

Mrs. Tom Sullivan (Wezzie)
Denham, Springs, Louisiana

GLORIA'S BAKED BEANS   6 servings

2 (15-ounce) can
  pork-n-beans
1 (10-ounce) can of canned
  pork
1 large onion, chopped

½ cup catsup
3 Tablespoons prepared
  mustard
½ cup dark corn syrup
Dash of Worcestershire sauce

Sauté onion in small amount of oil. Combine the remaining ingredients in a 2 quart casserole and bake at 400° for about an hour.

Note: Microwave on high for 30 minutes.

Mrs. Louis Campbell (Gloria)
Drew, Mississippi

HOPPING JOHN WITH HAM   6 to 8 servings

2 cups dried black-eyed peas
½ pound ham
2 quarts water
1 cup uncooked regular rice
1 cup chopped onion
1 cup chopped celery

2 teaspoons butter
1 teaspoon Italian seasoning
1 teaspoon sugar
2 teaspoons salt
¼ teaspoon pepper

Sort and wash peas. Place in a heavy saucepan. Cover with water and bring to a boil. Cook 2 minutes. Remove from heat. Cover and let soak 1 hour; drain. Combine ham and 2 quarts water in large Dutch oven. Bring to a boil. Reduce heat; cover and simmer 45 minutes. Add rice, onion, celery, butter, seasoning, sugar, salt, and pepper. Bring to a boil. Reduce heat; cover and simmer an additional 30 minutes or until black-eyed peas are done. Cut ham into small pieces. Stir ham into pea mixture.

Mrs. Donnie Deason (Missy)

JALAPEÑO BLACK-EYED PEA CASSEROLE 6 servings

2 (14-ounce) cans jalapeño
   black-eyed peas
1 (14-ounce) can stewed
   tomatoes
1 medium onion, sliced

1½ cups cooked white rice
2 Tablespoons bacon drippings
1 teaspoon salt
¼ teaspoon pepper

Combine all ingredients. Pour into casserole and bake in a moderate oven at 350° for 45 minutes or longer.

Mrs. E.A. Carlisle
Ocean Springs, Mississippi

MARINATED VEGETABLES 16 servings

¾ cup vinegar
½ cup vegetable oil
1 teaspoon salt
1 cup sugar
1 Tablespoon water
1 teaspoon pepper
1 (16-ounce) can French style
   green beans, drained
1 (16-ounce) can English peas,
   drained

1 (16-ounce) can whole kernel
   corn, drained
1 (2-ounce) jar chopped
   pimento
1 cup chopped celery
1 green pepper, finely chopped
1 bunch green onions, chopped

Combine first six ingredients and bring to a boil. Cool. Combine vegetables and vinegar mixture. Refrigerate 12 hours.

Mrs. Tim Haire (Debbie)

WILD RICE WITH MUSHROOMS AND ALMONDS 6 servings

¼ pound butter
1 cup wild rice
½ cup slivered almonds
2 Tablespoons chopped green
   onion or bell pepper

½ pound fresh mushrooms,
   sliced
3 cups chicken broth

Place all ingredients except broth into a heavy skillet. Cook 15 to 20 minutes on low heat. Put in casserole with broth. Cover and bake at 325° for 1 hour.

Mrs. Karl Horn (Ruth)
Moss Point, Mississippi

RICE SURPRISE
6 to 8 servings

2 cups Minute rice
2 cups chicken broth, canned
  or fresh
1 teaspoon salt
1 (8-ounce) carton sour cream
1 cup sliced water chestnuts
⅔ cup creamy Italian salad
  dressing

1½ Tablespoons seeded,
  chopped jalapeño peppers
1½ Tablespoons jalapeño
  pepper, juice
½ pound Monterey Jack
  cheese, grated

Cook the rice in chicken broth and salt. Mix sour cream, water chestnuts, salad dressing, peppers and pepper juice together with the rice. Bake at 400° for 25 to 30 minutes or until bubbly.

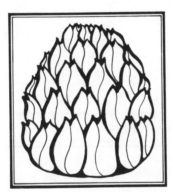

Mrs. Mike Robbins (Patty)
Mrs. Frank Canty (Libba)

FRIED RICE
6 to 8 servings

1½ cups rice
3 cups water
1½ teaspoons salt
4 slices bacon, chopped
3 eggs, beaten
⅛ teaspoon pepper
3 Tablespoons vegetable oil

2 teaspoons fresh grated ginger
8-ounces pork, cooked, cut into
  thin strips
1 cup cooked, chopped shrimp
8 green onions, chopped
1 to 2 Tablespoons soy sauce

Combine water, rice and salt. Cook 20 minutes. In a large skillet, cook bacon until crisp. Drain and set aside. Cook eggs and chop. Add remaining oil to skillet, stir in ginger and rice; cook and stir about 6 to 7 minutes. Stir in bacon, pork, shrimp, onions, eggs, and soy sauce. Cook and stir until hot. May garnish with extra chopped green onions.

Mrs. Howard Grittman (Ann)

RICE CASSEROLE   8 to 10 servings

2 cups rice
5 stalks celery, chopped
1 small onion, chopped
1 medium bell pepper,
   chopped
1 (12-ounce) package mild pork
   sausage, crumbled

2 (6-ounce) cans mushrooms,
   undrained
2 (10¾-ounce) cans beef
   consommé
1 cup margarine
2½ teaspoons curry powder
Salt and pepper to taste

Cook rice. Rinse with cold water and drain. Sauté celery, pepper and onions in butter. Fry sausage and drain. Combine all ingredients. Put into a buttered 9x12-inch casserole. Bake at 325° until hot.

Note: May be frozen before cooking.

Mrs. Roy L. Collins (Linda)

KATHRYN CAIN'S SPANISH RICE   6 servings

3 Tablespoons bacon
   drippings
1 large onion, chopped
1 cup rice
1 (14½-ounce) can tomatoes,
   roughly chopped, undrained
1 (10¾-ounce) can chicken
   broth
1 Tablespoon ground cumin
   seed

¼ teaspoon oregano
¼ teaspoon garlic powder
4 pinches saffron, broken into
   small pieces
1 teaspoon salt
Dash Tabasco
Dash Worcestershire sauce
Water to equal 1 quart
1 (10-ounce) package frozen
   green peas

In a heavy pan sauté onion until limp but not brown. Add rice and sauté until translucent to keep the grains separated. In a 1 quart pitcher, place tomatoes, broth, cumin, oregano, garlic powder, saffron, salt, Tabasco, Worcestershire and water. Add 1 quart of this mixture, and green peas to the rice mixture. Stir once. When liquid boils, cover. Reduce heat to a simmer for 30 minutes. Fluff rice once during this time. Further stirring will cause rice to stick. Uncover and continue to cook up to 30 minutes longer, if necessary, until dry— do not stir!

Mrs. Jim Tims (Frances)

HOT FRUIT
10 to 12 servings

1 (16-ounce) can sliced
  peaches
1 (16-ounce) can apricots
1 (16-ounce) can pears, sliced
1 (16-ounce) can pineapple
  chunks

1 (16-ounce) can bing cherries
12 soft maccaroons
¼ cup butter
⅓ cup brown sugar
½ cup cooking sherry
Slivered almonds

Drain fruit. Place maccaroons in bottom of shallow baking dish. Pour drained fruit over maccaroons. Melt butter and add brown sugar and cooking sherry. Pour over fruit. Top with toasted almonds. Bake for 30 minutes at 350°.

Variation: add sliced fresh bananas

Mrs. H.L. Dilworth (Anne)

SPICED APRICOTS
6 to 8 servings

2 (17-ounce) cans apricots,
  drained
1½ cups apricot syrup
½ cup red wine vinegar
1 teaspoon whole cloves

2 or 3 cinnamon sticks
¼ cup sugar
Dash of salt
1 teaspoon whole allspice

Heat to boiling, the syrup, vinegar, cloves, sugar, salt, allspice and cinnamon sticks; simmer for 5 minutes. Add apricots; cover; marinate overnight in refrigerator.

Mrs. Clarence Smith (Margaret Ann)

BAKED BANANAS
6 servings

6 or 7 bananas, split
  lengthwise
¼ cup butter
1 cup powdered sugar, sifted

2 Tablespoons brown sugar
½ teaspoon salt
Juice of ½ lemon

Mix above ingredients and spread over split bananas. Bake at 350° for 30 minutes.

Mrs. Paul Warrington (Pat)

Side Dishes

NUTTY FRUIT BAKE

6 servings

1 (8-ounce) can pineapple
  chunks
5 Granny Smith apples, peeled,
  cored, and sliced
½ cup chopped walnuts
½ cup chopped raisins

2 Tablespoons butter or
  margarine
⅓ cup sugar
2 Tablespoons all-purpose flour
1 teaspoon ground cinnamon
1 teaspoon vanilla

Drain chunks of pineapple and reserve ⅓ cup juice. Layer fruit and walnuts in 2 quart baking dish. Melt butter, add ⅓ cup juice and remaining ingredients. Mix well. Pour over fruit. Cover and bake 350° for 30 minutes. Remove cover and bake 15 to 30 minutes until liquid is cooked down.

Mrs. Robert Tibbs (Pat)

SCALLOPED PINEAPPLE

8 servings

4 cups fresh bread crumbs
1 (20-ounce) can pineapple
  chunks, drained

3 eggs, beaten
2 cups sugar
1 cup butter, melted

Toss together bread crumbs, and pineapple chunks and place in a greased 2 quart baking dish. Combine eggs, sugar, and butter and pour over pineapple. Bake at 350° for 30 minutes. Casserole can be made up and refrigerated overnight before baking. Reheats well. Good served with ham.

Linda Horton

CINNAMON APPLES

6 servings

Small or medium firm, tart
  apples
2 cups sugar
1 cup water

⅓ cup red cinnamon candy
  (red hots)
Drop or two of red food
  coloring

Pare and core apples. Cook until tender in syrup made with sugar, water, red cinnamon candy and red food coloring. Chill and serve around meat or as a salad.

Mrs. Troy Odom (Mary Ann)
Mrs. Donnie Deason (Missy)

Breads,
Pastry

ONE HOUR ROLLS
24 servings

2 packages dry yeast
1/4 cup warm water
1 1/2 cups warm buttermilk
1/4 cup sugar

1/2 cup shortening, melted
1 teaspoon salt
1/2 teaspoon soda
4 1/2 cups all-purpose flour

Dissolve yeast in warm water. Add milk, sugar, shortening, salt, soda and flour. Mix well and let stand 10 minutes. Roll out into desired shape. Allow to rise until doubled in size (about 30 minutes). Bake at 425° for 10 to 12 minutes.

Mrs. Larry York (Faye)

ROLLS
30 rolls

1/3 cup sugar
1/2 cup shortening
2 cups milk
2 packages dry yeast

1/4 cup warm water
6 cups self-rising flour
3 Tablespoons margarine

Combine first 3 ingredients in large boiler and mix. Heat to boiling point, then cool to lukewarm. Add yeast, dissolved in water, and mix well. Stir in 3 cups flour to make thin batter. Cover and let rise in warm place for 1 hour. Add 2 1/2 cups flour to make stiff dough. Roll moderately thin. Melt margarine in pie pan. Cut dough in circles, dip in margarine and fold in half to make rolls. Let rise 1 hour. Cook at 400° until golden brown.

Note: Dough may be kept in refrigerator in greased bowl for 2 to 3 days.

Mrs. Dan Hammett (Marcia)

EASY ROLLS
24 rolls

2 packages dry yeast
1 1/4 cups lukewarm water
1/2 cup butter, melted

1 package egg custard mix
3 1/2 cups all-purpose flour

Mix in order given. Knead and place in greased bowl in refrigerator or make into rolls and let rise 2 hours. Bake at 400° for 12 to 15 minutes.

Mrs. Vernon C. Hammett (Annette)

Breads

REFRIGERATOR ROLLS   6 dozen

1 quart milk
½ cup vegetable shortening
½ cup butter
1 cup sugar
1 package yeast

5 cups all-purpose flour
2 teaspoons salt
1 teaspoon baking powder
1 teaspoon soda
Flour

Bring milk to a boil; add to shortening and sugar. Stir to dissolve. Cool to lukewarm. Soften yeast in small amount of warm water, add to mixture. With a mixer, beat in about 5 cups of flour to make a thick batter. Cover and let rise until it doubles. Dissolve in a small amount of water, salt, baking powder and soda. Add to above mixture. Stir in enough flour to make bread dough consistency (not too stiff). Put in greased bowl; rotate to oil surface, cover and refrigerate. When ready to use, punch down, roll out, cut and bake at 425° until brown. Will freeze well before or after baking.

Mrs. Clarence Smith (Margaret Ann)

CRUSTY WHITE BRAIDS   2 loaves

4 to 4½ cups all-purpose flour
2 packages dry yeast
2 cups warm water

¼ cup cooking oil
2 Tablespoons sugar
1 Tablespoon salt

In a large mixing bowl, combine 2 cups flour and the yeast. Add water, cooking oil, sugar and salt to the dry mixture. Beat at low speed on mixer for ½ minute, scraping sides. Beat 3 minutes at high speed. By hand, stir in enough of the remaining flour to make a moderately stiff dough. Turn out onto a lightly floured surface; knead until smooth and elastic, 8 to 10 minutes. Shape into a ball. Place dough in a greased bowl, turning once to grease surface. Cover; let rise until doubled, about 1½ hours. Punch down dough. Divide in half. Divide each half into thirds; shape into 6 balls. Cover; let rise 10 minutes. Roll each ball into a 16-inch rope. Line up 3 ropes, 1 inch apart, on greased baking sheet. Braid very loosely, beginning in the middle. Pinch ends together and tuck under. Repeat with the remaining ropes. Cover; let rise in a warm place until almost doubled, about 40 minutes. Bake in a 375° oven for 30 minutes or until bread is done. Cool bread slightly before slicing. If desired, spread butter or margarine on bread immediately after removing from oven.

Mrs. Lanny Mosley (Nancy)

FRENCH BREAD
4 loaves

½ cup warm water (110° to
  115°)
2 packages active dry yeast
1½ cups lukewarm milk
¼ cup sugar

1 Tablespoon salt
3 eggs
¼ cup soft butter
7¼ to 7½ cups sifted
  all-purpose flour

Dissolve yeast in water. Stir in milk, sugar and salt. Add eggs, butter and half the flour. Knead. Add the rest of the flour. Knead until flour is blistery. Round up in a greased bowl. Cover with damp cloth. Let rise in a warm place until doubled (about 1½ to 2 hours). Punch down and let rise again until almost doubled (about 1 hour). Divide into 4 equal parts. Take each part and divide into 3 parts, making ropes. Braid. Put in large baking pan; let rise 30 minutes. Brush with 1 egg yolk and 2 tablespoons water beaten together. Sprinkle with sesame or poppy seeds. Bake at 325° until golden brown (about 25 minutes). Freezes well.

Mrs. Charles Billingsly, Jr. (Mitchie)

ARMENIAN FLAT BREAD
Four 10x14-inch sheets

1 cup warm water
  (approximately 100°-115°)
1 package active dry yeast
¼ cup butter or margarine,
  melted and cooled to
  lukewarm

1½ teaspoons salt
1 teaspoon granulated sugar
3¼ to 3¾ cups all-purpose flour

Pour the warm water into a large warm bowl, sprinkle in the yeast and stir until dissolved. After it has proofed, add the cooled butter, salt, sugar and two cups flour. Beat until smooth. Add enough additional flour to make a stiff dough. Turn out onto a lightly floured board and knead, adding remaining flour, until smooth and elastic, about 8 to 10 minutes. Place in a buttered bowl and turn to coat with butter. Cover and let rise in a warm spot until doubled in bulk. Punch the dough down, divide into flour equal pieces, and roll each piece into a rectangle 10x14 inches. Place on un-greased baking sheets and bake in preheated 350° oven about 20 minutes, or until golden brown. Cool on racks. Sesame seeds or poppy seeds may be sprinkled on before baking. Serve with cheese or other appetizers.

Mrs. H. L. Dilworth (Anne)

COMMUNION BREAD   2 large loaves

1 cup hot mashed potatoes	*2 packages yeast*
1 cup warm potato water	*1 cup soft butter*
1 cup scalded milk	*1 cup sugar*
7 cups or more of all-purpose	*1½ teaspoons salt*
flour	*4 large eggs*

Combine potatoes, liquids and 1 cup of flour; beat until thoroughly blended. Let cook until lukewarm, then stir in yeast. Cover bowl with damp cloth and let rise until light, about 30 minutes. When mixture is light, stir down with a wooden spoon. Cream butter and sugar, add salt and eggs and beat thoroughly. Stir into yeast mixture with the remaining flour. Use enough flour to make a firm dough. Knead. Place in a greased bowl and turn over until all sides are greased. Cover with damp cloth and let rise (about 1 hour or longer). After dough has risen, punch it down and turn onto floured board. Grease pans with vegetable shortening. Shape dough into loaves and place in bread pans. Let rise again, 45 minutes to an hour. Place in preheated 350° oven; check after about 15 minutes.

Variations:
1. May also pinch off dough and shape into dinner rolls. Let rise and bake.

2. May roll out part of dough for cinnamon rolls. Spread with soft butter. Sprinkle with brown sugar and cinnamon. Roll up like a jelly roll and slice. Put into a greased cake pan with edges slightly touching. Let rise and bake at 350° until brown. Cool. Drizzle with a mixture of milk and confectioners sugar.

Mrs. Delia Dunlap Blackstone

SWISS BREAD LOAF   10-12 servings

1 loaf unsliced French bread	*2 teaspoons Dijon mustard*
¾ cup margarine	*2 teaspoons season salt*
1 bunch green onions, chopped	*8 ounces Swiss cheese,*
2 teaspoons poppy seeds	*shredded*

Slice French bread lengthwise. Melt margarine, add next four ingredients and mix well. Spread this mixture evenly over the two pieces of French bread. Sprinkle with Swiss cheese. Bake for 20 minutes at 350°. Serve with a meal or cut in small strips for an appetizer.

Mrs. H. L. Dilworth (Anne)

SWEDISH RYE BREAD   4 loaves

3½ cups scalded milk
⅔ cup sugar
1 heaping Tablespoon salt
1 heaping Tablespoon caraway
  seed
1 heaping Tablespoon anise
  seed

½ cup plus 2½ Tablespoons of
  margarine
1 cup dark syrup (Ribboncane,
  Karo or sorghum)
2½ cups rye flour

Mix the above well and add to:

½ cup warm water
3 packages yeast (dissolved in
  water)

Add enough all-purpose flour to make a soft dough, about 9-11 cups. Let rise once, then make 4 loaves. Let rise until doubled in size. Bake at 350° for 60 minutes.

Mack Woolley

WENDY'S WHOLE WHEAT BREAD   2 loaves

2 cups milk
½ cup brown sugar, packed
1 Tablespoon salt
¼ cup butter
2 packages dry yeast

1 cup warm water
8 cups whole wheat flour
All-purpose flour to flour board
3 Tablespoons butter

Heat milk until bubbles form around the edge. Add sugar, salt and butter. Cool to lukewarm. Mix yeast and water to dissolve; stir into milk mixture. Add 4 cups flour and beat vigorously until smooth. Add rest of flour and knead 5 minutes. Turn into greased bowl and cover with a towel. Let rise 1 hour. Halve dough and let rest 10 minutes. Halve again and form into 12-inch strips. Twist two strips together 3 times. Pinch ends. Place in a greased loaf pan and brush top with butter. Repeat with remaining strips. Let rise 1 hour and bake at 400° for 30 to 35 minutes. Cover crust with foil after 20 minutes if too brown.

Mrs. Richard Cole (Wendy)

WHOLE WHEAT BREAD

3 loaves

3 cups whole wheat flour
½ cup non-fat dry milk

1 Tablespoon salt
2 packages dry yeast

Combine above ingredients in a large bowl.

3 cups water
½ cup molasses

2 Tablespoons oil

Heat above ingredients until warm (120° to 130°). Pour warm liquid over flour mixture. Blend at low speed 1 minute; medium speed, 2 minutes.

2 eggs
1 cup whole wheat flour

4½ cups all-purpose flour

Reduce to low speed and add eggs, whole wheat flour and all-purpose flour. Knead on floured surface about 5 minutes. Pour about 1½ tablespoons oil into bottom of large bowl. Put dough in and rotate to oil surface. Cover with cloth and let rise in a warm place (80° to 85°) for 1 hour or until doubled. (Tip: Put two fingers into dough ½ inch; if it doesn't bounce back it is ready.) Punch down and divide into thirds. Roll into rectangle. Roll up and tuck ends under. Place into pans sprayed with cooking spray. Cover and let rise 30 to 45 minutes until doubled. Bake at 375° for 30 to 40 minutes, or until it sounds hollow when tapped.

Mrs. Jimmy Sanders (Hazel)

CHEESE BISCUITS

48 servings

½ pound butter
1 pound sharp Cheddar
  cheese, shredded
1 teaspoon salt

½ teaspoon cayenne pepper
Approximately 4 cups
  all-purpose flour

Mix all ingredients, working in enough flour to make a stiff dough (about 4 cups). Roll out and cut with a shot glass. Prick with a fork. Bake at 400° on a cookie sheet until done (brown around edges). Sprinkle with paprika. Take up while warm. Store in tin.

Mrs. Eric Muir (Nan)

ANGEL BISCUITS
30-40 biscuits

5 cups all-purpose flour
¼ cup sugar
2 teaspoons baking powder
1 teaspoon soda
1 teaspoon salt
1 cup shortening

1 package dry yeast
2 Tablespoons warm water
2 cups buttermilk
½ cup margarine or butter,
melted

Sift dry ingredients together. Blend in shortening. Dissolve yeast in warm water, then let stand 4 minutes. Add yeast mixture to buttermilk. Add liquids to dry mix and mix well. Turn out on a floured board. Roll to desired thickness. Cut biscuits, dip in melted margarine, and put on greased cookie sheets or in 13x9x2-inch pans. Bake at 450° for 12 minutes.

Note: Biscuits may be baked now or refrigerated 2 weeks, if well covered. Once prepared, biscuits can be covered with foil and frozen. Also, the water for blending the yeast should be just slightly warm to the touch.

Mrs. Billy Latham (Sue)

BROWN AND SERVE BISCUITS
12 biscuits

2 cups all-purpose flour
½ teaspoon soda
1 well-rounded teaspoon baking
powder

1 teaspoon salt
3 well-rounded Tablespoons
shortening
1 cup buttermilk

Sift together dry ingredients; cut shortening in with 2 knives or pastry blender. Add buttermilk and mix well; turn out on floured board. Knead and roll to ¼ to ½-inch thickness. Cut with biscuit cutter. Bake at 425° for 10 to 12 minutes. If preparing biscuits to freeze, remove them from oven just before they brown. To serve (after freezing), heat and brown in 425° oven for about 10 minutes.

Mrs. S. R. Blakeman, Jr. (Mary James)

Breads

HOMEMADE BISCUIT MIX

24 biscuits

4 cups self-rising flour
1 rounded Tablespoon baking
  powder

1 rounded teaspoon salt
1 cup shortening

Cut together to powder texture. Refrigerate. To make biscuits, add ⅓ cup milk to 1 cup mix. (If you use buttermilk, add ¼ teaspoon soda.) Bake at 425° until golden brown.

Mack Woolley

LETHA'S CINNAMON ROLLS

24 rolls

1 package yeast
¼ cup lukewarm water
1 cup milk, scalded
¾ cup butter
3 eggs
4½ cups all-purpose flour

¼ cup sugar
Butter
Brown sugar
Cinnamon
Pecans, chopped (optional)

Mix yeast and water to dissolve. Mix milk, butter, eggs and half of the flour. Add yeast mixture. Add rest of flour and sugar. Refrigerate overnight, covered. Separate into orange-sized balls. Let dough rest a few minutes. Roll out into thin rectangle shape. Butter and sprinkle with brown sugar and cinnamon; add nuts if desired. Roll up jelly-roll fashion and cut in 1½-inch slices. Place on ungreased cookie sheet. Let rise, covered 1½ hours. Bake at 375° for 10 to 15 minutes. Ice while hot with glaze (recipe follows).

Note: These freeze well. Thaw, warm and enjoy.

Glaze
1 box powdered sugar
Enough whipping cream to
  make glaze spreadable

1 Tablespoon softened butter
½ teaspoon vanilla

Combine and spread on hot cinnamon rolls.

Mrs. Richard Cole (Wendy)

WHOLE WHEAT CINNAMON ROLLS
36 rolls

3 cups hot water
1 cup margarine, softened
1 cup honey
6 eggs
1½ teaspoons salt

⅔ cup powdered milk
8 cups whole wheat flour
3 packages dry yeast
Sugar-cinnamon mix

Pour hot water into a 4-quart mixing bowl and add margarine. Let the margarine soften. Add honey, eggs and salt to water. Combine the powdered milk with 2 cups whole wheat flour and sift into the other ingredients. Knead thoroughly. Add the yeast and blend. Add the rest of the whole wheat flour and knead for 10 minutes. Cover with towel and let rise for 2 hours. Divide dough into 2 sections and roll out on a lightly floured board. Brush with melted margarine and sprinkle with a generous amount of sugar and cinnamon. Roll up like a jelly roll and cut into ½-inch rolls. Place on a greased baking sheet and mash with palm of hand. Let rise until doubled. These rolls do not fall easily so let them rise to be very light, about 2 hours. Bake at 350° for 20 minutes.

Mrs. Felix Dean (Rowena)

ROSALIE'S EASY CORNBREAD
1 6-inch skillet

1 cup self-rising cornmeal
1 egg
¾ cup milk

Dash of salt
2 Tablespoons melted bacon
* grease*

Combine all ingredients except bacon drippings and mix well. In small (6-inch) iron skillet, heat bacon drippings until hot. Pour hot grease into cornmeal batter and mix quickly. Turn into hot skillet and bake at 400° for 20-30 minutes, or until done. For crisper top, I turn bread in pan and let set on counter until cool enough to eat.

Note: May be doubled for 10-inch iron skillet.

Mrs. Brady Cole (Rosalie)

Breads

MEMA'S MEXICAN CORNBREAD

1 cup cornmeal
1 teaspoon salt
½ cup milk
1 (8½-ounce) can cream-style
   corn
1 heaping cup of shredded
   Cheddar cheese

2 eggs
5 hot jalapeño peppers,
   seeded and chopped
1 medium onion, chopped
½ cup salad oil

Mix all ingredients well. Pour into greased 10-inch or 12-inch iron skillet and bake at 400° for 15 to 20 minutes, or until done.

Mrs. Joe Smith, III (Suellen)

MEXICAN SPOON BREAD

1 (16-ounce) can creamed corn
¾ cup milk
⅓ cup oil
2 slightly beaten eggs
1 cup cornmeal

½ teaspoon baking soda
1 teaspoon salt
1 (3-ounce) can green chiles
1½ cups cheese, shredded

Mix first 8 ingredients together. Pour ½ of batter into greased casserole dish. Sprinkle half of cheese over batter. Pour the remaining batter into casserole and top with remaining cheese. Bake at 350° for 45 minutes.

Alice Lee McIntosh

HUSHPUPPIES

1½ cups self-rising cornmeal
½ cup self-rising flour
1 egg
¼ teaspoon garlic powder
1 medium onion, finely
   chopped

1 (8-ounce) can cream style
   corn
¼ cup beer at room
   temperature

Mix well and drop from spoon into hot grease (275°). Cook until brown.

Mrs. Steve Brower (Jane)

CORNMEAL YEAST BREAD

3 loaves or 2 large loaves

5½ to 6 cups all-purpose flour
1 cup yellow cornmeal
2 packages dry yeast
2 cups milk
¾ cup butter

½ cup sugar
1½ teaspoons salt
2 eggs
Melted butter
Sesame seeds

In a mixing bowl, combine 2 cups flour, cornmeal and yeast. In a one-quart saucepan, combine milk, sugar, butter and salt; heat until warm (120° to 130°). Add to flour mixture. Add eggs. Beat ½ minute at low speed, scraping bowl. Then beat three more minutes at high speed. Add 1 cup flour and beat one minute longer. Stir in enough remaining flour to make a soft dough. Turn onto lightly floured surface; knead 5 to 10 minutes until smooth and satiny. Place in a buttered bowl, turning once to butter top. Cover bowl. Let rise on a rack over hot (boiling) water in oven until doubled, about 1 hour. Punch down. Divide into three pieces. Roll out into a 9-inch square. Roll it up lightly, seal ends and tuck under. Place into 9x5x3-inch buttered loaf pans, seam side down. Brush butter on top and sprinkle with sesame seeds. Cover and allow to stand in warm place (oven) until doubled, about 1 hour. Bake in preheated 375° oven 35 to 40 minutes until loaf sounds hollow. Turn out of pans onto wire rack to cool.

Mrs. Jimmy Sanders (Hazel)

FRIED CORN STICKS

20-25 servings

2 cups water
1¼ teaspoons salt
1½ cups cornmeal

1 cup shredded sharp Cheddar
cheese

Boil water and salt. Add meal and mix thoroughly. Cook until mixture separates from sides and bottom of pan. Remove from heat, add cheese and mix together. Take mixture out by teaspoonfuls and shape into balls. Roll balls to ½-inch thickness in shape of small cigars. Fry in deep fat at 375° for 2-3 minutes. Drain. Serve hot.

Mrs. Buster Young (Fane)
Drew, Mississippi

DOUBLE CORN 'N BACON DRESSING   12 servings

Cornbread

**2 cups self-rising cornmeal mix
  with hot rise**
¼ cup oil

1 cup milk or buttermilk
1 egg

Place oil into 10-inch or 12-inch iron skillet. Turn oven to bake at 400°. Preheat skillet in oven until temperature of 400° is reached. Meanwhile, mix cornmeal with milk; beat in egg. When oven is preheated, pour oil from skillet and mix with cornmeal mixture. Pour back into skillet and bake for 20 minutes. Proceed with dressing.

Dressing

**1 pan cornbread, cooled and
  crumbled**
6 cups soft ½-inch bread cubes
**1 (16-ounce) can whole kernel
  corn, drained**
2 teaspoons sage
**1 teaspoon crushed thyme
  leaves**
½ teaspoon salt

⅛ teaspoon pepper
1 chicken bouillon cube
1½ cups boiling water
**6 slices bacon, cut into ¾-inch
  pieces**
1 cup sliced green onions
2 cups sliced celery
3 eggs, boiled and diced
¼ cup butter, melted

Combine cornbread, bread, corn, sage, thyme, salt and pepper in a large bowl; mix chicken bouillon cube in boiling water and add. Cook bacon until crisp; remove bacon and drain on absorbent paper. Cook onions and celery in bacon drippings. Add vegetable mixture to cornbread mixture; toss lightly. Add drained bacon, diced boiled eggs and butter. Place in 3-quart casserole, cover lightly, and bake for 1 hour at 350°.

Mrs. John Denton (Becky)

CORNBREAD DRESSING
16 servings

1 (10-inch) skillet recipe for
  cornbread, crusts removed
Equal amount of white bread,
  crusts removed
6 eggs
2 or 3 large onions, finely
  chopped
4 or 5 stalks celery, finely
  chopped
8 to 10 cups homemade
  chicken broth, including fat
2 or 3 Tablespoons fat from
  broth

Combine all ingredients. Add enough broth to resemble cornbread batter. Pour into two (13½x8¾x1¾-inch) glass casseroles and bake at 400° for 25 to 30 minutes or until set. Stir while cooking. This may be frozen before baking. If frozen, thaw before baking.

Note: Mixing half duck broth and half chicken broth makes this dressing more moist and flavorful.

Mrs. M. T. Blackwood (Jauweice)

FRENCH TOAST WITH ORANGE BUTTER
6 servings

12 (1-inch thick) slices French
  bread
6 eggs
4 cups milk
½ teaspoon salt
½ teaspoon ground nutmeg
½ teaspoon vanilla extract
2 Tablespoons butter or
  margarine, divided
Orange butter

Place bread in a 13x9x2-inch pan. Combine eggs, milk, salt, nutmeg and vanilla; beat well. Pour mixture over bread; cover and refrigerate overnight. Melt 1 Tablespoon butter in an electric skillet at 300° or very low heat on stove. Remove as many slices as skillet will hold and cook in butter, 10 to 12 minutes on each side or until cooked through. Cook the rest in same manner. Serve hot with orange butter.

Orange Butter
2 cups

1 cup butter, softened
½ cup orange juice
½ cup powdered sugar

Cream butter until light and fluffy. Add orange juice and powdered sugar; beat until thoroughly blended.

Mrs. J. C. Gregory (Donna)

Breads

BEIGNETS

(French Market Doughnuts)

1 cup milk
¼ cup sugar
½ teaspoon salt
½ teaspoon nutmeg
1 package active dry yeast
2 Tablespoons water
  (lukewarm)

2 Tablespoons oil (plus 1 quart
  oil for frying)
1 egg
4 cups sifted all-purpose flour
Powdered sugar

Scald milk; add sugar, salt and nutmeg. Stir, then cool to lukewarm. Sprinkle yeast in water and add to milk. Add 2 tablespoons oil and 1 egg, beaten. Gradually add flour. Cover and let rise 2 hours. Knead and cut in 2x3-inch rectangles. Let rise 30 minutes. Deep fry at 375°. Drain and sprinkle with powdered sugar.

Mrs. Pete Baughman (Scarlet)

ZUCCHINI NUT MUFFINS

24 muffins or 12 giant muffins

This recipe is a specialty offering, courtesy of the Ullrhof Restaurant, Snowmass, Colorado.

3½ cups all-purpose flour
1½ teaspoons cinnamon
1 teaspoon baking soda
1 teaspoon salt
¼ teaspoon baking powder
3 eggs
2 cups sugar

1 cup vegetable oil
1 Tablespoon vanilla
2 cups grated zucchini, peeled
½ cup chopped nuts
1 teaspoon all-purpose flour
Cinnamon-sugar mixture

Mix flour, cinnamon, baking soda, salt and baking powder. Beat eggs well, gradually adding sugar and oil. Mix well. Add vanilla and dry ingredients to egg mixture. Blend well. Stir in zucchini. Combine nuts with 1 teaspoon flour and stir into batter. Put paper liners in muffin pan. Pour batter into cups, filling to ¾ full. Sprinkle cinnamon-sugar mixture over top of muffins and bake in oven preheated to 300° for about 25 minutes.

Mrs. Richard Cole (Wendy)

BLUEBERRY'S WORLD FAMOUS MUFFIN RECIPE — 14 muffins

Dry Ingredients

1¼ cups all-purpose flour
1 cup bran
¼ cup granulated sugar
½ teaspoon salt
½ teaspoon ginger

½ teaspoon nutmeg
¾ teaspoon cinnamon
¾ teaspoon baking powder
½ teaspoon baking soda

Wet Ingredients

½ cup heavy cream
¾ cup half-and-half
2 eggs

1 teaspoon vanilla
2 ounces butter
¾ cup blueberries

Preheat oven to 350°. Melt butter over low heat and set aside. Beat eggs well; add cream, half-and-half and vanilla and set aside. In another bowl, mix all dry ingredients. Add melted butter to dry ingredients. Add wet mixture to dry mixture and stir until blended. Add well drained blueberries. Grease muffin tin very well and spoon in batter, filling each cup approximately ¾ full. Bake for 18 minutes. For a delicious touch, sprinkle a cinnamon-sugar mixture on top of the muffins.

Blueberry's Restaurant
Snowmass, Colorado
The Editors

PRUNE MUFFINS — 3 dozen muffins

½ cup butter
2 scant cups sugar
2 eggs
2 cups all-purpose flour
1 teaspoon cinnamon
1 teaspoon cloves (ground)
⅛ teaspoon salt

1 teaspoon soda
1 cup buttermilk
1½ cups chopped prunes
1¼ cups chopped toasted pecans
1 teaspoon vanilla

Cream butter and sugar; add eggs one at a time. Beat well. Sift flour, spices and salt together and add to butter and sugar. Dissolve soda in milk and add to mixture. Stir in prunes, nuts and vanilla. Bake in a greased or paper lined muffin pans at 350° until done, about 20 to 25 minutes.

Mrs. Thomas H. Showers (Frances)
Drew, Mississippi

HOTEL PEABODY VANILLA MUFFINS 3 dozen muffins

½ cup butter or margarine, melted
4 cups all-purpose flour
2 cups sugar

2 cups milk
4 teaspoons baking powder
2 eggs
1 Tablespoon vanilla

Mix all ingredients thoroughly. Spoon into greased, hot muffin tins and bake at 400° for 20 minutes.

Note: Recipe may be halved.

Mrs. Joe Dakin (Hazel)
Mrs. Allen Pepper (Ginger)

SOUR CREAM MUFFINS 24 muffins

1 cup sour cream
1 cup self-rising flour

½ cup margarine, melted

Combine all ingredients in a bowl. Stir until well mixed. Bake in 1¾-inch, lightly greased muffin tins at 450° for 15 minutes.

Mrs. Terry Russell (Linda)

MAMA MACK'S BRAN MUFFINS 3 to 3½ dozen muffins

5 cups all-purpose flour
3 cups sugar
2 teaspoons salt
2 teaspoons soda

3 cups complete bran cereal
1 quart buttermilk
1 cup oil
4 eggs

Mix dry ingredients together in a large bowl. Add remaining ingredients and mix well. Refrigerated, this mixture will keep for several weeks. To bake, spoon into prepared muffin tins and bake at 400° until done, about 10 minutes.

Mrs. Richard Cole (Wendy)
Mrs. Billy Ratliff (SuSu)

YORKSHIRE PUDDING   12 muffins

2 cups all-purpose flour	*½ cup milk*
4 eggs	*1½ cups water*
1 teaspoon salt	*3 teaspoons oil*

Mix flour, eggs, salt, milk and water. Set aside for 2 hours at room temperature. Place ¼ teaspoon of oil in each of 12 muffin cups. Heat to very hot—smoking in 400° oven. Fill cups ¾ full with pudding mixture. Bake for 35 minutes at 400°. Serve with roast beef and gravy.

Note: This if first cousin to a popover.

Mrs. Brad Cole (Janet)

GRIDDLE CAKES   4-6 servings

1¼ cups all-purpose flour, sifted	*¾ teaspoon salt*
2½ teaspoons baking powder	*1 egg*
3 Tablespoons sugar	*1 cup milk*
	3 Tablespoons butter, melted

Sift dry ingredients. Add egg, milk and melted butter. Mix well. Drop by 2 to 3 tablespoons onto hot griddle.

Mrs. Don Blackwood (Suzan)

Variation: 1 tablespoon maple syrup added to batter.

Mrs. Pricilla White

EXTRA LIGHT PANCAKE OR WAFFLE MIX   4-6 servings

2 cups biscuit mix	*½ cup cooking oil*
1 egg	*1⅓ cups club soda*

Mix thoroughly and let batter rise without stirring for approximately 5 minutes. Be sure not to stir batter again. Pour onto a hot pancake griddle or waffle iron.

Mrs. Wiley Hilburn (Shirley)

CRUSTY POTATO PANCAKES 8-10 servings

Internationally Famous Kartoffel Puffers, served annually at the Wurstfest in NewBraunfels, Texas

6 medium potatoes, peeled
1 small onion, grated
3 eggs

¾ cup all-purpose flour
2 teaspoons salt
Oil for frying

Grate potatoes coarsely into a bowl with cold water. This keeps potatoes from turning dark and removes some of the excess starch, making the pancakes crisper. In another bowl, combine the onion, egg, flour and salt. Drain potatoes, pressing out all fluid. Beat potatoes into batter. Heat oil. Spoon heaping tablespoons of batter into oil, spreading batter with the back of the spoon into 4-inch rounds. Brown on one side, turn and brown on the other side. Brown the pancakes slowly so that potatoes will have a chance to cook through properly. Drain on absorbent paper. Serve hot with applesauce.

Mrs. Richard Cole (Wendy)

HERB BREAD 1 loaf

1½ cups whole wheat flour
1 teaspoon Italian dressing mix
½ teaspoon salt
1 Tablespoon minced onion
1 teaspoon garlic salt
¼ cup sugar

2 packages dry yeast
2½ cups white self-rising flour
1 cup water
1 cup milk
¼ cup oil

Mix all dry ingredients together. Heat the water, milk, and oil to lukewarm. Mix wet ingredients with the dry ingredients. Let rise for 50 minutes. Place in greased 2-quart casserole and bake at 375° for about 45 minutes or until done.

Mrs. J. C. Gregory (Donna)

NAVAJO FRY BREAD   10-12 servings

4½ cups all-purpose flour   1½ cups water
½ teaspoon salt   ½ cup milk
2 teaspoons baking powder   Cooking oil for frying

Mix dry ingredients in large mixing bowl. Stir in water and milk. Knead with hands on a floured board. Pat into circles a little bigger than your hands. Make a hole in the center of the dough with your finger. Drop into several inches of hot oil (about 375°). Dough will puff and bubble. Turn over when golden brown on first side. Fry to uniform golden brown. Drain on paper towels and serve hot with honey or butter.

Note: This is especially good with chili or with meals where Mexican dishes are served. Also good to make when teaching children to cook.

Mrs. Dan Hammett (Marcia)

APPLE BANANA NUT CAKE   2 loaves

2½ cups all-purpose flour   1 large banana, mashed
½ teaspoon salt   1 teaspoon vanilla
1 teaspoon baking powder   4 eggs
1 teaspoon soda   2 large tart apples, peeled and
2 cups sugar   grated
½ cup oil   1 cup chopped pecans

In a large bowl, combine dry ingredients. Add the next 5 ingredients and beat until creamy. Add pecans that have been mixed with 2 tablespoons of flour. Pour into 2 greased loaf pans and bake at 300° for 1 hour and 15 minutes.

Mrs. Elaine Hewlett

Breads

APPLE CHEDDAR WALNUT BREAD
1 loaf

2 cups self-rising flour
²/₃ cup sugar
½ teaspoon cinnamon
½ cup coarsely broken walnuts
  or pecans
2 eggs, slightly beaten
½ cup melted butter or salad
  oil

1½ cups finely chopped,
  peeled apples
½ cup shredded sharp
  Cheddar cheese
¼ cup milk

Preheat oven to 350°. Line a 9x5x3-inch loaf pan with waxed paper and grease paper well. Combine flour, sugar, cinnamon and nuts in a large bowl. Mix remaining ingredients and add to flour mixture. Stir just until blended; batter will be lumpy. Spoon batter into prepared loaf pan and bake for 60-70 minutes or until done. If top of loaf starts to get too brown, cover with foil the last 15 minutes of baking time. Remove from oven immediately and cool on wire rack.

Note: To test if bread is done, pierce the loaf just off center with a metal skewer or wooden toothpick. If it comes out clean and dry, the loaf is baked. Remove the bread from the oven, place it on a wire rack to cool slightly in pan, then turn out onto rack to complete cooling. This bread achieves better flavor and slices more easily if wrapped for one day.

Mrs. Richard Cole (Wendy)

STRAWBERRY BREAD
2 loaves

3 cups all-purpose flour
1 teaspoon salt
1 teaspoon soda
3 teaspoons cinnamon
2 cups sugar

3 eggs, well beaten
2 packages (10-ounces each)
  frozen strawberries
1¼ cups cooking oil
1¼ cups chopped pecans

Sift dry ingredients together in a large bowl, making a well in the center. Mix remaining ingredients and pour into the well. Stir enough to dampen all ingredients. Pour into two well-greased loaf pans. Bake at 350° for one hour. Cool at least 10 minutes before turning out.

Mrs. Tim Haire (Debbie)

PUMPKIN BREAD   4 loaves

3 cups sugar
3½ cups all-purpose flour
1 cup oil
¾ cup orange juice
1 cup chopped nuts
1 (16-ounce) can pumpkin

4 eggs
2 teaspoons soda
1 teaspoon nutmeg
1 teaspoon cinnamon
1½ teaspoons salt

Put all ingredients in a large bowl and mix. Bake in four greased one-pound coffee cans for one hour at 350°.

Mrs. Eric Muir (Nan)

PECAN CRUST   One 9-inch pie crust

1½ cups ground pecans
¼ cup butter at room
   temperature

6 Tablespoons sugar

Blend pecans with butter and sugar. Spread and pat firmly into a lightly greased 9-inch pie pan. Bake at 400° for 10 minutes. Watch closely as it scorches easily. Freezes well.

Mrs. Milton Robinson (Patricia)

FOOLPROOF PIE CRUST   4 7-inch crusts or 2 11-inch crusts

4 cups all-purpose flour
1¾ cups vegetable shortening
1 Tablespoon sugar
½ cup water

2 teaspoons salt
1 Tablespoon vinegar
1 egg

With a fork, mix together first four ingredients. In a separate bowl, beat the remaining ingredients. Combine all together and stir until moistened. With hands, make dough into ball. Chill for 15 minutes before rolling or freeze until ready to use. Dough will remain soft in the refrigerator and can be rolled at once.

Note: No matter how much you handle this dough, it will always be flaky and handle easily.

Mrs. J. C. Gregory (Donna)

MARGARET ANN'S PIE CRUST
Two 7-inch crusts

2 cups all-purpose flour
½ teaspoon salt
Pinch of sugar
½ cup butter, chilled

3 Tablespoons shortening,
 chilled
4 to 5 Tablespoons cold water

Put all ingredients except water in a bowl and crumble with your fingers until mixture resembles coarse meal. Add water, 1 tablespoon at a time—should not be sticky. Chill several hours or may be refrigerated for days. Roll out to ⅛-inch thickness and 3 inches larger than your pan. Prick bottom of crust and cover with buttered foil weighted with dried beans in order to prevent shrinkage. Bake at 400° for 8 to 10 minutes. Cool.

Mrs. Ben Mitchell (Margaret Ann)

OH SO GOOD PIE SHELL
One 9-inch pie crust

3 egg whites
¼ teaspoon cream of tartar
1 cup sugar
1 teaspoon vanilla

20 round, butter crackers,
 rolled into crumbs
1 cup chopped nuts

Beat eggs and cream of tartar until peaks begin to form. Add sugar, one tablespoon at a time, while beating. Add vanilla, crackers and nuts. Blend. Spread into greased 9-inch pie pan and shape as for pie shell. Bake at 300° for 30 minutes.

Note: This shell may be filled with fruit filling and topped with whipped cream or whipped topping.

Mrs. J. C. Gregory (Donna)

Desserts

NEW YORK DREAM CHEESE CAKE   12 servings

¼ cup butter, melted
1 cup graham cracker crumbs
1 teaspoon cream of tartar
6 eggs, separated
3 Tablespoons sugar
19-ounces cream cheese

1½ cups sugar
3 Tablespoons all-purpose flour
½ teaspoon salt
2 cups sour cream
1 teaspoon vanilla

Have all ingredients at room temperature. Butter a 9 inch springform pan. Mix butter and crumbs well and press on bottom of pan. Add cream of tartar to egg whites. Beat until foamy. Gradually add 3 Tablespoons sugar and beat until stiff. Set aside. Beat cheese until soft. Mix together 1½ cups sugar, flour and salt. Gradually beat into cheese. Add egg yolks one at a time beating after each addition. Add sour cream and vanilla. Mix well. Fold in egg whites and pour in pan. Bake in slow oven 350° for 1¼ hours or until firm. Turn off oven, open door and leave cake for 10 minutes. Remove and let stand away from drafts until cool. Then put in refrigerator.

Mrs. Karl Horn (Ruth)
Moss Point, Mississippi

CHOCOLATE CHEESECAKE

1⅓ cups chocolate wafer
    crumbs
2 Tablespoons sugar
¼ teaspoon ground cinnamon
¼ cup butter, softened
1½ cups semisweet chocolate
    morsels
2 eggs

½ cup sugar
2 teaspoons rum
1 (8-ounce) carton sour cream
2 (8-ounce) packages cream
    cheese, cubed and softened
2 Tablespoons butter, melted
Whipped cream
Chocolate leaves

Combine wafer crumbs, 2 tablespoons sugar, cinnamon, and ¼ cup butter; mix well. Firmly press into bottom of a 10 inch springform pan; set aside. Melt chocolate morsels over hot water in top of a double boiler. Set aside. Combine eggs, ½ cup sugar, rum, and sour cream in container of an electric blender; process 15 seconds. Continue blending, and gradually add chocolate and cream cheese. Add melted butter; blend well. Pour cheese mixture into chocolate crust. Bake at 325° for 45 minutes or until cheesecake is set in center. Cool at room temperature for at least 1 hour. Chill at least 6 hours. Remove sides of pan. Garnish with whipped cream and chocolate leaves.

Mrs. Ben Mitchell (Margaret Ann)

PRALINE CHEESE CAKE

1 cup graham cracker crumbs
3 Tablespoons sugar
3 Tablespoons butter, melted
3 (8-ounce) packages cream
  cheese, softened
1¼ cups packed dark brown
  sugar

2 Tablespoons all purpose flour
3 eggs
½ cup sour cream
1½ teaspoons vanilla
Maple syrup

Preheat oven to 350°. Combine graham cracker crumbs, sugar and butter; press into bottom of 9 inch springform pan. Bake for 10 minutes. Combine cheese, brown sugar and flour beating with electric mixer at medium speed until well blended. Add eggs, one at a time, mixing well after each addition. Beat in sour cream. Blend in vanilla. Pour mixture over crumbs. Bake for 50 to 55 minutes. Cool and loosen cake from rim of pan. Chill in pan. Brush with maple syrup and top with praline topping.

Praline Topping
2 Tablespoons butter
¼ cup packed brown sugar
½ cup chopped pecans

Stir butter and sugar in small skillet over medium heat until bubbly. Add pecans and cook 2 minutes, stirring constantly. Pour onto aluminum foil. Cool and crumble over cheesecake.

Mrs. Roy Cole (Gail)

AUNT EMILY'S FUDGE CAKE   48 squares

1 cup butter
3 squares unsweetened
  chocolate
1½ cups all purpose flour,
  sifted

2 cups sugar
4 eggs, large
1 teaspoon vanilla
2 cups chopped pecans

Preheat oven to 325°. Melt butter and chocolate over low heat while stirring. Sift sugar and flour together. Beat eggs until foamy and thick. Add sugar and flour to the eggs. Add butter and chocolate. Add salt and vanilla. Stir in pecans by hand. Bake in greased and floured (or spray with cooking spray) 15½x10½x1-inch pan at 325° for 35 minutes. Pan must be this size.

Mrs. Kirkham Povall (Hilda)

ICING FOR FUDGE CAKE

6 Tablespoons half-and-half
6 Tablespoons margarine
4 Tablespoons cocoa

1 pound powdered sugar
Pinch of salt
1 teaspoon vanilla

Melt margarine in milk over low heat. Put cocoa and sugar in small mixing bowl. Add heated mixture while beating. Add salt and vanilla. Spread over cooled cake still in pan. Slice cake into 48 squares. (This icing is also great for cupcakes)

Mrs. Kirkham Povall (Hilda)

CHOCOLATE SOUR CREAM SHEET CAKE

1 cup margarine, softened
1 cup water
4 Tablespoons cocoa
2 cups cake flour
2 cups sugar

½ teaspoon salt
2 eggs, beaten
½ cup sour cream
1 teaspoon soda
1 teaspoon vanilla

Preheat oven to 375°. In a saucepan, heat water, cocoa and margarine to boiling. In a large bowl, mix flour, sugar, and salt. Combine with hot liquid mxture and beat with electric mixer at medium-high speed for 1 minute. Continue beating, but reduce speed to medium and gradually blend in eggs, sour cream, soda and vanilla. Afterwards, turn speed back to medium-high and beat for 2 to 3 minutes. Pour batter into greased and floured 11x16x1-inch sheet pan and bake about 20 minutes or until cake "springs back" when touched. Remove from oven, cool and ice.

Chocolate Icing
½ cup margarine
1 pound box powdered sugar
4 Tablespoons cocoa
6 Tablespoons evaporated milk

1 teaspoon vanilla
Dash of salt
1½ cups walnuts or pecans,
chopped

Melt margarine in small saucepan with cocoa. Add milk. Stir and cook on low heat until mixture slightly thickens. Remove from heat. Add powdered sugar, salt and vanilla. Beat with mixer until smooth and creamy. Stir in nuts and spread on cake.

Mrs. Russell Day (Bobbie)

PINKIE MAXWELL'S CHOCOLATE CAKE

2 cups sugar
2 cups all purpose flour, sifted
½ cup margarine
1 cup water
½ cup vegetable shortening

4 Tablespoons cocoa
2 eggs
½ cup buttermilk
1 teaspoon soda
1 teaspoon vanilla

Combine sugar and flour in a large bowl. Set aside. In a saucepan, bring to a boil margarine, water, shortening and cocoa. Pour over flour and sugar. Dissolve soda in buttermilk. Add eggs, buttermilk mixture and vanilla. Pour batter into a 9x13-inch sheet cake pan and bake at 325° for 30 minutes. Do not remove cake from pan.

Chocolate Icing
¾ cup margarine
4 Tablespoons cocoa
6 Tablespoons buttermilk

1 pound box powdered sugar
1 teaspoon vanilla
1 cup chopped nuts

Bring first 3 ingredients to a boil. Add powdered sugar, nuts and vanilla. Pour over cake while hot.

Mrs. Jeff Levingston (Barbara)

CHOCOLATE SOUR CREAM CAKE

1½ cups margarine, softened
3 cups sugar
5 eggs
3 cups all purpose flour
½ cup cocoa

1 teaspoon baking soda
¼ teaspoon salt
8-ounces sour cream
1 cup boiling water
2 teaspoons vanilla

Cream butter; add sugar and beat until light. Add eggs, one at a time beating until light and fluffy. Combine dry ingredients. Add to creamed mixture alternately with sour cream beginning and ending with dry ingredients. Add cup of boiling water and vanilla. Stir until well blended. Pour into greased and floured tube pan. Bake at 350° until done.

Mrs. Robert Tibbs (Pat)

FRENCH CHOCOLATE CAKE

6 squares semi-sweet chocolate	3 cups all-purpose flour
2 egg yolks (well beaten)	1½ teaspoons salt
1 cup buttermilk	1½ teaspoons soda
½ cup butter	1 cup very strong coffee
2 cups sifted brown sugar	2 teaspoons vanilla

Rum Glaze

¼ cup butter	½ cup rum
⅔ cup sugar	

Cream Filling

6-ounces semi-sweet chocolate chips	4-ounces evaporated milk
	1 egg, beaten

Topping

2 cups whipping cream	Shaved chocolate

Grease 2 (9-inch) pans; then line with waxed paper and flour pans. Melt semi-sweet chocolate in double boiler. Add egg yolks. Slowly stir in buttermilk. Mix well. Cook until thick. Cool. Cream together butter and brown sugar. Sift flour with salt and soda. Add this to butter mixture with the coffee. Add chocolate mixture and vanilla. Bake at 325° about 30 minutes. Mix ingredients for rum glaze. Cook over low heat until sugar is dissolved. Pour evenly over warm cakes. Let stand in pans until cool. Mix chocolate chips and evaporated milk. Stir over low heat until smooth. Do not boil. Add one whole beaten egg. Mix well and chill. (If sauce is too thin add a beaten egg yolk). To assemble: Remove cakes from pans and generously spread a layer of filling between layers and on top. Whip the cream and ice the entire cake. Shave chocolate over top of iced cake.

Mrs. John Tatum (Carol)

SPICE CAKE

1½ cups sugar
3 eggs
1 cup oil
¾ cup buttermilk
½ cup bourbon
2½ cups sifted all purpose flour

1 teaspoon baking powder
1 teaspoon baking soda
1 teaspoon cinnamon
½ teaspoon all spice
½ teaspoon cloves
¼ teaspoon salt

Mix eggs, sugar and oil. Combine dry ingredients. Add to first mixture alternately with buttermilk and bourbon. Bake at 350° for 40 to 50 minutes. Cool 10 minutes. Poke holes in top of cake. Cover with glaze.

Glaze
¼ cup margarine
¼ cup water

1 cup sugar
½ cup bourbon

Heat all ingredients except bourbon until slightly thick. Add bourbon. Pour over hot cake.

Mrs. R.W. Atkinson (Miriam)

BUTTERMILK POUND CAKE

1¼ cups butter-flavored
   shortening
3 cups sugar
6 eggs
3 cups cake flour, sifted
1 cup buttermilk

¼ teaspoon baking soda
¼ teaspoon salt
½ teaspoon vanilla extract
½ teaspoon lemon extract
1 teaspoon butter extract

Preheat oven to 325°. Grease and flour 1 large Bundt pan or 3 (9-inch) layer cake pans or 3 small loaf pans. Cream shortening and sugar. Add eggs, one at a time, beating well after each addition. Combine buttermilk with soda, salt, and flavorings. Add flour alternately with buttermilk mixture; end with flour. Bake at 325° for 1½ hours.

Mrs. Warren Williamson (Sallie Sanders)
Greenville, Alabama

BROWN SUGAR POUND CAKE

3½ sifted all-purpose flour
½ teaspoon baking powder
1 cup butter, softened
½ cup vegetable shortening
1 pound plus 1 cup firmly
    packed light brown sugar

5 eggs, room temperature
1 cup milk, room temperature
Butter Pecan Frosting

Preheat oven to 325°. Grease and flour a 10-inch tube pan. Sift flour and baking powder onto waxed paper. Beat butter, shortening and sugar until smooth. Beat in eggs, one at a time until fluffy. Add flour ⅓ at a time, alternately with milk, just until blended. Pour into pan. Bake for 1½ hours or until top springs back. Cool on rack 15 minutes. Turn out on rack and cool completely.

Butter Pecan Frosting
1 cup chopped pecans
½ cup butter

2 cups powdered sugar
Milk

Brown pecans in butter in medium saucepan. Let cool. Stir in powdered sugar and enough milk to make frosting creamy. Spread icing over top of cake, allowing to drip down sides and center.

Note: It is especially good if you warm the slices in the microwave.

Marietta Smith Melvin

COCONUT POUND CAKE

1 cup shortening
½ cup margarine
3 cups sugar
6 eggs
1 cup milk

3 cups cake flour, sifted three
    times
1 teaspoon coconut extract
1 teaspoon almond extract
1 can of flake coconut

Cream shortening and margarine, mixing at medium speed. Add sugar a little at a time while continuing to beat. Add eggs, one at a time, beating one minute after each one is added. Add milk and flour, a little at the time. Add the flavorings and coconut. Pour the cake into a greased and floured tube pan. DO NOT PREHEAT THE OVEN. Put the cake in a cold oven and bake at 300° for 1 hour and 45 minutes.

Dr. Daisy Howell

PINEAPPLE POUND CAKE

½ cup margarine
1 cup butter
2¾ cups sugar
6 extra large eggs
3 cups all-purpose flour

1 teaspoon baking powder
¾ cup crushed pineapple and juice
1 teaspoon vanilla
¼ cup milk

Cream butter, margarine and sugar. Add eggs, one at a time, beating well after each. Add flour and baking powder, a small amount at a time, alternating with milk. Add pineapple and vanilla and blend well. Pour into greased and floured 10-inch tube pan and place in a cold oven. Turn oven to 325° and bake for 1½ hours. Remove from oven and let stand for a few minutes before adding glaze.

Glaze
¼ cup melted butter
1½ cups powdered sugar

1 cup crushed pineapple, drained

Mix and pour over hot cake.

Mrs. H.L. Dilworth (Anne)

BEST EVER POUND CAKE

Have all ingredients at room temperature.

½ cup real butter
½ cup shortening
3 cups sugar
5 eggs
1 cup milk
3½ cups sifted cake flour

½ teaspoon baking powder
¼ teaspoon salt
1 teaspoon almond flavoring
1 teaspoon vanilla extract
1 teaspoon lemon flavoring

Cream butter, shortening and sugar till fluffy. Add eggs one at a time. Add milk and dry ingredients alternately. Add flavorings. Bake in greased and floured tube pan at 325° for one hour.

Mrs. Gerald Burnside (Eugenia)

MILLION DOLLAR POUND CAKE   1 bundt cake

3 cups sugar
1 pound butter, softened
6 eggs
1 Tablespoon vanilla extract

1 teaspoon almond extract
4 cups all purpose flour
¾ cup milk

Cream sugar and butter. Add eggs, beating after each one. Add extracts. Add flour and milk alternately, beating well after each addition. Grease and flour Bundt pan. Bake at 325° for 1½ hours.

Mrs. Milton Wilder (Cathy)

ORANGE CAKE DELIGHT

¾ cup shortening
1½ cups sugar
3 beaten egg yolks
2¼ cups cake flour
1 Tablespoon grated orange
   rind

3 stiffly beaten egg whites
¾ cup cold water
¼ cup orange juice
½ teaspoon salt
3½ teaspoons baking powder

Cream sugar and shortening; add egg yolks and beat well. Add sifted dry ingredients alternately with water, orange juice and rind. Fold in egg whites. Bake in 2 waxed paper lined 9 inch pans for 30 to 35 minutes in 350° oven. Put together with orange filling below:

2 Tablespoons butter, melted
¼ cup cornstarch
1 cup sugar
½ teaspoon salt

2 Tablespoons grated orange
   rind
1 cup orange juice and pulp
1½ Tablespoons lemon juice

Blend butter and cornstarch together. Add sugar, salt, rind, juice and pulp; mix well. Cook in double boiler until thick. Remove from heat. Add lemon juice. Let cool completely before using. Frost with Favorite White Icing (Check Index)

Mrs. C.L. Beckham (Marie)

COCONUT CAKE

⅔ cup shortening
2 cups sugar
1 cup warm water
3 teaspoons baking powder*

3 cups all purpose flour*
8 egg whites, beaten
1 teaspoon orange extract

*Best results are when flour and baking powder are combined and refrigerated overnight!

Cream shortening and sugar. Add water, ¼ cup at a time. Alternate flour mixture and egg whites. Add flavoring. Bake in 3 layers. Place in a cold oven. Bake at 350° until done. May also bake in a sheet cake pan. When cool, frost.

Divinity Frosting
4 cups sugar
2 cups hot water or coconut
   juice
4 egg whites, beaten

1 teaspoon orange extract
Coconuts (2 large or 3 small),
   grated

Boil sugar and water in large pot rapidly (400°) until reaches a soft ball stage. Pour ½ syrup very slowly over beaten whites while mixer is running on medium-high. Do not turn mixer off! Continue to cook the remainder of syrup to a hard-crack stage (should be a short time - watch closely), then pour the syrup slowly over whites until peaks form. Add orange extract. May turn mixer to high after last syrup addition to reach peaks. Spread on cake and sprinkle coconut on top and sides. May be frozen.

Note: This icing is a wonderful divinity candy. Omit orange extract and add vanilla and chopped pecans.

Mrs. Sis Manning
Drew, Mississippi

AUNT ROGERS' JAM CAKE

2 cups sugar
1 cup butter
4 cups all purpose flour
1 cup buttermilk
4 eggs
1 teaspoon nutmeg

1 teaspoon allspice
1 teaspoon cloves
1 teaspoon cinnamon
1½ cups blackberry jam
2 teaspoons soda

Cream butter and sugar. Add flour then buttermilk, eggs, spices and jam. Last, add soda dissolved in a little water. Bake in layers. Use caramel filling between layers and on top.

Caramel Filling
4 cups sugar
1½ cups sweet milk
2 teaspoons all purpose flour

2 Tablespoons butter
1 teaspoon vanilla

Caramelize 1 cup sugar in heavy skillet. Set aside. In a saucepan, mix 3 cups sugar, milk and flour. Cook and stir until sugar melts and let boil 5 minutes. Add caramelized sugar. Cook to soft ball stage. Remove from heat and add butter. Cool. Add vanilla and beat until spreading consistency is reached.

Mrs. Buster Young (Fane)

APPLE SAUCE CAKE   1 large tube pan

1½ cups shortening
2 cups sugar
5 eggs
3½ cups sifted all-purpose flour
2 teaspoons soda
2 teaspoons nutmeg
1 teaspoon salt
1 teaspoon cloves
1 teaspoon cinnamon

2 cups applesauce
2 cups raisins
1 pound candied diced fruit mix
1 cup candied chopped
  pineapple
1 cup candied chopped
  cherries
1 box dates, chopped
2 cups chopped pecans

Soak raisins in warm water and drain. Cream shortening and sugar. Add eggs one at a time. Add applesauce alternately with sifted dry ingredients. Blend in fruit and nut mixture. Use lined stem pan. Bake 300° for 2 to 2½ hours.

Mrs. E.F. Farrish (Stell)

MY FAVORITE APPLE CAKE

¾ cup raisins
½ cup bourbon
1¾ cups corn oil
2½ cups sugar
4 eggs
2½ cups all-purpose flour,
  sifted
1 cup cake flour, sifted
1 teaspoon baking soda

1 teaspoon nutmeg
1 teaspoon cinnamon
1 teaspoon salt
⅛ teaspoon ground cloves
1 teaspoon mace
3½ cups chopped peeled
  apples
¾ to 1 cup chopped toasted
  pecans

Combine raisins and bourbon. Let stand for 15 to 20 minutes. Prepare a 10-inch pan 3 inches deep or a 10-inch spring form pan. In large bowl, beat oil and sugar about 5 minutes. Beat in eggs, one at a time. Combine dry ingredients and stir well. Add dry ingredients to oil mixture. Stir in apples, raisins, and any remaining bourbon. Scrape into prepared pan, pushing batter to sides. Bake in a 325° oven for 1 to 1½ hours until a toothpick inserted in center comes out clean. Cool in pan for 5 minutes. Remove sides of spring form pan; invert, remove, bottom of pan. Invert again and cool right side up on rack. Spoon warm caramel sauce onto dessert dish. Place slice of cake and scoop of ice cream next to it. Drizzle additional warm sauce over cake and ice cream if desired.

Caramel Sauce
1 cup dark brown sugar
⅓ cup granulated sugar
¼ cup maple syrup

¼ cup light corn syrup
1 cup heavy cream

Combine all ingredients in medium-sized heavy saucepan. Cook over high heat, stirring occasionally to dissolve sugar. Cook until candy thermometer reaches 210°. Maple syrup may be omitted if so desired and ½ cup light corn syrup used instead.

Mrs. Robert Tibbs (Pat)

LINDA HORTON'S WHITE CAKE

Linda uses a white Pillsbury Plus ® cake mix and bakes it in layers. She freezes the layers and frosts them frozen. The texture is similar to a petite fore. Linda says the texture is not the same if you frost before freezing.

Frosting

1 cup vegetable shortening	**1 pound box powdered sugar**
1 teaspoon salt	**¼ cup water**
1 teaspoon butter extract	**1 pound box powdered sugar**
2 teaspoons almond extract	**¼ cup water**

Beat well shortening, salt and flavorings. Add 1 pound powdered sugar and ¼ cup water; then add another box of powdered sugar and ¼ cup water. Beat 5 minutes.

Note: This requires a sturdy mixer.

Absolutely Delicious!

Linda Horton
County Extension Agent
502 South Walnut
Greensboro, Georgia

PEACHES AND CREAM CAKE

1 (18.5-ounce) butter flavor cake mix	**2 to 3 Tablespoons powdered sugar**
1½ cups sugar	**1 cup sour cream**
4 Tablespoons cornstarch	**Fresh sliced peaches**
4 cups chopped fresh peaches	**2 cups whipping cream**
½ cup water	

Prepare cake mix in 2 layers. Cool and split each layer. Combine sugar and cornstarch in saucepan. Add peaches and water. Cook over medium heat, stirring constantly. Cook until smooth and thickened. Cool. Combine whipping cream and powdered sugar in mixing bowl. Beat until stiff peaks form. Spoon ¼ of peach filling over split layer of cake. Spread ¼ cup sour cream over filling. Repeat. Frost with sweetened cream and garnish with peaches.

Mrs. H.L. Dilworth (Anne)

POPPY SEED CAKE

1 box yellow cake mix without added pudding
1 (3½-ounce) box butter pecan instant pudding
4 eggs
½ cup vegetable oil
1 cup hot water
2 teaspoons maple extract
2 Tablespoons poppy seeds

Mix cake mix and pudding mix together. Add eggs, oil, water, maple extract and poppy seeds. Beat well. Grease a large tube pan. Bake at 350° for 30 minutes. Test with straw to be sure cake is done. Cool slightly, then remove from pan.

Glaze
¼ cup butter, melted
⅓ cup brown sugar
½ box powdered sugar
1 teaspoon maple extract
Cream
Chopped pecans

Combine melted butter and brown sugar. Bring to a boil. Add confectioners' sugar, maple extract and enough cream to make a fairly runny glaze. Pour over the cake a little at a time to completely cover the top and let it run down the sides. Sprinkle with chopped pecans. This cake freezes well.

Mrs. Toby Michael (Eleanor)

PINA COLATA CAKE

1 box yellow cake mix (with pudding)
1 (14-ounce) can condensed milk
1 (8-ounce) can cream of coconut
1 (20-ounce) can crushed pineapple, drained
1 (8-ounce) carton non dairy whipped topping
1 (6-ounce) bag frozen coconut

Bake cake according to package directions in a 9x13-inch cake pan. Leave cake in pan. While hot, prick with fork. Mix condensed milk, cream of coconut, and pineapple. Pour over hot cake. Let cool and cover with whipped topping. Sprinkle with coconut.

Mrs. Johnny Hobbs (Carolyn)

PUMPKIN CAKE

2 cups sugar
1½ cups oil
3 teaspoons cinnamon
1 teaspoon allspice
2 Tablespoons baking powder
1 teaspoon salt
2 teaspoons soda

2 cups canned pumpkin
1 cup chopped pecans
1 cup white raisins
3 cups all purpose flour
4 eggs
2 teaspoons vanilla

Mix sugar, oil, spices, baking powder, salt, soda and pumpkin together. Mix nuts and fruit with flour. Add to pumpkin mixture, one cup at a time. Beat in eggs one at a time. Add vanilla. Bake in greased and floured tube pan at 350° for 1 hour.

Buttermilk Glaze
1 cup sugar
½ teaspoon baking soda
½ cup buttermilk

1 Tablespoon light corn syrup
1 teaspoon vanilla

Leave cake in pan for 20 minutes after baking. While cake is cooling boil sugar, soda, milk, corn syrup and vanilla for about 3 minutes, stirring constantly. Pour glaze over cake while it is in pan. Let cool completely before taking cake from pan.

Mrs. Joe Garrison (Joyce)

FRUIT CAKE

4 cups all purpose flour
1 Tablespoon cinnamon
1 teaspoon allspice
1 cup butter
2 cups brown sugar
6 eggs
1 teaspoon soda

1 cup buttermilk
1 cup peach preserves
1 cup pear preserves
1 cup jam (your favorite)
1 (15-ounce) box raisins
1 pound figs or dates
1 pound nuts

Sift together flour and spices. Cream butter and sugar. Add eggs, one at a time. Beat well. Add soda to buttermilk. Alternately add flour and buttermilk mixture. Add preserves and jam. Cut raisins, nuts and dates in small pieces and add to mixture. Mix well. Bake in a greased and floured tube pan for 1 hour at 350° or until done.

Sarah Logsdon
Louisville, Kentucky

MINCEMEAT FRUITCAKE   2 large bundt pans

1 pound jar mincemeat
2 cups pecans
2 cups raisins
1 cup sugar
2 eggs, separated
½ cup butter, melted

2 cups all purpose flour
1 teaspoon vanilla
1 teaspoon baking soda
  (dissolved in 1 Tablespoon
  boiling water)

Separate eggs. Beat whites until stiff. Set aside. Mix all other ingredients in a large bowl. (I use my hands. Batter is very stiff.) Bake in greased Bundt pans or angel food pans at 300° to 325° for 1 to 1½ hours or until cake springs back when touched with finger.

Suggestion: When cake is cool, pour grape juice over it, wrap it well, and store several weeks.

Mrs. Dan Hammett (Marcia)

FAVORITE WHITE ICING

2 egg whites
1½ cups sugar
¼ cup water

¼ teaspoon cream of tartar
1 teaspoon vanilla

In top of double boiler combine all ingredients except vanilla. Beat with portable mixer 1 minute. Place over boiling water (not to touch bottom of icing container) and heat 7 minutes. Remove from heat and add vanilla and beat 3 minutes.

Note: Will ice and fill a 3 layer cake. Also excellent for coconut cake, lemon cake or orange cake. A pleasant change to use with chocolate layers. Allow iced cake to stand uncovered 1 to 2 hours to let thin layer of icing dry a bit.

Mrs. Robert Tibbs (Pat)

DECORATOR FROSTING

2 boxes powdered sugar
1⅓ cups vegetable shortening
1 egg white
½ teaspoon butter flavoring
1 teaspoon vanilla extract
12 to 14 Tablespoons hot milk

Mix shortening, flavorings, and egg white until creamy. Next add sugar and hot milk. Mix on low speed, then beat on high speed for 10 minutes. Excellent for birthday cakes or cupcakes. I cut the recipe in half and it will generously ice 2 to 3 dozen cupcakes. Add food coloring for desired icing color.

Mrs. Louis Radicioni (Lynn)

MRS. W.J. PARKS' CHOCOLATE ICING

2½ cups sugar
Dash salt
1 cup cream or half-and-half
4 Tablespoons cocoa
½ cup butter
1 teaspoon vanilla

Mix together. Bring to a boil while stirring. Cook to soft ball. Let cool and add 1 teaspoon vanilla. Beat until spreading consistency.

Mrs. Eric Muir (Nan)

CHRISTMAS FILLING FOR SPICE CAKE

3 cups sugar
¼ cup butter
1½ cups milk
Pinch soda
1 teaspoon baking powder
1 grated coconut
1 cup chopped pecans
1 cup raisins
1 orange, sectioned
Grated rind of 1 orange
1 teaspoon vanilla

Cook to soft ball stage the sugar, butter, milk, soda and baking powder. Add remaining ingredients. Put on cake while hot.

Note: This makes enough filling and topping for a 3 layer cake.

Mrs. Thomas H. Showers (Frances)
Drew, Mississippi

CARAMEL ICING

2½ cups sugar	Pinch salt
2 scant Tablespoons all purpose flour	¼ cup sugar
	¼ cup hot water
½ cup sweet milk	2 Tablespoons butter
½ cup half-and-half	1 teaspoon vanilla

In a saucepan combine 2½ cups sugar, flour, sweet milk, half-and-half, and salt. Start cooking over low heat. Take ¼ cup sugar, stir in skillet over low heat until melted and the sugar is brown and foamy. Add ¼ cup hot water and stir until melted sugar makes a syrup. Add a little more hot water if necessary,. Pour syrup into cooking mixture. Cook until it forms a soft ball in cold water. (or use candy thermometer) Remove from heat and add butter and vanilla. Let cool and then beat until consistency to spread. If it gets too thick while spreading, add milk, a little at a time and beat. Keep adding a little milk and continue beating until icing can be spread. If grainy, add ½ cup milk, stir and cook again.

Note: As the icing cooks, after adding syrup to cooking mixture, the flour rises to the top and collects around the sides of the boiler. Take a spoon and run around sides. Put whatever you scrape from sides back in the boiling mixture. I try not to stir mixture any more than I have to. Sometimes the flour sticks to the bottom of the boiler but I've never had it burn. When you mix the sugar, flour, and milk, stir often until it begins to boil. Be sure all the lumps of flour are mixed with milk. I never add the vanilla until mixture cools and I begin to beat. I put the boiler in a pan of cold water to cool mixture. Change water two or three times before you begin beating. If it is grainy, and you cook it over, it will be darker.

Mrs. Emily Lucas
Lexington

PINEAPPLE FILLING AND FROSTING   2 - 9 inch layers

1 (20-ounce) can crushed pineapple	2 cups sugar
2 eggs yolks, beaten	2 Tablespoons all purpose flour

Beat egg yolks well. Add pineapple to this. Combine sugar and flour and add to pineapple and egg yolks. Let mixture come to boil and cook 5 to 10 minutes, stirring to prevent sticking.

Mrs. Helen Boozer
Amory, Mississippi

VANILLA FUDGE

6 cups sugar
2 cups cream
¼ teaspoon soda

1 teaspoon vanilla
½ cup butter
2 cups chopped nuts

Caramelize 2 cups sugar in a heavy pan until light brown. Into another pan, add 4 cups sugar and cream and cook while sugar browns. When sugar is brown, pour the first mixture into second mixture in a very thin stream. Cook to a firm ball (238°). Remove from heat and add soda. When all is foamy, add vanilla and butter. Cool 10 minutes and beat until thick. Takes a lot of beating. Add nuts and pour into greased pan. Cut when cool.

Mrs. James Beard (Patty)

DIVINITY CANDY
35 to 40 pieces

2½ cups of sugar
½ cup light corn syrup
½ cup water

2 egg whites
½ teaspoon vanilla extract
nuts to taste (optional)

Mix sugar, syrup, and water in a sauce pan. Bring to boil, stirring constantly. Cook until syrup mixture forms a firm ball when dropped into cold water. Beat egg white until stiff. Continue beating as hot syrup is poured into egg white mixture. Add vanilla and continue beating until mixture is thick. Nuts may be added. Drop by spoonful on buttered platter (waxed paper) or pour into a 9x13-inch dish to set. May garnish with pecan halves or sprinkle ground nuts on top. After dish candy has cooled, cut into squares.

Variation: Omit nuts; garnish with green cake decorator icing making 2 leaves on each piece of candy. Press 2 or 3 cinnamon flavored candies where leaves are joined to look like holly and berries.

Mrs. James Hobby (Julia)
Drew, Mississippi

Mrs. Frank Whisman (Elaine)

Candies

SOUR CREAM CANDY

2 cups sugar
2 Tablespoons butter

¼ teaspoon salt
8-ounces sour cream

Stir together until sugar is dissolved. Cook slowly to soft ball stage. Cool. Beat until creamy. Add ¾ cup toasted pecans and drop on waxed paper.

Mrs. Thomas H. Showers (Frances)
Drew, Mississippi

CREAM CHEESE FUDGE   2 pounds

1 (8-ounce) package of
**   cream cheese**
1 (16-ounce) box of powdered
**   sugar**

1 teaspoon vanilla
1 cup finely chopped pecans,
**   toasted in butter**

Melt cream cheese over very low heat, stirring constantly. Just as cream cheese reaches a smooth consistency, quickly stir in powdered sugar. Add vanilla and pecans and mix well. Pour out onto buttered platter and refrigerate until serving time. Cut into squares for serving.

Mrs. Keith Griffin (Leslie)

SPICY PRALINES   2 dozen

1 cup evaporated milk
1 (16-ounce) package dark
**   brown sugar**
¼ cup butter or margarine

12 large marshmallows
1 teaspoon ground cinnamon
2 cups chopped pecans

Combine milk and sugar in a heavy black skillet or Dutch oven; bring to a boil, stirring constantly. Cook over medium heat, stirring constantly, until mixture reaches soft ball stage (238°). Remove from heat. Stir in butter, marshmallows, and cinnamon. Beat with a wooden spoon until mixture is creamy and begins to thicken. Quickly stir in pecans. Drop by rounded tablespoonfuls on wax paper. Cool.

Mrs. David Taylor (Mary)

CREAM PRALINES
20 (2-inch) pralines

1 pound light brown sugar
¾ cup evaporated milk
Few grains salt

Pinch of soda
2 cups pecan halves

Combine all ingredients and cook over low heat, stirring constantly. Cool slightly, then beat until mixture begins to thicken. Drop candy rapidly from a tablespoon on a sheet of aluminum foil or a well buttered baking sheet.

Mrs. Ray Thornton (Kate)

PEANUT BRITTLE

2 cups sugar ·
1 cup light corn syrup
½ cup cold water
¼ teaspoon salt
2 cups, 12 ounces, raw spanish
  peanuts

4 Tablespoons butter
2 teaspoons soda
1 teaspoon vanilla

Cook sugar, syrup and water to soft ball stage or 238°. Add salt and peanuts and cook to hard crack stage or 290°, stirring constantly. Remove from heat and add butter, soda and vanilla and stir with wooden spoon to mix.

Note: Cook in large 1 gallon pot and do all stirring with wooden spoon. Pour into a buttered 13x15-inch cookie sheet with sides. Tip back and forth quickly to spread mixture. Let cool completely and break into pieces.

Mrs. Paul M. Belenchia (Donna)

PEANUT BUTTER CANDY

2 cups sugar
¾ cup milk
1 Tablespoon butter

1 teaspoon vanilla
1 Tablespoon peanut butter,
  heaping

Mix sugar, milk, butter and vanilla in large sauce pan. Cook until soft ball stage using candy thermometer. Then add peanut butter. Pour into buttered pyrex dish (6x9). Cool, cut, serve.

Mrs. Barry Sullivan (Betty)

Candies

COCONUT MOUNDS

¾ cup light corn syrup
2½ cups flaked coconut
½ teaspoon almond flavoring

1 (12-ounce) package
   chocolate chips, melted

Bring corn syrup to rolling boil. Add coconut and almond flavoring. Stir and set aside. Cool. Melt chocolate in double boiler. Shape coconut with your hands into balls or logs. Dip in chocolate. Place on waxed paper and chill.

Mrs. Charles Fioranelli (Vicki)

TOFFEE CANDY

1 pound butter
2 cups sugar
1 cup nuts, finely chopped

12 plain chocolate bars
½ cup chopped nuts

Combine butter, sugar and 1 cup chopped nuts and boil until light brown with dark brown streaks (cook slowly). Pour mixture into a 12x18-inch cookie sheet. Lay chocolate bars on top. When they begin to melt, spread candy evenly to cover top. Sprinkle with ½ cup nuts. Cut or break into pieces.

Mrs. Clarence Smith (Margaret Ann)

FOOL PROOF FUDGE

1 stick oleo
1 cup whipping cream
4 Tablespoons cocoa

2 cups sugar
1 cup broken pecans

Mix all ingredients and cook to soft ball stage. Let cool. Beat until mixture loses the gloss. Add pecans and pour into desired pan. Cut in one inch squares.

Mrs. Joe Smith (Bill)

OLD-FASHIONED FUDGE
1¼ pounds

2 cups granulated sugar
1 cup milk
½ teaspoon salt
2 squares unsweetened
  chocolate

2 Tablespoons light corn syrup
2 Tablespoons butter or
  margarine
½ teaspoon vanilla
½ cup chopped nuts (optional)

In saucepan, combine sugar, milk, salt, chocolate squares, corn syrup and stir over low heat until sugar dissolves. Cook gently, stirring occasionally, to 238° on candy thermometer, or until a little mixture, dropped into cold water, forms soft ball. Remove from heat, drop in butter; DO NOT STIR. Cool without stirring to 110°, or until outside of saucepan feels lukewarm to hand. Add vanilla. With spoon, beat until candy loses gloss and small amount dropped from spoon holds its shape. Add nuts. Turn into greased pan or plate. Cool and cut.

Note: Use peanut butter for a different taste. Crunchy peanut butter does great. Add about ¼ to ½ cup after candy cools a bit.

Mrs. Robert Denton (Martha)

DATE LOAF

2 cups sugar
1 cup light cream
2 Tablespoons light corn syrup
1 cup pitted, chopped dates

2 cups chopped pecans
1 Tablespoon butter
1 teaspoon vanilla

Put sugar, cream and corn syrup in saucepan and stir until sugar has dissolved. Turn heat down low and let cook until mixture forms soft ball. Put in dates and butter and cook 5 minutes longer, stirring so that dates won't stick. Remove from heat, add vanilla and cool. Beat well and add pecans. Beat until mixture is cold, then pour on a slightly dampened cloth. Shape into long loaf. Roll cloth over loaf and let stand 30 minutes or more. Slice and serve.

Mrs. Eric Muir (Nan)

CHOCOLATE TRUFFLES

½ cup whipping cream
8-ounces real chocolate chips
1 teaspoon Amaretto

Dash of salt
2 Tablespoons cocoa for dusting

Line a 9x9-inch cake pan with heavy foil. Grease well. In heavy saucepan heat cream. When it begins to boil remove from heat and add chocolate. Cover and let stand 5 minutes. Mix with a wooden spoon. Add Amaretto and salt. Pour onto foil. Chill 30 minutes. Cut in squares. Dust with cocoa. Store in refrigerator. Truffles are soft.

Mrs. Charles Fioranelli (Vicki)

MARTHA WASHINGTON CANDY

2 (16-ounce) boxes powdered
   sugar
½ cup margarine or butter
1 (14-ounce) can sweetened
   condensed milk
1 teaspoon vanilla

4 cups pecans, chopped
1 (½ pound) package
   semi-sweet chocolate
   squares
1 block paraffin

Cream first 4 ingredients. Add nuts. Roll into balls the size of a walnut. Use powdered sugar to dip hands into as you roll the balls. Melt the chocolate and paraffin over low heat. Dip balls into this mixture, one piece at a time, holding each with a toothpick. Drop on waxed paper.

Mrs. Phillip Gaither

SANTA'S WHISKERS COOKIES   5 dozen

1 cup butter
1 cup sugar
2 Tablespoons milk
1 teaspoon vanilla
2½ cups all-purpose flour

¾ cup red and green cherries,
   finely chopped
½ cup nuts, finely chopped
¾ cup flaked coconut

Cream butter and sugar well. Blend in milk and vanilla. Stir in flour, cherries, and nuts. Form into 2 rolls, each 2 inches by 8 inches. Roll in coconut. Wrap in foil and chill overnight. Slice ¼ inch thick and place on ungreased cookie sheet. Bake in 375° oven about 12 minutes or until edges are golden.

Mrs. Tommy Naron (Memorie)

THE ABSOLUTE BEST CHOCOLATE CHIP COOKIES   4 dozen

1 cup butter
1 teaspoon salt
1 teaspoon vanilla extract
¾ cup granulated sugar
¾ cup light brown sugar, firmly
  packed
2 eggs, large
2¼ cups unsifted all-purpose
  flour

1 teaspoon baking soda
1 teaspoon hot water
8-ounces (2 generous cups)
  walnuts or pecans, chopped
12-ounces (2 cups) semi-sweet
  chocolate morsels

Preheat oven to 375°. Cut aluminum foil to fit cookie sheets. In a large bowl with an electric mixer cream the butter. Add the salt, vanilla, and both sugars. Beat well. Add eggs and beat well. On low speed add ½ of the flour. Beat only until incorporated. In a small cup stir the soda into the hot water to dissolve. Mix into dough. Add the remaining flour. Beat only to mix. Stir in nuts and morsels. Drop by teaspoons onto cookie sheets. Bake for about 12 minutes.

Note: Beth won a blue ribbon at the Bolivar County Fair and the Mississippi State Fair with these cookies.

Beth Blackwood

CREAM CHEESE COOKIES   7 dozen

1 cup butter or margarine,
  softened
1 (3-ounce) package cream
  cheese, softened
1 cup sugar

1 egg yolk
2½ cups all-purpose flour
1 teaspoon vanilla extract
Candied cherries or pecan
  halves

Cream butter and cream cheese; gradually add sugar, beating until light and fluffy. Add egg yolk, beating well. Add flour and vanilla; mix until blended. Chill dough at least one hour. Shape dough into 1-inch balls, and place on greased cookie sheets. Gently press a candied cherry or pecan half into each cookie. Bake at 325° for 12 to 15 minutes.

Note: These are great at Christmas done with red and green cherries.

Mrs. Jimmy Goodman (Carolyn)

REMA'S ROYAL CHIP COOKIES   15 to 17 dozen

4½ cups all-purpose flour
2 teaspoons baking soda
1 teaspoon salt
1½ cups sugar
1½ cups brown sugar
2 cups vegetable shortening (1
    cup plain; 1 cup butter
    flavored)
2 teaspoons vanilla

2 teaspoons squeezed orange
    juice
Grated peel of 1 orange
    (orange part only)
4 eggs
1 (12-ounce) package
    chocolate chips
2 cups chopped pecans

Combine flour, soda, and salt; set aside. In separate bowl, combine sugars, shortening, vanilla, and juice. Beat until mixture is creamy; beat in eggs. Add flour mixture, ½ cup at a time, mixing well after each addition. Stir in chocolate chips, nuts, and grated orange peel. Refrigerate dough several hours or overnight. Drop the dough by teaspoonfuls on to lightly greased insulated cookie sheet. Bake at 325° for 10 to 12 minutes. Allow cookies to cool 2 to 3 minutes before removing from sheet.

Mrs. C.E. Dunlap (Jane)

BACHELOR BUTTONS   3½ dozen

¾ cup butter, softened
1 cup dark brown sugar,
    packed
1 egg
2 cups all-purpose flour
1 teaspoon soda

¼ teaspoon ground ginger
¼ teaspoon ground cinnamon
¼ teaspoon salt
1 teaspoon vanilla
1 cup chopped pecans
⅓ cup granulated white sugar

Cream butter and brown sugar until light and fluffy. Add egg and beat well. Combine the dry ingredients, stir to mix, and add to creamed mixture. Stir in the vanilla and nuts. Chill in the refrigerator covered for several hours. Shape into small balls, dip in sugar and place on a greased cookie sheet. Gently press flat with a fork. Bake at 350° for 17 minutes. Let cool 2 minutes before removing from cookie sheet.

Mrs. Bob Tibbs (Pat)

LEBKUCHEN (GERMAN HONEY COOKIES) 5 dozen

4 cups all-purpose flour,
  sifted
¼ teaspoon baking soda
¾ teaspoon cinnamon
⅛ teaspoon nutmeg
⅛ teaspoon cloves
⅔ cup honey
½ cup brown sugar, packed

2 Tablespoons water
1 egg, beaten
¾ cup chopped candied
  orange peel
¾ cup chopped candied citron
1 cup chopped and blanched
  almonds

Sift flour, then add soda and spices. In a large saucepan, combine honey, sugar, and water and boil for 5 minutes. Cool. Add flour mixture, egg, orange peel, citron, and almonds. Press dough into a cake-like shape and wrap in waxed paper. Store in refrigerator 2 or 3 days to ripen. Roll ¼ to ½ inch thick or floured surface and cut into 1x3-inch strips. Bake on greased cookie sheet at 350° for 15 to 20 minutes. When cool spread with Transparent Glaze. Store at least one day before serving.

Transparent Glaze
2 cups powdered sugar
3 Tablespoons water, boiling

1 teaspoon vanilla

Combine ingredients and beat thoroughly. Spread on cookies while warm.

Note: Cookies are hard and chewy and develop better flavor upon storage of 2 weeks or longer. I usually bake these several weeks before Christmas.

Mrs. Jim Brown (Pat)

PATTY'S MOLASSES COOKIES 4½ dozen

¾ cup shortening
1 cup sugar
¼ cup molasses
1 egg
2 teaspoons baking soda

2 cups sifted all-purpose flour
½ teaspoon cloves
½ teaspoon ginger
1 teaspoon cinnamon
1 teaspoon salt

Melt shortening and let cool. Add sugar, molasses, and egg. Beat well. Add the remaining dry ingredients and mix. Refrigerate for 1 hour or more. Roll into balls. Then roll balls into sugar. Bake on greased cookie sheet at 350° for 8 to 10 minutes.

Mrs. James Taylor (Bev)

JUBILEE JUMBLES (OLDE TYME DROP COOKIES)   4 dozen

½ cup shortening
1 cup brown sugar, packed
½ cup white sugar
2 eggs
1 cup evaporated milk
1 teaspoon vanilla

2¾ cups all-purpose flour,
  sifted
½ teaspoon soda
1 teaspoon salt
1 cup chopped walnuts or
  pecans

Mix thoroughly shortening, sugars, eggs; stir in evaporated milk and vanilla. Sift together flour, soda, and salt; stir into the above mixture. Blend in chopped nuts and chill 1 hour. Drop by rounded tablespoonfuls 2 inches apart on greased baking sheet. Bake at 375° about 10 minutes until delicately browned. While still warm, frost with Burnt Butter Glaze and garnish with pecan or walnut halves.

Burnt Butter Glaze
2 Tablespoons butter
2 cups powdered sugar, sifted

¼ cup evaporated milk

Heat butter until golden brown. Beat in powdered sugar and milk until smooth.

Mrs. Inez McCain

LOVE LETTERS   4 dozen

2 cups all-purpose flour
½ cup sugar
1 cup butter or margarine
2 teaspoons finely grated lemon
  rind

Finely grated rind of 1 orange
½ cup sour cream
Candied cherries

Heat oven to 475°. Measure flour and blend with sugar. Cut in butter and rinds until mixture resembles coarse meal. Blend sour cream in evenly. Shape dough into firm ball. Divide in half. Roll on well-floured board to ⅛ inch thickness. Cut into 3x2-inch pieces. Fold ends to center, overlapping slightly; seal with tiny piece of candied cherry. Place on ungreased baking sheet. Brush tops with water; sprinkled with sugar. Bake 6 to 8 minutes.

Note: This is an adaptation of an old German cookie. Perfect for Valentine's Day, engagement parties, or bridal showers.

Mrs. J.C. Gregory (Donna)

TEA CAKES
6 dozen

2 cups sugar
1 cup margarine
4 Tablespoons milk
1 teaspoon soda
2 teaspoons baking powder

2 eggs
1 teaspoon vanilla
3½ to 4 cups all-purpose flour
Pinch of salt
Pinch of nutmeg (optional)

Cream sugar and margarine, add remaining ingredients. (Add flour slowly). Mix thoroughly. Spoon out dough with large spoon onto cookie sheet. Take glass or quart jar and cover bottom with a towel. Secure with a rubber band. Wet bottom of jar and fill a bowl with sugar. Press jar in sugar, then press cookie. Repeat for each cookie. Bake 5 to 6 minutes at 375°. (Just until bottom browns.) Sprinkle with sugar.

Mrs. Johnny Hobbs (Carolyn)

NONNIE'S VANILLA NUT COOKIES
7 dozen

4 cups all-purpose flour,
  sifted
3 teaspoons baking powder
¼ teaspoon salt
1 cup butter or margarine
½ cup brown sugar, firmly
  packed

2 cups granulated sugar
2 eggs, well beaten
1 cup pecans, chopped
1 Tablespoon vanilla

Sift flour once, measure, add baking powder and salt, and sift again. Cream butter and sugars until light and fluffy—add eggs, nuts and vanilla. Add flour gradually, mixing well. Shape into rolls, 1½ inches in diameter, and roll in waxed paper. Chill overnight, or until firm enough to slice. Cut in ⅛ inch slices. Bake on ungreased baking sheet at 425° for 5 minutes, or until done.

Mrs. Rex Shannon, Jr. (Leslie)

MUFF PUFFS 3 dozen

1 cup butter (no margarine!),
   softened
4 Tablespoons powdered sugar

1 teaspoon vanilla
2 cups all-purpose flour, sifted
1 cup chopped pecans

In medium bowl cream butter; add sugar and continue to beat until light and fluffy. Add vanilla. Add sifted flour and mix well; fold in chopped nuts. Shape into small balls and bake on an ungreased baking sheet for 15 to 18 minutes at 350°. Sprinkle with powdered sugar while hot.

Mrs. Richard Spehr
Marietta, Georgia

SOUR CREAM COOKIES

2 cups granulated sugar
½ cup shortening
½ cup butter
2 eggs

1 cup thick cream
1 teaspoon soda
4 cups all-purpose flour
1 teaspoon vanilla

Allow cream to sour at room temperature and mix in soda. Cream sugar with shortening and butter, add eggs, then add cream alternately with flour. Stir in vanilla. Chill. Roll out ¼ inch thick and cut with cookie cutter. Bake on ungreased cookie sheet in 400° oven until lightly brown.

Mrs. Mark Ambrose (Frances)
Billings, Montana

BROWN SUGAR DROP COOKIES 4 to 5 dozen

½ cup shortening
½ cup butter
2½ cups brown sugar
2 eggs

2½ cups all-purpose flour
½ teaspoon soda
¼ teaspoon salt
1 cup chopped pecans

Cream shortening, butter, and sugar. Add eggs, beating well. Sift together flour, soda, and salt and add to creamed mixture. Stir in pecans. Drop by teaspoon on ungreased cookie sheet and bake at 350° for 6 to 7 minutes for soft, chewy cookies; 8 to 10 minutes for crisp cookies.

Mrs. Brady Cole (Rosalie)

CHOCOLATE PEANUT BUTTER BARS   3 dozen

*1 (12-ounce) package milk
   chocolate chips*

Filling
1½ cups powdered sugar   *1½ cups creamy peanut butter*
¾ cup pecans, finely chopped   *1 teaspoon vanilla*
¼ cup butter, melted

Crust
1½ cups all-purpose flour   *¼ teaspoon baking soda*
⅔ cup packed brown sugar   *⅔ cup butter, softened*
½ teaspoon baking powder   *2 egg yolks, slightly beaten*
½ teaspoon salt   *1 teaspoon vanilla*

Filling: Combine sugar and pecans. Add remaining filling ingredients and stir. Set aside.

Crust: Preheat oven to 350°. Combine crust ingredients and beat at low speed until crumbly, use pastry blender or fork.

Press crumbs into bottom of ungreased 13x9-inch baking pan. Bake 12 to 15 minutes or until golden brown. Remove from oven. Turn oven off. Let crust cool 2 to 3 minutes. While still warm, spread filling evenly over crust. Sprinkle chocolate chips over filling. Return pan to warm oven for 2 to 3 minutes or until chocolate softens. Remove from oven and spread chocolate evenly. Cool on wire rack. Cut into bars.

Mrs. Terry Barron (Lynn)

REFRIGERATOR OATMEAL COOKIES   2 dozen

1 cup butter   *¼ teaspoon salt*
1 cup powdered sugar   *1 cup oatmeal*
2 teaspoons vanilla   *Chocolate Sprinkles*
1½ cups cake flour

Cream butter and powdered sugar. Add vanilla, cake flour, salt, and oatmeal; mix well. Chill dough. Roll into 4 rolls about the size of a quarter. Roll in chocolate sprinkles. Chill again. Can roll in waxed paper and freeze at this point. When ready to cook, slice and bake at 325° for 15 minutes. Do not brown.

Mrs. Ben Mitchell (Margaret Ann)

OATMEAL COOKIES

1 cup shortening
1 cup brown sugar
1 cup granulated sugar
2 eggs
1 teaspoon vanilla
1½ cups all-purpose flour

1 teaspoon soda
1 teaspoon cinnamon
½ teaspoon salt
3 cups rolled oats
1 cup nuts, chopped (optional)
1 cup raisins (optional)

Cream shortening and sugars. Add eggs and beat well. Add vanilla. Sift dry ingredients and add oats. Stir in raisins and nuts. The batter will be so stiff that you will have to stir by hand. Bake at 350° for 10 to 12 minutes. (You may refrigerate this batter and bake as you want.)

Variation: Add ½ teaspoon baking powder
Add 1 small package chocolate chips

Mrs. Jim Adams (Signe)

SOUR CREAM OATMEAL COOKIES   6 dozen

1 cup butter
1½ cups sugar
2 cups oatmeal
1 teaspoon soda
1 cup sour cream

½ teaspoon baking powder
2 cups all-purpose flour
2 teaspoons cinnamon
1 cup chopped nuts
1 cup raisins

Mix in order given. Add a little more flour if dough is too soft. Drop onto greased cookie sheet and bake at 350° for 15 to 18 minutes.

Mrs. Terry Barron (Lynn)

TOFFEE BARS   2 to 3 dozen

1 cup butter
1 cup light brown sugar
1 egg yolk, slightly beaten
1 cup all-purpose flour

¼ teaspoon salt
1 teaspoon vanilla
6 milk chocolate candy bars
1 cup pecans, chopped

Cream butter and sugar. Add the egg yolks, mixing well. Add flour, salt, and vanilla. Cream well. Spread in a 9x13x2-inch pan and bake at 350° for 20 minutes. Immediately after removing from oven, top with chocolate candy bars and spread these as they melt. Sprinkle this with pecans. Refrigerate at least overnight. Cut into squares and place in a tin.

Mrs. Leo McGee (Judy)

VIENNESE ALMOND SANDWICH COOKIES
2 dozen

1 (4½-ounce) can whole
 almonds
1¼ cups all-purpose flour
½ cup butter

⅓ cup sugar
¼ teaspoon salt
¼ cup apricot preserves
Chocolate Glaze

Grind almonds in food processor very fine. Into large bowl, measure flour, butter, sugar and salt; add ground almonds. With hands, knead until well blended (dough will be very dry).

Preheat oven to 350°. Between two sheets of waxed paper, roll ½ of dough ⅛ inch thick. Cut out cookies with 2 inch round cutter. Place cookies ½ inch apart on ungreased cookie sheets. Repeat with all dough. Bake 8 minutes. Remove to racks and cool.

Note: dough is difficult to roll out. Do not become discouraged becauce cookies are worth the trouble!!!

On half of cookies, spread ½ teaspoon preserves evenly on each cookie. Top with remaining cookies.

Chocolate Glaze

½ cup semi-sweet chocolate
 pieces
1 Tablespoon butter

1 Tablespoon milk
1½ teaspoons light corn syrup

In double boiler over hot, not boiling, water, melt chocolate pieces and butter. Remove from heat. Stir in milk and corn syrup until blended. Dip filled cookies, edgewise, into chocolate mixture to cover half of cookie. Place cookies on waxed paper to dry. Store in refrigerator.

Mrs. John Tatum (Carol)

DONNA'S KOOKIE POPS

12 to 15 cookies

¾ cup margarine
1 cup sugar
2 eggs
¼ teaspoon vanilla

2½ cups all-purpose flour
1 teaspoon baking powder
1 teaspoon salt
12 popsicle sticks

Mix together margarine, sugar, egg, vanilla, flour, baking powder, and salt. Chill dough. Roll out to ¼ inch thick. Cut in large shapes, such as hearts, trees, or circles. Press a stick into each dough shape. Bake at 400° for 8 to 10 minutes. Cool and frost.

Frosting
⅓ cup margarine
Dash of salt
1 teaspoon vanilla

3 cups powdered sugar
2 to 3 Tablespoons milk

Beat above ingredients until light and fluffy.

Mrs. Dan Hammett (Marcia)

PEANUT BUTTER COOKIES

4 dozen

½ cup butter
½ cup peanut butter
½ cup granulated sugar
½ cup brown sugar
1 egg

½ teaspoon vanilla
1¼ cups sifted all-purpose flour
¾ teaspoon soda
¼ teaspoon salt
Peanut halves (optional)

Thoroughly cream butter, peanut butter, egg, sugars, and vanilla. Sift together dry ingredients. Blend into creamed mixture. Shape into 1-inch balls. Roll in granulated sugar. Place 2 inches apart on ungreased cookie sheet. Press peanut halves on top of each cookie or crisscross cookie with fork tines. Bake at 375° for 10 to 12 minutes. Cool slightly. Remove from pan.

Brittany Baughman

GERMAN CHOCOLATE BARS   35 bars

1 box German Chocolate   1 cup pecans
  cake mix   1 (15-ounce) bag caramels
¾ cup margarine   ½ cup milk
⅓ cup milk
1 (12-ounce) package
  semi-sweet chocolate pieces

Mix cake mix, margarine, and milk together and spread half of the cake mixture in a thin layer on the bottom of a 9x13-inch pan. Bake 6 minutes at 350°. Sprinkle chocolate pieces and pecans on cake. Next, mix together the caramels and milk. Cool on low heat until the caramel is dissolved. Pour the caramel mixture on the cake. Spread the other half of the cake mix onto the top and bake at 350° for 15 to 18 minutes. Cool and cut into bars. Delicious.

Mrs. J.D. Mathis (Rose Ann)

CHOCO CHEWY BARS   35 bars

1 (12-ounce) package   2 eggs
  chocolate chips   2 cups all-purpose flour
1 (15-ounce) can sweetened   ½ teaspoon salt
  condensed milk   1 teaspoon vanilla
2 Tablespoons margarine   ½ cup chopped pecans
1 cup margarine, melted and   ½ cup flaked coconut
  cooled   1 teaspoon vanilla
1 (1 pound) box brown sugar

In top of double boiler over boiling water, melt chips with milk and 2 tablespoons margarine. Stir until smooth and set aside. Combine 1 cup margarine, brown sugar, and eggs. Add flour and salt. Stir in pecans, coconut, and vanilla. Blend well, then spoon into quart container in order to measure. Spread half the dough in an ungreased 10x15-inch jelly roll pan. Drizzle chocolate mixture over dough in pan. Dot top of chocolate mixture with remaining brown sugar dough and spread carefully. Swirl top slightly with a knife. Bake at 350° for 30 to 35 minutes or until golden brown. Cool. Cut into bars using knife dipped frequently in hot water. Lift from pan carefully so layers will remain intact—a small spatula is helpful. These cookies are tedious to make—each step seems more difficult than the last—but they are well worth the effort.

Mrs. Jim Tims (Frances)

Cookies

NUTTY COCOA BROWNIES

2 cups sugar
2 cups self-rising flour
1 teaspoon soda
¼ cup plus 1 Tablespoon cocoa
1 cup butter

1 cup water
½ cup buttermilk
2 eggs, beaten
1 teaspoon vanilla

Combine sugar, flour, soda, and cocoa. Stir well and set aside. Melt butter over low heat and add water. Pour over the dry ingredients and beat on medium speed for 1 minute. Add buttermilk, eggs, and vanilla. Stir until blended. Pour into a floured and oiled 18x12-inch pan. Drop filled pan several times on the countertop to remove bubbles. Spread mixture evenly to the sides of the pan. Bake at 400° for 15-20 minutes. While warm, ice with icing.

Chocolate Icing
1 package confectioners' sugar
Dash of salt
¼ cup cocoa
½ cup butter

⅓ cup milk
1 teaspoon vanilla
1 cup chopped, toasted pecans

Combine sugar, salt, and cocoa. Stir well. Combine butter and milk in a heavy saucepan and cook until butter melts. Pour over the cocoa mixture and beat until smooth. Stir in pecans and vanilla. Pour over the cake as it is removed from the oven.

Mrs. Bob Tibbs (Pat)

SAUCEPAN BROWNIES   16 servings

½ cup butter or margarine
1-ounce unsweetened
   chocolate
1 cup sugar

2 eggs, slightly beaten
¾ cup self-rising flour
1 teaspoon vanilla extract
½ cup chopped pecans

Melt butter and chocolate over low heat. Add remainder of ingredients. Pour into well-greased 8x8x2-inch pan. Bake 30 to 35 minutes in 350° oven.

Mrs. Evelyn G. Brown

BUTTERSCOTCH BROWNIES
16 brownies

½ cup margarine
1 cup light brown sugar
½ cup granulated sugar
1 cup sifted all-purpose flour
1 teaspoon baking powder

2 eggs
1 teaspoon vanilla
½ teaspoon salt
1 cup chopped pecans

Melt margarine and add to brown and white sugars. Cool slightly and blend in eggs. Sift dry ingredients and add to sugar mixture, stirring until thoroughly blended. Add vanilla and nuts. Bake in a 9-inch square pan at 350° for 30 minutes.

Mrs. Wylie Hilburn (Shirley)

CARROT COOKIES
4 dozen

¾ cup sugar
¾ cup shortening
1 egg
1 cup cooked and mashed
  carrots

2 cups all-purpose flour
1 teaspoon baking powder
¼ teaspoon salt
1 teaspoon vanilla

Mix above ingredients. Drop by teaspoonfuls on greased cookie sheet. Bake at 350° until done, about 12 minutes. They do not brown on top but do brown around the edges. Cool.

Icing
1 cup powdered sugar
Orange juice

Pinch of grated orange rind

Add orange juice to powdered sugar until icing is of good spreading consistancy. Add grated rind. Ice cookies.

Mrs. S.R. Blakeman (Mary James)

GINGERBREAD

10 to 12 servings

1 cup oil	4 teaspoons cinnamon
1 cup buttermilk	2 teaspoons ginger
1 cup dark corn syrup	1 teaspoon nutmeg
2 eggs	1 teaspoon salt
1 teaspoon baking soda	2 cups all-purpose flour
1 teaspoon vanilla	1 cup sugar

Mix all ingredients together. Bake at 325° for 40 minutes in greased 9x13-inch pan. Cut in squares and serve with Lemon Butter Sauce (see index).

Mrs. Joe Smith, III (Suellen)

PECAN STRIPS

4 dozen bars

1 cup butter	1 teaspoon baking powder
1 cup sugar	1 teaspoon vanilla
1 egg, separated	1½ cups chopped pecans
1 teaspoon cinnamon	2 cups flour

Cream butter, sugar, and egg yolk; add cinnamon, baking powder, vanilla, ½ cup of the pecans, and flour. Mix. Spread over greased cookie sheet. Beat egg white lightly. Spread over cookie mixture. Sprinkle rest of pecans on top. Bake at 300° for 1 hour. Cut into strips while warm.

Mrs. Dan Hammett (Marcia)

DATE CAKE SQUARES

16 servings

4 eggs, separated	1 package dates, chopped
1 cup sugar	½ cup broken pecans
1 heaping teaspoon vanilla	½ cup all-purpose flour

Cream egg yolks with sugar and vanilla. Toss dates and nuts with flour. Mix with eggs and sugar. Beat egg whites until stiff but not dry. Fold in other mixture. Pour into 8-inch square pan. Bake at 350° about 30 minutes. After cake cools, sprinkle top of cake with powdered sugar and cut into squares.

Mrs. Leonard Rubenstein (Bettie)

LOUISE'S LEMON BAR   15 to 18 servings

2 cups all-purpose flour   **½ cup powdered sugar**
1 cup butter

Mix flour, butter, and sugar and press into 13x9x2-inch pan. Bake at 350° for 20 minutes.

Filling
4 eggs   **½ Tablespoon baking powder**
2 cups sugar   **¼ cup all-purpose flour**
⅓ cup lemon juice

Beat eggs, sugar, lemon juice, flour, and baking powder. Pour over crust. Bake 25 minutes at 350°. Sprinkle with powdered sugar. Slice into bars. These are delicious!

Louise Kleier
Louisville, Kentucky

HUNGARIAN PECAN TRIANGLES   64 triangles

2 cups all-purpose flour   **¼ cup light brown sugar,**
1 cup granulated sugar   **packed**
1 cup butter or margarine,   **4 cups finely chopped pecans**
** softened**   **1½ teaspoons ground cinnamon**
2 egg yolks   **4 egg whites**
1 Tablespoon brandy or water   **Powdered sugar (optional)**

Mix flour and ½ cup granulated sugar in medium size bowl. Cut in butter until particles resemble small peas. With fork, stir in egg yolks and brandy. With hand, press mixture to make a dough. Press evenly and firmly into a jelly-roll pan. Bake in preheated 350° oven 15 minutes or until firm to touch. Meanwhile, in a heavy 3-quart saucepan, mix the remaining ½ cup granulated sugar, brown sugar, pecans, cinnamon, and egg whites. Stir over low heat about 5 minutes until sugar dissolves. Spread evenly over prebaked dough. Bake 25 minutes or until topping is lightly brown and glazed. Cool 5 minutes; cut in four long strips, then cut each strip in eight pieces. Cut each piece in half diagonally in 2 triangles. Dust with powdered sugar. Store tightly covered with waxed paper between layers.

Mrs. J.D. Mathis (Rose Ann)

GINGERBREAD MEN - CHRISTMAS TRADITION

1½ cups sugar
1 cup margarine
1 egg
2 Tablespoons dark corn syrup
4 teaspoons grated orange rind
3 cups all-purpose flour

2 teaspoons baking soda
2 teaspoons ground cinnamon
1 teaspoon ground ginger
½ teaspoon salt
½ teaspoon ground cloves
Raisins, plumped and drained

Cream sugar and margarine. Add egg and beat until light and fluffy. Add corn syrup and orange peel; mix well. Stir together flour, soda, cinnamon, ginger, salt, and cloves. Mix well and chill thoroughly. Use ⅓ or ½ of dough at a time. Roll on lightly floured surface either ⅛ to ¼ inch thick depending on thickness desired. Cut with a gingerbread man cookie cutter. Place on ungreased cookie sheet (5 large ones on one cookie sheet). Use a raisin for each eye and 3 down his tummy for buttons. Dip the raisins in water and press into the dough. Bake at 375° for 8 to 10 minutes. Cool 1 minute before removing from pan. Cool completely on rack. These freeze well in zip-lock bags. If desired after removing from freezer, ice by piping icing at neck for collar, wrists, and across center raisin on tummy for belt.

Icing
1 cup sifted confectioners'
  sugar
1 Tablespoon softened butter
⅛ teaspoon vanilla or ⅛
  teaspoon almond flavoring

1-2 Tablespoons milk
Food coloring

Beat together sugar, butter, vanilla, and flavoring of choice. Add 1-2 tablespoons milk for desired consistency. Icing may be tinted with color of choice.

Mrs. Robert Tibbs, (Pat)

PINEAPPLE CHEESECAKE BARS   16 servings

Crumb Mixture
½ cup butter, softened
1¼ cups all-purpose flour
⅓ cup sugar

1 Tablespoon grated orange
   peel

Combine all ingredients and press into a 8 or 9-inch square pan, reserving ½ cup of crumb mixture. Bake in a 350° oven for 12 to 17 minutes until edges are lightly browned.

Cheesecake Mixture
1 (8-ounce) package cream
   cheese, softened
¼ cup sugar
1 egg

1 Tablespoon lemon juice
½ cup chopped candied
   pineapple

Combine first 4 ingredients. Beat till smooth, scraping sides of bowl often. Stir in pineapple. Pour over hot crust, sprinkle with reserved crumb mixture. Bake at 350° 15 to 20 minutes until edges are lightly browned. Cool completely. Cut into bars. Cover and store in refrigerator. (Chop pineapple fine. Large pieces make it difficult to slice.)

Mrs. Robert Tibbs (Pat)

CHOCOLATE CREAMY CUPCAKES   20 to 24 cupcakes

1 egg
1 (8-ounce) package cream
   cheese
⅓ cup sugar
⅛ teaspoon salt
6-ounces chocolate chips
1 cup sugar
1¼ cups all-purpose flour

¼ cup cocoa
1 cup water
1 teaspoon soda
⅓ cup oil
½ teaspoon salt
1 Tablespoon vinegar
1 teaspoon vanilla

Combine egg, cream cheese, ⅓ cup sugar and ⅛ teaspoon salt. Stir in chocolate chips and heat well. Combine remainder of ingredients in another bowl. Mix well. Batter will be runny. Put half of this batter in muffin cups. Top with first mixture. Bake at 350° for 30 minutes.

Mrs. James Beard (Patty)

BROWNIE CUPCAKES   2 dozen

4 squares semi-sweet
   chocolate
1 cup butter or margarine
1 cup all purpose flour, unsifted

4 eggs,
1¾ cups sugar
2 teaspoons vanilla
2 cups chopped pecans

Mix butter and chocolate in top of double boiler. Stir until chocolate is melted. Set aside to cool. Mix flour and sugar. Add eggs one at a time. Stir as little as possible. Add vanilla and chocolate mixture along with pecans. Pour into muffin cups. Bake 20 to 25 minutes at 325°. Be sure not to overbake because cupcakes will stick to paper muffin liners.

Mrs. Travis Tribble (Jeri)

PAT CLARK'S CUPCAKES   2 dozen

1½ cups all-purpose flour
2 Tablespoons baking powder
½ teaspoon salt
½ cup butter

1 cup sugar
1 teaspoon vanilla
2 eggs, separated
½ to ⅔ cup milk

Sift dry ingredients, set aside. Cream butter and sugar. Add vanilla and 2 egg yolks, beat well. Add flour mixture alternately with milk. Beat egg whites stiff and fold into batter. Bake at 375° for 15 to 20 minutes. These are wonderful iced.

Note: May be baked in layers at 350° for 30 minutes.

Mrs. Roy Clark (Pat)
Bay St. Louis, Mississippi

LEMON CHEESE CAKE PIE   6 servings

1 (8-ounce) package cream
   cheese
2 Tablespoons soft butter or
   margarine
1 egg
½ cup sugar
2 Tablespoons all-purpose flour

⅔ cup milk
¼ cup lemon juice
2 Tablespoons grated lemon
   rind
1 graham cracker crust pie
   shell

Mix all ingredients and pour into graham cracker crust. Bake at 350° for 35 minutes.

Mrs. James Taylor (Bev)

BANANA CREAM PIE
6 to 8 servings

½ cup sugar
5 Tablespoons all-purpose flour
¼ teaspoon salt
2 cups milk

2 eggs, divided
1 Tablespoon butter
½ teaspoon vanilla
3 ripe bananas

Combine sugar, flour, and salt in top of double boiler. Add milk slowly, mixing thoroughly. Cook over rapidly boiling water until thick, stirring constantly. Cool 10 minutes stirring occasionally. Stir small amount of hot mixture into egg yolks that have been beaten. Pour egg yolks back into remaining hot mixture while beating. Cook 1 minute longer. Remove from heat. Add butter and vanilla. Cool. Slice bananas into baked 9-inch pie crust. Cover with filling. Top with meringue and brown in oven at 350°.

Mrs. George Fortenberry (Jerry)

GRANNY'S DUTCH APPLE PIE
6 servings

6 large York or Granny Smith
   apples
½ cup sugar
4 Tablespoons cold water

Cinnamon
¾ cup brown sugar
1 cup all-purpose flour
½ cup margarine

Peel, core, and slice apples (thinly) into a large casserole dish. Sprinkle the sugar, water, and cinnamon on the apples as you slice them. Cream together the brown sugar, flour, and margarine. Spread over apple mixture. Bake at 300° for 1 hour. Serve warm with vanilla ice cream.

Mrs. Roger Dicks (Sallie)

FRENCH COCONUT PIE
6 to 8 servings

½ cup butter, softened
1½ cups sugar
3 eggs, slightly beaten
1 Tablespoon vinegar
1 teaspoon coconut extract

1 teaspoon vanilla extract
Pinch of salt
1 (6-ounce) package frozen
   coconut
1 (9-inch) pie shell, unbaked

Cream butter and sugar. Add eggs and beat slightly. Add vinegar, coconut, extracts, and salt. Mix well. Add frozen coconut and mix. Pour into a 9-inch unbaked pie shell. Bake at 325° for 40 to 50 minutes.

Mrs. Paul Belenchia (Donna)

IMPOSSIBLE COCONUT PIE
6 to 8 servings

4 eggs
1¾ cups sugar
½ cup all-purpose flour
Pinch of salt

2 cups milk
½ cup margarine, melted
1½ teaspoons vanilla
7-ounces flaked coconut

Grease and flour 2 9-inch pie pans. Beat eggs well. Add sugar, flour, salt, milk, margarine, vanilla and coconut. Divide the mixture between pans (needs no crust). Bake at 350° for 25 minutes or until done.

Mrs. Frank Gaither

PEAR CRUMBLE PIE
6 to 8 servings

6 medium pears, pared,
    cored, and cut in eighths
1 teaspoon grated lemon peel
½ cup sugar
3 Tablespoons lemon juice
1 (9-inch) pie shell, unbaked
½ cup all-purpose flour

½ teaspoon ginger
¼ teaspoon mace
½ cup sugar
½ teaspoon cinnamon
⅓ cup butter or margarine
Whipped cream

Mix pears, sugar, lemon peel, and lemon juice. Arrange in pie shell. Next combine flour, sugar, and spices. Cut in butter until crumbly and sprinkle over pears. Bake in preheated 400° oven for 45 minutes or until pears are tender. Serve warm with whipped cream.

Mrs. Phillip Adams (Mona)

SWEET POTATO PIE
12 servings

2 (9-inch) pie shells, unbaked
1 (8-ounce) package cream
    cheese
1 (12-ounce) carton non-dairy
    whipped topping
2 cups sugar

3 cups cooked, mashed sweet
    potatoes
1 egg, beaten
1 teaspoon vanilla
3 Tablespoons all-purpose flour
½ cup margarine

Brown pie shells and let cool. Mix together cream cheese, whipped topping, and 1 cup of sugar. Place in bottom of crust and chill. Mix 1 cup of sugar, potatoes, egg, vanilla, flour and margarine in skillet on top of stove and heat. Let cool. Put on top of chilled pie. Chill entire pie before serving.

Mrs. Gerald Burnside (Eugenia)

HAZIE'S PEACH PIE

6 to 8 servings

1 (9-inch) pie shell
2 cups sliced fresh peaches
½ cup sugar
2 Tablespoons all-purpose flour

⅛ teaspoon salt
¼ teaspoon nutmeg
½ cup heavy cream
½ teaspoon vanilla extract

In a pie shell place sliced peaches. Mix sugar, flour, salt, nutmeg, cream, and vanilla and stir until well-blended. Pour over peaches. Bake at 400° for 45-55 minutes.

Note: You may want to serve this as a cobbler because it doesn't hold its shape very well, but it is truly delicious.

Quick and easy

Mrs. Jimmy Sanders (Hazel)

SOUR CREAM PEACH PIE ✓

6 to 8 servings

2 cups fresh sliced peaches
¾ cup sugar
2 Tablespoons all-purpose flour
¼ teaspoon salt

1 cup sour cream
1 egg
½ teaspoon vanilla
1 (9-inch) unbaked pie shell

Topping
½ cup sugar
½ cup all-purpose flour

1 teaspoon cinnamon
½ cup margarine

Peel and thinly slice enough peaches to make 2 cups. Set aside. Mix sugar, flour, and salt in bowl. Add sour cream, egg, and vanilla. Mix well. Add peaches to sour cream mixture and stir with spoon to mix. Pour into pie shell and bake in preheated 400° oven for 15 minutes. Reduce heat to 350° and bake for 20 minutes. While baking, prepare topping by mixing sugar, flour, and cinnamon together. Add margarine and mix with fork until crumbly. Sprinkle on top of pie and bake an additional 10 minutes.

Mrs. Paul Belenchia (Donna)

OLD-FASHIONED LEMON PIE

6 to 8 servings

1 cup sugar
¼ cups cornstarch
1¼ cups hot water
3 egg yolks
1 teaspoon grated lemon rind

1 Tablespoon butter
6 Tablespoons lemon juice
3 egg whites
6 Tablespoons sugar
1 (8 or 9-inch) pie shell, baked

Combine 1 cup sugar, cornstarch, and water. Cook over medium heat in double boiler, stirring constantly. Mix egg yolks, lemon rind, and butter. Add to double boiler and keep stirring until thick. Add lemon juice and cook until thick. Cool. Put in baked and cooled pie shell. Beat egg whites until they peak. Add sugar, 1 tablespoon at a time, beating well after each addition. Put on pie and bake in 325° oven for 15 minutes.

Mrs. Frank Canty
Mrs. W.S. Boland

LEMON CHESS PIE

6 to 8 servings

1 Tablespoon all-purpose
    flour
1 Tablespoon cornmeal
2 cups sugar
¼ teaspoon salt
¼ cup melted butter or
    margarine

¼ cup lemon juice
¼ cup milk
4 eggs
1 (9-inch) pie crust, unbaked

Combine dry ingredients—flour, cornmeal, sugar, and salt. Mix butter, lemon juice, and milk with the dry ingredients. Add eggs, one at a time, beating well. Pour into unbaked pie crust. Bake at 350° for 50 minutes.

Mrs. James Hobby (Julia)
Drew, Mississippi

Variation: Add 3 Tablespoons grated lemon peel.

Mrs. Paul Belenchia (Donna)

MILLIONAIRE PIE
12 servings

2 cups powdered sugar	**2 baked pie shells**
¼ pound butter, softened	**1 cup whipping cream**
1 large egg	**½ cup chopped nuts**
¼ teaspoon salt	**1 cup drained, crushed**
½ teaspoon vanilla	**pineapple**

Cream together powdered sugar and butter. Add egg, salt, and vanilla. Beat until fluffy and chill. Whip cream with a dash or two of sugar. Fold in pineapple and nuts. Spoon powdered sugar and butter mixture into pie shells. Top with whipped cream mixture. Very rich and delicious. Keep refrigerated!

Note: This recipe was a guarded secret of Farr's Cafeterias in Texas for decades! It was published one time in my hometown's daily newspaper.

Mrs. Richard Cole (Wendy)

CUSTARD PIE
6 to 8 servings

1 (9-inch) unbaked pie crust	**1 teaspoon vanilla**
1 Tablespoon butter or	**½ teaspoon salt**
margarine, softened	**¼ teaspoon ground nutmeg**
2½ cups milk	**Chopped nuts, ground nutmeg,**
½ cup sugar	**or whipped cream for garnish**
3 eggs	

Rub unbaked crust with softened butter; refrigerate. Preheat oven to 425°. In medium bowl with a wire whisk or hand beater, beat all ingredients except garnish. Place pie plate on an oven rack and pour mixture into pie crust. Bake for 35 to 40 minutes until a knife inserted about 1 inch from edge comes out clean. Cool. Garnish with whipped cream, ground nutmeg, or chopped nuts.

Mrs. Leigh Sanders (JoAnn)
Merigold

Pies

LEMON-EGG CUSTARD PIE   6 to 8 servings

4 eggs
¾ cup sugar
2 cups milk

1 teaspoon vanilla
1 teaspoon lemon juice
1 (9-inch) deep dish pie shell

Beat eggs, sugar and milk together. Add vanilla and lemon juice. Pour into pie shell. Bake at 350° for 40 minutes or until set.

Mrs. Paul Mullins (Libba)
Merigold, Mississippi

SUPER SPECIAL EGG CUSTARD   6 to 8 servings

5 eggs
3 cups scalded milk
1 teaspoon vanilla

1 cup sugar
1 unbaked 9-inch pie shell

Combine ingredients and pour into uncooked pie crust. Bake until a knife will come out clean. Cook at 300° for 1 hour.

Note: This recipe does not call for butter. I searched for 20 years for this recipe.

Mrs. W.P. Skelton (Louise)
Pace, Mississippi

PUMPKIN PIE   6 to 8 servings

¾ cup sugar
½ cup biscuit mix
2 Tablespoons butter
1 (13-ounce) can evaporated
   milk

2 eggs
1 (16-ounce) can pumpkin
2½ teaspoons pumpkin pie
   spice
2 teaspoons vanilla

Preheat oven to 350°. Grease a 9-inch pie plate. Beat all ingredients until smooth in blender on high for 1 minute or by hand, 2 minutes. Pour into plate and bake 50 to 55 minutes at 350°.

Mrs. Don Blackwood (Suzan)

STRAWBERRY-BANANA PIE
6 to 8 servings

1 (6-ounce) package
   strawberry gelatin
1 cup hot water
⅓ cup sugar
1 small package frozen
   strawberries, thawed

3 bananas, sliced
1½ pints ice cream (vanilla),
   softened
1 (9-inch) vanilla wafer or
   graham cracker pie crust

Combine first three ingredients and let cool. Add strawberries and bananas, mixing gently. Pour over softened ice cream which has been set aside in large bowl over five minutes. Fold together until blended. Let set to gel awhile before pouring into pie shell. May be frozen or refrigerated until firm.

Mack Woolley
Mineola, Texas

FRESH STRAWBERRY PIE
6 servings

4 Tablespoons cornstarch
3 Tablespoons strawberry
   gelatin
1 cup water
1 cup sugar

1 quart fresh strawberries
   (washed and stemmed)
1 (9-inch) baked pie shell
Whipping cream

Mix cornstarch, water, and sugar in saucepan. Cook till clear over medium heat (stirring constantly). Cool until lukewarm. Add strawberry gelatin. Pour over fresh strawberries in a baked pie shell. Chill and serve with whipped cream.

Emma Jane Myers

EXTRA RICH PECAN PIE
6 to 8 servings

5 eggs
¾ cup sugar
1½ cups white corn syrup
½ cup butter, melted

1½ cups chopped pecans
1 (9-inch) deep-dish pie shell,
   unbaked

Beat by hand or with mixer the first 4 ingredients. Add pecans. Pour into pie shell and bake at 400° for 5 minutes—then reduce heat to 350° and bake about 30 minutes or until pie is set.

Mrs. Don Blackwood (Suzan)

Pies

BOURBON PECAN PIE
6 to 8 servings

3 eggs, beaten
1 cup sugar
½ cup light corn syrup
½ cup dark corn syrup
⅓ cup butter, melted

2 Tablespoons bourbon
⅛ teaspoon salt
1 cup chopped pecans
1 (9-inch) pastry shell, unbaked

Combine first seven ingredients. Mix well. Place pecans in bottom of shell and pour mix over. Bake at 375° for 35 to 40 minutes.

Mrs. Robert Tibbs (Pat)

CHOCOLATE PECAN PIE
6 to 8 servings

1 cup sugar
½ cup self-rising flour
2 eggs, beaten
½ cup margarine, melted
1 cup nuts, chopped

1 cup semi-sweet chocolate chips
1 teaspoon vanilla
1 (9-inch) pie shell, unbaked

Mix sugar and flour. Add beaten eggs, then cooled margarine, nuts, chocolate chips and vanilla. Pour into unbaked pie shell and bake 30 minutes at 350°. Serve warm or cold with ice cream on top.

Mrs. Bob Buchanan (Sharon)

FROZEN PEANUT BUTTER PIE
2 pies

1 (8-ounce) package cream cheese
¾ cup powdered sugar
1 cup crunchy peanut butter
1 cup milk

1 (16-ounce) carton prepared whipped topping
2 prepared graham cracker crust pie shells

Cream powdered sugar and cream cheese. Add peanut butter and milk, mixing well. Fold in whipped topping and pour into graham cracker pie shells. Freeze. To serve, top with your favorite fudge sauce.

Note: A crust made of crushed chocolate cookies and margarine is very good.

Mrs. H.T. Miller, Jr. (Dotty)

BUTTERSCOTCH PIE   6 to 8 servings

6 Tablespoons butter
2 cups brown sugar
½ cup cream
2 cups milk
¼ cup cornstarch
3 Tablespoons all-purpose flour

⅛ teaspoon salt
3 eggs, separated
¼ teaspoon vanilla
1 baked 9-inch pie shell
6 Tablespoons sugar

Melt butter; add sugar and cream; boil 4 minutes, stirring constantly. Scald 1 cup milk. Mix cornstarch, flour, salt; add the other cup milk. Add scalded milk to butter-sugar mixture. Add cornstarch-milk mixture. Cook until thick. Beat egg yolks and add. Cook 2 to 3 minutes. Remove from heat; add vanilla. Cool. Pour into pie shell. Beat egg whites with 6 tablespoons sugar for meringue. Put on top of pie. Bake at 350° until lightly browned.

Brenda Jo Hoop

MOOSE CHIP PIE   10 to 12 servings

Crust
3 cups chocolate wafer crumbs   *½ cup unsalted butter, melted*

Filling
1 pound semi-sweet chocolate   *2 cups whipping cream*
2 eggs   *6 Tablespoons powdered sugar*
4 egg yolks   *4 egg whites, room temperature*

Crust: Combine crumbs and butter. Press on bottom and completely up sides of a 10-inch springform pan. Refrigerate 30 minutes or chill in freezer while preparing filling.

Filling: Soften chocolate in top of a double boiler over simmering water. Let cool to lukewarm (95°). Add whole eggs and mix well. Add yolks and mix until thoroughly blended. In another bowl whip cream with sugar until soft peaks form. In another bowl beat egg whites until stiff, but not dry. Stir a little of the cream and whites into chocolate mixture to lighten. Fold in remaining cream and whites until thoroughly incorporated, or leave a few "chips" of chocolate in mixture. Turn into crust and chill at least 6 hours, preferably overnight. Cover top of pie with whipped cream rossettes and chocolate shavings. Loosen crust on all sides using a very sharp knife. Remove springform.

Mrs. Allen Findley (Shirley)

FUDGE PIE

6 to 8 servings

3 eggs
2 cups sugar
5 Tablespoons cornstarch
¼ cup cocoa
1 cup evaporated milk

6 Tablespoons margarine,
melted
1 teaspoon vanilla
1 (9-inch) unbaked pie shell

Beat eggs until lemon colored. Add sugar, cornstarch, cocoa, evaporated milk, melted margarine, and vanilla. Beat and pour into pie shell. Bake for 30 minutes at 350°. This can be made into two thin pies, using 2 9-inch pie shells.

Mrs. Curtis Lofton (Janice)
Merigold, Mississippi

OUT OF THIS WORLD PIE

6 to 8 servings

1 (9-inch) unbaked pie shell
2 large eggs
½ cup all-purpose flour
1 cup sugar
1 teaspoon vanilla extract
½ cup melted butter

1 cup pecans, chopped
1 cup semi-sweet chocolate
chips
Whipped cream or ice cream
for garnish

Preheat oven to 325°. In a medium mixing bowl, beat eggs until thick and lemon-colored. Add flour and sugar; continue beating for 2 minutes. Add vanilla, butter, pecans, and chocolate chips. Pour into pie shell and bake at 325° for 60 minutes. Serve warm or at room temperature. Garnish with whipped cream or ice cream.

Note: Do not put pie in refrigerator until after serving. When cold, the texture changes. Before serving any leftover pie, take it out of the refrigerator and warm in a 200° oven and serve when warmed. Watch closely because pie will dry out.

Mrs. Jimmy Yeager (Neysa)

MARTHA ANNE'S PRALINE PIE

2 eggs
1 cup sugar
½ teaspoon cornstarch
½ cup butter, melted
2 ounces Praline Liqueur

1 cup finely chopped pecans
6 ounces package semi-sweet
    chocolate chips
1 (9-inch) unbaked pastry shell

Beat eggs slightly. Combine sugar and cornstarch and gradually add to eggs. Mix well. Stir in melted butter. Add Praline Liqueur, pecans and chocolate chips. Pour into unbaked shell. Bake at 275° 40 to 45 minutes. Cool. Serve with whipped cream or ice cream. May spoon 1 tablespoon Liqueur over topping.

Mrs. Bill Simmons (Evelyn)
Starkville, Mississippi

BLACK BOTTOM PIE

14 chocolate cookies
5 Tablespoons butter, melted
1½ Tablespoons cornstarch
½ cup sugar
4 beaten egg yolks
2 cups scalded milk
1½ squares unsweetened
    chocolate
1 teaspoon vanilla

4 egg whites, beaten
½ teaspoon cream of tartar
Pinch of salt
½ cup sugar
1 teaspoon rum
Whipped cream
1 Tablespoon powdered sugar
1 Tablespoon unflavored gelatin
4 Tablespoons cold water

Make crumbs of cookies; add butter to form crust. Press into pie pan and bake 10 minutes. Cool. Add cornstarch and ½ cup sugar to beaten egg yolks. Slowly add scalded milk to this mixture. Cook in top of double boiler for 20 minutes. Remove a cup of custard and add chocolate and vanilla. Stir until chocolate is melted. Pour into crust and chill. Beat 1 egg white, cream of tartar, salt, and ½ cup sugar until soft peaks are formed. Into remaining custard dissolve gelatin and fold in meringue. Add rum. Pour this over chocolate layer. Cover with sweetened whipped cream. Garnish with either chopped pecans or chocolate shavings. Chill and serve.

Mrs. J.R. Taylor
Pace, Mississippi

CHOCOLATE-AMARETTO MOUSSE PIE   6 to 8 servings

2 (1.5-ounce) envelopes
  whipped topping mix
1½ cups milk
2 (4⅛-ounce) packages
  chocolate instant pudding
  and pie filling mix

⅓ cup Amaretto
1 (9-inch) deep-dish pie crust,
  baked and cooled
1 (8-ounce) container frozen
  whipped topping, thawed
Chocolate candy bar, shaved

Prepare topping mix according to package instructions. Add milk, pudding mix, and Amaretto; beat with electric mixer 2 minutes at high speed. Spoon mixture into pastry shell. Top with whipped topping. Chill 4 hours. When ready to serve, shave candy bar over topping.

The Editors

GRASSHOPPER PIE   6 to 8 servings

1 (6-ounce) package
  chocolate morsels
1 Tablespoon shortening
1½ cups finely chopped nuts
½ pound marshmallows (about
  35 large)
⅓ cup milk

¼ teaspoon salt
3 Tablespoons green creme de
  menthe
3 Tablespoons white creme de
  cocoa
1½ cups heavy cream, whipped

Line a 9-inch pie pan with aluminum foil. Combine over hot (not boiling) water, chocolate morsels and shortening; stir until morsels are melted and smooth. Add chopped nuts; mix well. Spread evenly on bottom and up sides of foil-lined pie pan. Chill in refrigerator until firm, about one hour. Lift chocolate shell out of pan; peel off foil and replace shell in pie plate; chill in refrigerator until ready to use. Combine over hot (not boiling) water, marshmallows, milk, and salt; heat until marshmallows melt. Remove from heat. Add liqueurs; stir until blended. Chill in refrigerator until slightly thickened (about one hour). Gently fold in whipped cream. Pour into shell and chill in refrigerator until firm (about one hour). Makes one 9 inch pie.

Mrs. Allen Findley (Shirley)
Gunnison, Mississippi

KAHLUA PIE
6 servings

32 large marshmallows, or 3
   cups small
½ cup milk

¼ to ½ cup Kahlua
1 cup whipped topping
1 (9-inch) baked pie crust

In saucepan combine marshmallows and milk. Simmer until marshmallows melt. Cool, add Kahlua and whipped topping. Mix well and put in a baked pie crust and chill.

Mrs. Howard Grittman (Ann)
Drew, Mississippi

DATE PECAN PIE
6 to 8 servings

3 egg whites
1 cup sugar
½ cup graham cracker crumbs
1 cup pecans, chopped

½ cup dates, chopped
1 teaspoon vanilla
Whipped cream, for topping

Preheat oven to 350°. Beat the egg whites until stiff; continue beating while gradually sprinkling in the sugar. Fold in the graham cracker crumbs followed by the pecans and dates. Stir in the vanilla. Spread the mixture evenly in a buttered pyrex pan, round or square, and bake 30 minutes. Serve warm, topping each serving with whipped cream.

The Editors

APRICOT NECTAR DESSERT
10 to 12 servings

1½ cups sugar
7 Tablespoons cornstarch
1 Tablespoon gelatin
1 quart apricot nectar

1 Angel Food cake
2½ pints heavy cream
Coconut
Strawberries

Mix first 3 ingredients together; add apricot nectar. Cook in double boiler about 10 minutes or until spoon is coated. Tear cake into bite-sized pieces and place in 9x13-inch pan. Pour nectar mixture over cake. Chill for 2 hours. Whip cream and spread over mixture. Sprinkle with coconut. Garnish with strawberries.

Mrs. J.C. Darby (Dorothy Lynn)

Desserts

BANANAS FOSTER

2 servings

1 large ripe banana
3 Tablespoons brown sugar
3 Tablespoons butter
1 Tablespoon lemon juice

⅛ teaspoon cinnamon
2 Tablespoons banana liqueur
2 ounces light rum
Vanilla ice cream

Peel and slice banana lengthwise. Sauté in sugar and butter until tender. Sprinkle with lemon juice and dust with cinnamon. Heat liqueur and rum. Add to banana mixture and ignite, baste the banana until the flame dies out. Serve over ice cream.

Mrs. Joe Smith, III (Suellen)

BANANA PUDDING

12 to 15 servings

2 (3-ounce) packages of
    instant vanilla pudding
1 (14-ounce) can condensed
    milk
1 (8-ounce) carton whipped
    topping

1 teaspoon vanilla
1 (12-ounce) medium box
    vanilla wafers
6 to 8 bananas, sliced

Mix pudding according to package directions. Add condensed milk and fold in whipped topping. Into a 9x13-inch dish put a layer of vanilla wafers, layer of bananas, and a layer of pudding mixture. Repeat and end with pudding mix. Refrigerate until serving time.

Mrs. Howard Grittman (Ann)

BING CHERRY PARFAIT

10 to 12 servings

1 (16-ounce) can pitted bing
    cherries
½ cup bourbon
½ gallon vanilla ice cream

2 dozen almond macaroons,
    crumbled
1 cup chopped pecans
16-ounces heavy cream

Soak cherries in juice and bourbon for 24 hours. Cut cherries in half. Mix cherries, juice and bourbon mixture with softened ice cream. Add crumbled macaroons and nuts to above mixture. Put into parfait glasses; cover with plastic and freeze. Just before serving, whip cream and serve on top.

Mrs. Jimmy Sanders (Hazel)

CHERRY CREPES JUBILEE
6 servings

Crepes

1 egg	1 Tablespoon melted butter
1 cup milk	1 cup sifted all-purpose flour

Beat egg slightly. Add rest of ingredients and beat until smooth. Cook in lightly greased crepe pan on one side only. Stack onto paper towels until ready to use.

Almond cream filling

1 cup sugar	½ cup finely chopped toasted
¼ cup all-purpose flour	almonds
1 cup milk	3 Tablespoons butter
2 eggs	2 teaspoons vanilla
2 egg yolks	¼ teaspoon almond extract

Combine sugar and flour. Add milk. Cook, stirring until thick and bubbly. Then cook and stir 2 minutes longer. Beat eggs and yolks slightly. Stir a little hot mixture into eggs and add eggs back to mixture. Cook and stir just to boiling and remove from heat. Beat smooth and stir in rest of ingredients. Cover with wax paper and cool.

Brandied Cherry Sauce

1 can cherry pie filling	½ teaspoon grated lemon peel
2 to 4 Tablespoons brandy	1 Tablespoon fresh lemon juice
2 Tablespoons butter	

Combine all ingredients and heat in saucepan.

To put together:
Spread almond cream filling on crepes. Roll and put in baking dish (can be prepared ahead and refrigerated at this point). Bake at 350° for 20 to 25 minutes. Spoon hot cherry sauce over crepes. Heat 4 tablespoons brandy, flame and pour over cherries.

Mrs. John Tatum (Carol)

CHERRIES JUBILEE

2 (16-ounce) cans pitted dark
  sweet cherries
2 Tablespoons corn starch
2 Tablespoons sugar
Grated rind of 1 orange

2 dashes lemon juice
¾ to 1 cup brandy, warm
  (Kirsch may be substituted)
Vanilla ice cream

Mix sugar, cornstarch, orange peel, lemon juice, and cherry juice. Cook until thick. Add cherries and brandy. Ignite and serve over vanilla ice cream.

Note: May serve without flaming.

Mr. Frank Farrish (Wynell)
Fayetteville, Arkansas

LEMON CHARLOTTE RUSSE   8 to 10 servings

1 Tablespoon unflavored
  gelatin
½ cup cold water
4 large eggs, separated
1 cup sugar

½ cup fresh lemon juice
1 lemon rind, grated
1 pint heavy cream
2 dozen ladyfingers
½ cup toasted slivered almonds

Soften gelatin in cold water and dissolve over hot water. Set aside. Beat egg yolks until thick and lemon colored. Add sugar slowly while continuing to beat stiff. Add lemon juice and grated rind. Continue beating. Add gelatin to egg mixture. Beat egg whites until light and fluffy. Fold into lemon mixture. Whip cream and fold half into lemon mixture. Pour into springform pan lined with ladyfingers and add rest of custard. Top with remaining whipped cream and toasted almonds. Refrigerate 24 hours. Tastes like a lemon cloud!

Mary Lynn Peyton

CHARLOTTE RUSSE   10 to 12 servings

2 envelopes unflavored
  gelatin
¾ cup sugar
¼ teaspoon salt
4 eggs, separated
2 cups milk, scalded

⅓ cup brandy
12 ladyfingers, split
2 cups heavy cream, whipped
9 strawberries
Heavy cream, whipped, for
  garnish

Combine first 3 ingredients in double boiler. Add egg yolks and slowly stir in milk. Cook, stirring constantly, until mixture coats spoon. Cool. Add 3 tablespoons brandy and refrigerate until mixture congeals slightly. Sprinkle remaining brandy over ladyfingers and line mold. Fold gelatin mixture into beaten egg whites. Fold in cream and pour into lined mold. Refrigerate at least 8 hours. Unmold and garnish with strawberries and whipped cream.

The Editors

RASPBERRY-STRAWBERRY BAVARIAN   9 servings

6-ounces strawberry-flavored
  gelatin
2 cups boiling water
1 cup sour cream
1 pint strawberry ice cream
1 Tablespoon lemon juice

2 (10-ounce) packages frozen
  raspberries (whole berries
  packed in syrup)
1 (10-ounce) package frozen,
  sliced strawberries (halves
  packed in syrup)

Dissolve gelatin with boiling water in large bowl. Add sour cream and beat with wire whisk or egg beater until smooth. Cut the frozen ice cream into the gelatin mixture, into about ten pieces. Stir until melted and smooth. Add lemon juice and frozen fruit. Use a fork to break up the frozen fruit a bit, then use your hands until there are no pieces larger than a single piece of fruit. (Adding the fruit while it is frozen helps to set the gelatin mixture.) Pour into nine 9-ounce glasses. Refrigerate. Do not freeze. This will be ready to serve in an hour or two, or it may stand overnight. Top with the following:

2 cups heavy cream, whipped
1½ teaspoons vanilla

½ cup powdered sugar

In a chilled bowl with chilled beaters, whip above ingredients until cream holds a shape. Place a large spoonful on each dessert.

Mrs. Allen Findley (Shirley)

CHOCOLATE ECLAIRS   10 servings

1 cup water
½ cup butter
1 cup all-purpose flour
4 eggs

3-ounce package French
Vanilla pudding, cooked
according to package
directions

Heat oven to 400°. Heat water and butter to rolling boil. Stir in flour. Stir over low heat about 1 minute or until mixture forms a ball. Remove from heat. Beat in eggs, all at one time; continue beating until smooth. Shape dough by ¼ cupfuls into "fingers" 4½ inches long and 1½ inches wide. Bake 35 to 40 minutes on an ungreased baking sheet until puffed and golden or until they sound hollow when tapped with spoon or finger. Cool thoroughly. Split eclair lengthwise with a sharp knife. Fill generously with chilled pudding.

Chocolate Glaze
1-ounce of unsweetened
  chocolate
1 teaspoon butter

1 cup powdered sugar
2 Tablespoons boiling water
1 teaspoon vanilla

Melt chocolate and butter over low heat. Remove from heat; stir in sugar and hot water. Add vanilla. Spoon on glaze.

Note: It is best to prepare and serve these the same day.

Mrs. Richard Spehr
Marietta, Georgia

HEATH BAR PIE   8 to 10 servings

1 (16-ounce) package Oreo
  cookies
10 to 12 Heath bars, crushed

½ gallon vanilla ice cream,
  softened

Place cookies in a plastic sack and crush with a rolling pin. Pour into bottom of 2 pie pans. Place heath bars in a plastic sack and crush with a hammer. Mix crushed Heath bars with ice cream and pour in cookie crust. Freeze for at least 1 hour.

Note: May be served with Hot Fudge Sauce. (See Index)

Mrs. Mert Toler (Debbie)

AMBROSIA
8 servings

10 to 12 large oranges
10-ounces crushed pineapple
(½ of 20-ounce can,
undrained)

2 to 3 (6-ounce) bags frozen
coconut
Whipped cream for topping

Mix the above ingredients. If the ambrosia is not juicy enough, add orange juice. This freezes well. Serve with whipped cream on top.

Mrs M.T. Blackwood (Jauweice)
Drew, Mississippi

ANN'S STRAWBERRIES IN SCALLOP SHELLS
6 servings

Pastry
2 cups all-purpose flour
½ teaspoon salt

⅔ cup vegetable shortening
¼ cup cold water

Filling
1 cup whipping cream
3-ounces cream cheese
½ cup sugar
1 Tablespoon fresh lemon juice

2 pints strawberries, washed,
hulled and cut in half
2 Tablespoons Cointreau or
Grand Marnier

Combine flour and salt. Cut in shortening until it resembles coarse meal. Sprinkle water over mixture and mix until it can be gathered in a ball (use additional water if necessary). Divide dough in 2 balls; wrap in wax paper and chill. Roll out 1 ball at a time on lightly floured surface. Cut circles to fit shells. Press dough on ungreased back of scallop shell. Pierce dough with a fork. Arrange shells, dough side up on baking sheet. Bake 12 minutes at 400°. Remove dough from back of shells and put inside of shells until cool. Combine whipping cream, cream cheese, sugar and lemon juice. Fill shells. Combine strawberries and Grand Marnier. Use as glaze over filling.

Mrs. Howard Grittman (Ann)
Drew, Mississippi

STRAWBERRY SQUARES   10 servings

2 cups sifted all-purpose flour
1 cup pecans, finely chopped
½ cup brown sugar
1 cup melted margarine
2 egg whites
1 cup sugar

1 package gelatin
1 Tablespoon lemon juice
1 (16-ounce) package frozen
   whole strawberries, sliced
1 cup whipping cream

Mix flour, pecans, brown sugar, and margarine together. Spread above mixture in shallow pan and bake at 350° for 20 minutes. Stir often. In a large mixing bowl, beat egg whites until stiff. Slowly add sugar, gelatin, lemon juice, and sliced strawberries. Beat all this together until it stands in stiff peaks. Whip whipping cream and fold into mixture. Spread ⅔ of the baked, crumbled mixture on bottom of 9x13-inch pan. Spread the strawberry mixture over this. Sprinkle remaining crumbs over top and freeze 6 hours or overnight. Cut into squares when ready to serve.

Mrs. James Elmore (Evelyn)

INDIVIDUAL STRAWBERRY SHORTCAKES   6 servings

2 pints fresh strawberries
¼ cup sugar or to taste
2 cups unsifted all-purpose flour
¼ cup sugar
1 Tablespoon baking powder

½ teaspoon salt
½ cup butter or margarine, cut
   into chunks
⅔ cup milk
Whipped cream

Prepare strawberries several hours before making the shortcakes. Clean, hull, and slice berries; toss with sugar. Refrigerate berries until serving shortcakes. To make shortcakes, combine flour, ¼ cup sugar, baking powder, and salt in a large bowl. With a pastry blender or 2 knives using a short cutting motion, cut ½ cup margarine into flour until the mixture resembles coarse cornmeal. In the center of mixture make a well, pour in milk. Mix with a fork until flour is moistened. Dough will be lumpy. Turn dough out onto a floured pastry cloth. Knead 8 to 10 times. Roll dough ½ inch thick. With floured 2-inch round cookie or biscuit cutter, cut out cakes. Place 1 inch apart on an ungreased cookie sheet. Bake 11 to 13 minutes or until light brown. Split warm cakes. Spread with butter (optional); spoon strawberries on half, top with other half cake. Spoon berries over top. Garnish with whipped cream.

Mrs. James Taylor (Bev)

DAFFODIL LAYERS
10 servings

1½ teaspoons unflavored
  gelatin
¾ cup sugar
3 beaten egg yolks
¾ teaspoon grated lemon peel
⅓ cup lemon juice

3 egg whites
1 (10-inch) tube angel food
  cake
Food coloring (optional)
2 cups whipped cream

Mix gelatin and ½ cup of sugar. Add next 3 ingredients. Cook and stir over hot water until slightly thick and gelatin dissolves, 5 to 8 minutes. Cool until partially set. Beat egg whites to soft peaks, gradually add remaining ¼ cup sugar, beating to stiff peaks. Fold into gelatin mixture. (May tint with few drops of yellow food coloring.) Cut cake into 3 layers. Spread bottom with half the gelatin mixture. Add second layer. Repeat, ending with cake. Chill. Frost with whipped cream.

Variation: Ice with confectioners sugar glaze.

Mrs. Lyle Dilworth (Mary Lou)
Memphis, Tennessee

ELOISE'S FOUR LAYER LEMON DESSERT
10 to 12 servings

1 cup chopped nuts
2 cups all-purpose flour
1 cup margarine
8-ounces cream cheese
1 cup powdered sugar
3 cups non-dairy whipped
  topping

2 cans condensed milk
1 cup lemon juice
½ teaspoon lemon extract
2 egg yolks

Combine flour, margarine, and chopped nuts and pack in the bottom of a 9x13-inch baking dish. Bake at 350° for about 30 minutes and cool thoroughly. Cream the cheese and powdered sugar. Add 1 cup of whipped topping and spread on the baked layer. Combine the condensed milk, lemon juice, lemon extract, and egg yolks. Spread on top of the cheese layer. Spread 2 cups of whipped topping on top. Refrigerate. This dessert keeps well.

Mrs. Mike Davis (Sheryl)

FROZEN LEMON BISQUE

6 to 8 servings

6 eggs, separated (room
temperature)
2 (14-ounce) cans condensed
milk
1 cup lemon juice

1 (13½-ounce) box graham
cracker crumbs
¼ cup margarine, melted
2 Tablespoons sugar

In a large bowl, combine egg yolks, milk, and lemon juice. Blend well and
set aside. In a 9x13-inch glass dish, combine crumbs and sugar with
melted margarine. Press to cover bottom. Bake at 300° for 8 minutes.
Remove and cool completely. In a large bowl, beat egg whites until stiff.
Fold egg whites into lemon mixture. Pour into glass dish. Garnish by sprinkling a few crumbs on top. Freeze until completely set (overnight
preferably). Serve with whipped topping and fruit, such as strawberries or
blueberries as garnish. Keep pie in freezer.

Mrs. Paul Mullins (Libba)

NANCY'S LEMON TARTS

24 tarts

½ cup margarine or butter,
softened
1 (3-ounce) package cream
cheese, softened
1 cup all-purpose flour
1 egg

1 Tablespoon all-purpose flour
1 cup sugar
Juice and grated rind of 1½
lemons
1 Tablespoon melted butter

Blend softened margarine with softened cream cheese. Add 1 cup flour
and mix thoroughly. Shape into small balls and press into small greased
muffin cups. Beat egg and add 1 tablespoon flour and remaining ingredients. Pour into pastry shells; fill ⅔ full. Bake at 350° for 20 minutes or
until filling is almost set. Reduce oven temperature to 250°. Bake for 10
minutes longer or until filling is firm. Cool in muffin cups.

Mrs. Jim Adams (Signe)

CHOCOLATE ICEBOX CAKE

8-ounces German Sweet Chocolate	*Pinch of salt*
4 eggs, separated	*1 teaspoon vanilla*
2 cups cream	*12 ladyfingers*
	Whipped cream for topping

Melt the chocolate in the top of a double boiler. Separate the eggs and add the yolks, one at a time, to the chocolate. Allow this mixture to cool. In a medium-sized mixing bowl, whip the egg whites until they form stiff peaks, then fold them into the chocolate. Next, whip the cream until soft peaks are formed; add the salt and vanilla. Whip briefly to mix. Add the whipped cream into the chocolate mixture, folding gently. Split the lady-fingers in half lengthwise. Line a 1½-quart round mold with wax paper. Arrange half of the split ladyfingers on the bottom and sides of the dish, then pour in half of the chocolate mixture. Arrange half of the remaining ladyfingers on top of this, to form a middle layer, and pour in the rest of the batter. Top with the remaining ladyfingers. Refrigerate the cake overnight. The next day, unmold carefully, remove the wax paper, top with whipped cream and serve.

The Editors

CHOCOLATE MOUSSE   6 servings

6-ounces semi-sweet chocolate bits	*2 eggs plus 2 egg yolks*
2 Tablespoons Kahlua	*1 teaspoon vanilla*
1 Tablespoon orange juice	*½ cup sugar*
	1 cup heavy cream

Melt chocolate bits in 2 tablespoons Kahlua in top of double boiler. In blender, mix orange juice, eggs, egg yolks, vanilla, and sugar. Add heavy cream to chocolate mixture (chocolate mixture will be like a large clump). Blend all together in blender. Pour into serving dishes and refrigerate 4 to 6 hours. Top with whipped cream.

Variation: Substitute Kahlua with 2 Tablespoons rum.

Mrs. Sid Blockstone (Delia)

Desserts

WHITE CHOCOLATE MOUSSE   6 servings

6-ounces white chocolate
2 Tablespoons unsalted butter
3 egg yolks

3 Tablespoons sugar
1½ ounces rum or amaretto
1 cup heavy cream, whipped

Break chocolate into coarse pieces. Melt in double boiler over very low heat. Add butter in small pieces to chocolate and melt. Cool. Beat egg yolks, sugar, and rum until foamy. Add to chocolate mixture. Fold whipped cream slowly into chocolate mixture. Chill in parfait glasses.

Mrs. Bob Aylward (Betsy)
Baltimore, Maryland

CHOCOLATE PARFAIT   4 to 6 servings

1 (8-ounce) package
  chocolate drops
1¼ cups light cream
1 egg
Dash of salt

1 teaspoon vanilla extract
8-ounces heavy cream,
  whipped
Chocolate shavings

Put chocolate into blender jar. Heat cream to boiling and pour over chocolate in blender and turn to speed 7 for 30 seconds. Add eggs, salt, and vanilla. Cover and run at high speed until it is smooth. Pour into parfait glass and chill. Serve topped with whipped cream, sprinkle with shavings.

Mrs. Jimmy Sanders (Hazel)

ANGEL DISH DELIGHT   20 servings

¼ cup butter
2 teaspoons vanilla
2 eggs
2 cups powdered sugar
1 pint cream, whipped until stiff

1 (18-ounce) angel food cake,
  torn into pieces
6 Butterfingers, chilled and
  crushed

Cream butter, vanilla, and eggs. Add sugar and fold in whipped cream. In a greased 3 quart pyrex dish, layer cake, cream mixture, and candy. Repeat. Refrigerate overnight.

Mrs. Donald Aylward (Lee)

BAVARIAN CREAM DESSERT

4 servings

1 envelope unflavored gelatin
½ cup sugar, divided
⅛ teaspoon salt
2 eggs, separated

1¼ cups milk
½ teaspoon vanilla
1 cup heavy cream, whipped

Mix gelatin, ¼ cup sugar, and salt together in top of double boiler. Beat egg yolks and milk together. Add to gelatin mixture. Cook over boiling water, stirring constantly until gelatin is dissolved, about 5 minutes. Remove from heat, add vanilla. Chill mixture to unbeaten egg white consistency. Beat egg whites until stiff. Beat in remaining ¼ cup sugar. Fold into gelatin mixture. Then fold in whipped cream. Turn into 4-cup mold. Chill until firm. Unmold and garnish with fresh fruit.

Nancy Therrell
Jackson, Mississippi

BAKED ALASKA PIE

½ cup margarine
1-ounce square unsweetened
** chocolate**
1 cup sugar

2 beaten eggs
⅓ cup all-purpose flour
1 teaspoon vanilla

Melt margarine and chocolate together. Combine sugar, eggs and flour; heat. Add to chocolate mixture. Add 1 teaspoon vanilla. Pour into greased 9-inch dish. Bake 35 minutes for 325°. Cool. Loosen all around to facilitate serving later. Mound ½ gallon ice cream over cake. Mound should resemble a beehive. Freeze.

Meringue
12 egg whites, beaten
¼ teaspoon cream of tartar

Salt
1 cup sugar

Combine egg whites, cream of tartar, salt; gradually add sugar while beating. Beat until glossy peaks form. Completely cover ice cream sealing at edges. Freeze. To serve bake at 350° just until meringue is golden. Let stand 5 to 10 minutes before serving. Drizzle with hot fudge sauce.

Mrs. Robert Tibbs (Pat)

BREAD PUDDING (MICROWAVE)   6 to 8 servings

6 slices white bread
2 cups milk
1 Tablespoon margarine
2 eggs
1¼ cups sugar

¼ teaspoon salt
½ teaspoon cinnamon
1 teaspoon vanilla
½ cup raisins

Place bread (including crust), torn in small pieces, in 9-inch round glass dish. Heat milk and margarine on high for 3 minutes in 4-cup measure. Beat eggs. Stir small amount of hot milk into beaten eggs. Return eggs to milk. Add sugar, salt, cinnamon, vanilla, and raisins. Pour mixture over bread pieces. Cook on high for 7 minutes. Cook 2 minutes longer if center is not firm. Serve with rum, lemon, or orange sauce.

Mrs. Eric Muir (Nan)

TRIFLE   12 to 15 servings

10 cups milk (or ½ gallon)
2 cups sugar
7 or 8 Tablespoons all-purpose
   flour
2 teaspoons vanilla
1 teaspoon almond extract
10 eggs, beaten
1 (10-ounce) tube Angel Food
   cake

1 small jar of raspberry jam,
   seedless
¼ cup sherry
Pecan shortbread cookies
1 cup heavy cream
Almonds or pecan pieces
Cherries for garnish

Combine first 6 ingredients and cook until thick in a heavy saucepan. Chill well. Tear the Angel Food cake into large bite-sized pieces. Spread each piece with jam. In a trifle bowl, make one layer of cake. Sprinkle with sherry; crumble several cookies over cake and add enough custard to cover well. Add a sprinkle of pecan pieces or almonds and proceed layering until all is used. Before serving, whip cream and spread over top, garnish with cherries and nuts.

Note: This is a versatile recipe. You may use any combination of liqueur, jam, and cookies. It also may be halved.

The Editors

FROZEN CARAMEL DESSERT

12 to 15 servings

2 (14-ounce) cans condensed
  milk
1 Angle Food cake
1 cup pecans, chopped or
  sliced, toasted almonds

1 (10-ounce) carton non-dairy
  whipped topping

Place 2 unopened cans of milk in large boiler or Dutch oven. Cover with water. Bring to a rolling boil and continue boiling for 3 hours. Watch carefully and never let water get low. Cool. The milk will caramelize. Tear or cut cake in inch-size cubes. Place cake cubes in bottom of 9x13-inch dish. Spread caramel over cake. Sprinkle half of nuts over caramel. Top with whipped topping. Sprinkle more nuts over whipped topping. Cover and freeze. Take out of freezer 30 minutes before serving so that it will thaw slightly.

Mrs. Billy Nowell (Ann)

CARAMEL ICE CREAM DESSERT

12 to 15 servings

Crust
2 cups all-purpose flour
½ cup oatmeal
½ cup brown sugar

1 cup margarine, melted
1 cup chopped pecans

Combine all ingredients and crumble on a cookie sheet. Bake at 400° for 15 to 20 minutes, stirring to brown evenly. Press ½ of crumbs on the bottom of a greased 9x13-inch pan.

Filling
½ gallon vanilla ice cream,
  softened

1 (12.25-ounce) jar caramel ice
  cream topping

Layer ice cream and then caramel sauce on top of crumb crust. Sprinkle top with remaining crumbs. Freeze. Cut in squares and top each square when serving with caramel sauce.

Variation: Use an additional jar of fudge topping.

Mrs. Don Aylward (Lee)

TRILBY
24 servings

2 cups cranberry juice
2 cups half-and-half
1 cup orange juice
1 cup whipping cream

2 cups sugar
1 bag of cranberries, puréed
Sweet milk
Red food coloring

Mix the first 6 ingredients. Put into a gallon ice cream freezer. Pour milk to line. Add a drop or two of food coloring. Freeze.

Note: This is a holiday tradition during Thanksgiving and Christmas. Serve in footed dishes during meal.

Mrs. Vernon Shelton, (Pam)
Drew, Mississippi

AUNTIE'S PINEAPPLE SHERBET
10 to 12 servings

Juice of 4 lemons
1 (20-ounce) can crushed
   pineapple

3 cups sugar, divided
1 quart milk
1 pint heavy cream

Combine lemon juice, pineapple, and 1 cup sugar. Stir to dissolve sugar. Put this mixture in ice cream freezer can; freeze until slushy. Combine milk and 1 cup sugar; stir to dissolve sugar. Whip cream with 1 cup sugar. Add milk and cream mixtures to freezer can. Continue freezing until frozen. Remove blade. Pack freezer with salt and ice.

Note: The sugar will not dissolve while stirring. It doesn't matter. Scrape any sugar not dissolved into the freezer can.

Mrs. Emily P. Lucas
Lexington, Mississippi

GRAPE SHERBET

1 scant cup sugar
2 cups grape juice
1 cup orange juice

¼ cup lemon juice
1 cup heavy cream

Dissolve sugar in juices. Add 1 cup unwhipped cream. Freeze in freezer. Stir when mixture becomes icy.

Mrs. Charles Lawrence (Mary Kathryn)

BANANA ICE CREAM   4 quarts

6 eggs, separated
1 quart milk
2 cups sugar

2 teaspoons vanilla
4 ripe bananas

Separate eggs. Beat whites until stiff. Beat egg yolks and add to milk; stir in sugar. Fold in egg whites. Add vanilla. Peel bananas and mash; add to ice cream mixture. Pour into a gallon ice cream freezer and finish filling freezer bucket with milk. Freeze until firm.

Mrs. W.G. Jeffcoat (Melissa)

GRANDMOMMA'S PEACH ICE CREAM   5 quarts

1 quart homogenized milk
1 (14-ounce) can sweetened
   condensed milk
1 (5-ounce) can evaporated
   milk
½ pint heavy cream, whipped

1 pint coffee cream
2 cups sugar
2 Tablespoons vanilla
Juice from one lemon
3 cups of mashed peaches

Combine first five ingredients, then add sugar, vanilla, and juice from lemon. Stir in peaches. (Best when prepared a day ahead of time.) Freeze in 4-quart freezer.

Mrs. James M. Gatling (Jennifer)

CANDY BAR ICE CREAM   1 gallon

6 Milky Way bars
2 (13-ounce) cans evaporated
   milk

1 (14-ounce) can condensed
   milk
Water

Melt bars and ½ cup evaporated milk in top of double boiler. Stir until smooth. Add remaining milk and up to 2 cans of water. Pour mixture into freezer and freeze in usual manner using 8 parts ice to 1 part rock salt.

Mrs. Jimmy Goodman (Carolyn)

Desserts

TORTONI

16 to 18 servings

½ gallon vanilla ice cream, softened
1 cup pecans, chopped, toasted, and salted
½ cup chopped maraschino cherries
1 cup crushed coconut macaroons
1 Tablespoon almond extract

Mix together and spoon into fluted, paper cups placed in muffin tins; freeze. Store in plastic bags in freezer or after mixing you may freeze in a plastic container and scoop with ice cream scoop. Garnish with one cherry and mint leaves. Light and refreshing after a heavy meal.

Mrs. Bill Profilet (Mary)

COFFEE LIQUEUR SAUCE

1 cup

1½ Tablespoons sugar
2 teaspoons cornstarch
⅓ cup cold strong coffee
2 Tablespoons coffee liqueur
1 Tablespoon fresh lemon juice
¼ teaspoon vanilla
2 Tablespoons blanched and slivered almonds

Combine the first five ingredients in the top of a double boiler and bring to a boil. Cook until thick and clear, stirring constantly. Add vanilla and almonds. Use as a sauce over ice cream.

Mrs. Bob Buchanan (Sharon)

RUM SAUCE

½ cup sugar
1 Tablespoon all-purpose flour
1½ cups milk
3 eggs, beaten
1 Tablespoon crushed pineapple, squeezed dry
2 or 3 bottle caps of rum (white or dark)

Combine sugar and flour in a heavy saucepan. Add rest of the ingredients and stir on stove until thick. Chill and pour over bread pudding.

Mrs. M.T. Blackwood (Jauweice)
Drew, Mississippi

HOT FUDGE SAUCE I

1 (14-ounce) can condensed
  milk
1 (5½-ounce) can chocolate
  syrup

½ cup butter
1 teaspoon vanilla

Melt butter in a saucepan; add other ingredients and bring to a boil for 4 minutes. Remove from heat and add vanilla. Stores well in a quart jar in refrigerator. Reheat as needed. Serve over Heath Bar Pie, Baked Alaska, or ice cream.

Dianne Crews

HOT FUDGE SAUCE II   4 cups

½ cup margarine
4 (1-ounce) squares
  unsweetened chocolate or 8
  Tablespoons cocoa and 2 to
  3 Tablespoons margarine

3 cups sugar
½ teaspoon salt
1 (13-ounce) can evaporated
  milk

Combine margarine and chocolate in double boiler. Cook over hot (not boiling) water until melted. Gradually stir in sugar—about ¼ cup at a time—stirring well. Mixture will be very thick. Add salt and evaporated milk slowly, stirring constantly.

Mrs. Doug Wheeler (Lynn)

LEMON BUTTER SAUCE   3 cups

¾ cup sugar
3 Tablespoons cornstarch
Dash of salt
2 cups boiling water
2 Tablespoons lemon juice

½ teaspoon grated lemon rind
  (optional)
2 Tablespoons butter
½ teaspoon nutmeg

Mix sugar, salt and cornstarch in saucepan. Add boiling water gradually. Boil for 5 minutes, stirring constantly, until thickened. Remove from heat and add remaining ingredients. Serve hot on gingerbread or pound cake.

Mrs. W. C. Cox, Jr. (Mary Elizabeth)
Jackson, Mississippi

RASPBERRY SAUCE   2¼ cups

2 (10-ounce) packages frozen raspberries, thawed
6 fresh strawberries

1 Tablespoon cornstarch
2 Tablespoons lemon juice
2 Tablespoons Kirsch liqueur

Purée berries and juice in blender. Mix cornstarch with lemon juice and add to berries. Place this mixture in a saucepan and bring to a boil. Cook until slightly thickened. Add liqueur.

Note: Keeps for weeks. Serve over raspberry sherbert, vanilla ice cream, or cake.

Mrs. Karl Horn (Ruth)
Moss Point, Mississippi

PEANUT BUTTER ICE CREAM SAUCE   1¼ cups

1 cup firmly packed brown sugar
⅓ cup milk

¼ cup light corn syrup
1 Tablespoon butter, softened
¼ cup creamy peanut butter

Combine first 4 ingredients in a medium saucepan. Cook over medium heat, stirring until sugar dissolves. Remove from heat; add peanut butter, beating until smooth. Serve warm over ice cream.

Mrs. Mark Routman (Terry)

CHOCOLATE SYRUP

½ cup cocoa
1 cup water
2 cups sugar

⅛ teaspoon salt
2 teaspoons vanilla

Cook together cocoa and water. Add sugar and salt. Stir until dissolved. Boil for 3 minutes. Add vanilla. Use for milk or over ice cream.

Mrs. Dane Johnson (Patricia)
Jackson, Mississippi

A Man's Taste

BUTTERMILK PANCAKES

4 to 6 servings

1 egg
1 cup buttermilk
½ teaspoon baking soda
1 cup all-purpose flour

1 Tablespoon sugar
1 Tablespoon cooking oil
1½ teaspoons baking powder
½ teaspoon salt

Beat egg; add buttermilk and soda. Add flour, sugar, oil, baking powder, and salt. Stir until blended. Bake on a lightly greased hot griddle until brown. Turn only once.

Scott Horton

HUSHPUPPIES

100 servings

Mix in 30 quart pan:
5 pounds self-rising flour
5 pounds self-rising meal
1 dozen eggs
1 cup cooking oil

1 cup chopped onions
1 cup chopped bell pepper
½ gallon buttermilk
1 Tablespoon baking powder

Mix well. Let set for 10 minutes at room temperature. Use small ice cream scoop to drop small amounts in deep fryer, temperature set at 330°. Cook for 5 minutes or until golden brown.

Wiley Hilburn

BATTER FOR SEAFOOD

1½ cups all-purpose flour,
  divided
½ cup corn meal

1 (12-ounce) can of beer
1 Tablespoon salt
1 Tablespoon paprika

In bowl combine ½ cup flour and corn meal. In another bowl combine remaining flour, beer, salt, and paprika. Dip oysters, shrimp, or fish into dry mixture first and then into beer mixture. Fry in hot grease.

Robert Milbrand

EASY BROCCOLI SOUP

2 (10-ounce) boxes chopped
   broccoli or broccoli spears,
   chopped
¼ cup butter
2 (10¾-ounce) cans mushroom
   soup
3 soup cans milk

1 (6-ounce) roll jalapeño
   cheese
1 (6-ounce) roll nippy sharpe
   cheese or 1 jar Old English
   Cheddar
Salt to taste

Cook broccoli according to package directions, drain. In Dutch oven, sauté onions in butter; add cheese to onions; add soup, milk, broccoli, and salt. Simmer 15 to 20 minutes or until ingredients are thoroughly heated. Place in blender and mix well. Reheat if necessary.

Bill Powell

DELTA FISH CHOWDER
12 cups

¼ pound salt pork, cut in
   chunks
2 cups uncooked fish, boned,
   skinned and cut in chunks
6 small potatoes, diced

2 onions, finely chopped
3 cups boiling water
2 cups milk
1 Tablespoon all-purpose flour
Salt and pepper to taste

Fry salt pork in a deep iron pot or similar pot. When crisp, remove pieces of pork and put in fish, potatoes and onion. Cover with boiling water and simmer for ½ hour or until potatoes are tender. Mix flour and milk, add to chowder and cook 5 minutes longer. Season to taste with salt and pepper.

Note: This is a good way to use your fish other than frying. Most fish will do and this includes all local fish. It can be easily frozen for later use.

Milton Smith

QUICK CLAM CHOWDER   6 servings

2 Tablespoons butter
¼ cup finely chopped onions
½ cup finely chopped celery
2 cans potato soup
1 soup can milk
1 soup can water

1 (7½-ounce) can chopped
   clams (undrained)
1 (7-ounce) can tuna, drained
   and flaked
1 (8-ounce) can baby tomatoes
   or tomato sauce

Sauté onions and celery in butter. Stir in all other ingredients. Heat, stirring occasionally. DO NOT BOIL.

Charlie Whittington

STUFFED ARTICHOKES

2 fresh artichokes
3 pounds extra lean ground
   beef
1 pound ground pork
4 cloves fresh garlic, chopped
   very fine

6-ounces seasoned bread
   crumbs
4 Tablespoons cooking sherry

Boil artichokes fully covered, until leaves just begin to become tender. Do not over cook. Take out and cool. Combine all remaining ingredients, mixing well to season all the meat. Place artichokes on a dinner plate. Starting at the bottom of the artichoke, pull down leave and place 1 teaspoon of meat mixture on each leaf, continuing until all leaves are stuffed. Artichoke should be the size of dinner plate when finished. Place artichoke on a piece of foil (double wrap) and make a basket of foil around the bottom of artichoke. Seal with another piece of foil. Place artichoke in pie pan and cook for 30 minutes at 350°. Take foil off top of artichoke and brown meat 10 to 15 minutes more until done. Serve hot with tooth picks as a great hors d'oeuvre.

Deb Gee

A Man's Taste

SAUTÉED MUSHROOMS

3 Tablespoons butter
3 Tablespoons olive oil
3 pounds fresh mushrooms, sliced
1 Tablespoon fresh minced garlic

Juice of 2 lemons
1 Tablespoon of chopped parsley
Salt and pepper to taste
1 teaspoon whole thyme

Heat butter and olive oil over medium high heat. Add mushrooms and cook for 2 minutes. Add garlic and cook 1 minute. Add salt, pepper, thyme, parsley and lemon juice and sauté an additional minute. Serve on chunks of French bread.

Todd Warrington

POTATOES ALA "WHITT"   6 to 8 servings

6 large red potatoes
6 large onions
1 cup margarine

8-ounces mild Cheddar cheese
Salt, and pepper to taste

Peel, wash and slice potatoes and onions into ¼-inch slices. Line 10-inch pan with aluminum foil large enough to leave 1-inch above sides of pan. Rub bottom of pan with ½ cup margarine to keep from sticking. Alternate layers of potatoes, onions, sliced cheese and pats of margarine until all ingredients are used. Salt and pepper each layer to taste. Seal with another piece of foil. Bake for 1 hour at 325°. Good with char-broiled steak.

Charles Mosley

CUCUMBER DRESSING   6 cups

1 quart mayonnaise
1 large onion, quartered for blending
1 large cucumber, sliced for blending

1 teaspoon MSG
1 small clove of garlic
Juice of 1 lemon
Dash of Worcestershire sauce
Salt to taste

Blend ingredients in blender. Refrigerate until ready to use.

Robert Milbrand

BIG RIVER BARBECUE SAUCE

2 onions, chopped	6 Tablespoons red pepper
1 pint honey	1 Tablespoon dry mustard
2 quarts barbecue sauce	1 pint beer
2-ounces lemon juice	2 Tablespoons marjoram
1 cup butter	½ pint vinegar
2-ounces chili powder	1 Tablespoon cinnamon

Big River Basting Sauce

1 quart Worcestershire sauce	1 cup butter
1 quart Italian dressing	2 Tablespoons red pepper
1-ounce chili powder	1 Tablespoon garlic
4 Tablespoons lemon juice	

First—make your favorite drink. Get out of direct sunlight. Place ingredients of barbecue sauce in a large pot and the ingredients of the basting sauce in another large pot. Boil and simmer barbecue sauce one hour, basting sauce 15 minutes. When cooking meat, baste with basting sauce every 30 minutes until the last ½ hour, then change over to barbecue sauce and baste every 10 minutes. Save remaining barbecue sauce to eat with meat.

F.R. Armstrong

BARBECUE SAUCE

½ cup barbecue sauce	½ teaspoon garlic salt
½ cup catsup	½ teaspoon Tabasco salt
¼ cup brown sugar	
1 Tablespoon Worcestershire sauce	

Mix catsup and barbecue sauce in boiler. Warm over low heat. Add brown sugar and stir until melted. Add remaining ingredients. Simmer 5 minutes. Sauce is now ready to be poured over meat to be grilled or cooked in oven.

Mike Robbins

BASIC SAUCE RECIPE FOR MEATS   1½ cups

1 cup water
½ cup margarine
1 teaspoon sugar
1 teaspoon salt

1 teaspoon Worcestershire
   sauce
1 Tablespoon vinegar

Place the above ingredients in a small saucepan (or small pot) and heat on low until the margarine melts. Baste meat before cooking.

Note: Excellent on steak. Sauce may be prepared in a microwave also.

Dr. Frank Young

CHEF LONG'S MARINADE

1 cup Worcestershire sauce
1 cup steak sauce
¼ cup fresh lemon juice

1½ teaspoons MSG
1½ teaspoons garlic powder
1 teaspoon oil

Mix above ingredients in bowl. Rub in salt and pepper liberally on meat. Mop sauce regularly over 5 to 7 pounds eye of round over drip pan at end of charcoal grill opposite charcoal for 3 to 5 hours.

Note: Add hickory chips to charcoal briquettes.

Ben Griffith, misappropriated from
James Long

SWEET-AND-SOUR SAUCE   1½ cups

1 cup sugar
½ cup white vinegar
½ cup water
1 Tablespoon finely chopped
   green pepper

1 Tablespoon finely chopped
   pimento
½ teaspoon salt
1 teaspoon paprika

Mix above ingredients in saucepan and simmer 5 minutes. Combine: 2 teaspoons cornstarch and 1 tablespoon cold water; add to hot mixture. Cook and stir until sauce thickens and bubbles; cool. Add 1 teaspoon paprika. Great with egg rolls, won ton, rumaki, etc.

Ben Griffith

BROILED SHRIMP

In a 9-inch skillet:
¼ cup butter
Shrimp (shelled)
3 cloves garlic, minced

Beau Monde seasoning
Juice of 1 lemon

Arrange shrimp in a single layer in melted butter. Sprinkle with remaining ingredients. Turn shrimp when they are pink on the bottom and cook until they curl. Remove and pour butter over to serve. Additional lemon juice may be squeezed over all if desired.

Note: Do not over cook shrimp.

Dr. Frank Branch

CHAR-BROILED SHRIMP

Shrimp (15 to 20 count per pound) peeled
3-ounces Italian dressing

1-ounce rice vinegar
Juice of 1 lemon
Tony's creole seasoning

Marinate shrimp in above ingredients. Cook on the grill 3 minutes on each side.

Dip
2 Tablespoons butter
Juice of 1 lemon

2-ounces Worcestershire sauce
Pepper to taste

Heat and serve hot with shrimp and French bread.

Roy Clark
Pass Christian, Mississippi

SAUCE OF SHRIMP   4 servings

2 green onions, chopped
½ cup butter
Garlic salt to taste
4 Tablespoons of Sherry
Juice of 1 lemon

2 pounds of peeled, raw shrimp
1 pound fresh mushrooms,
  sliced
Grated Parmesan cheese

In skillet sauté onions in butter, season with garlic salt; add sherry, lemon juice, shrimp, and mushrooms. Sprinkle with Parmesan cheese, simmer until shrimp are done. Serve with or without rice. Freezes well after cooked.

Robert Milbrand

BRAISED SHRIMP AND VEGETABLES   6 servings

2 pounds fresh peeled shrimp
8 to 10-ounces fresh broccoli,
  chopped
1 (8-ounce) can sliced water
  chestnuts
3 Tablespoons cooking oil

½ teaspoon pepper
½ teaspoon salt
2 Tablespoons cooking sherry
1 Tablespoon cornstarch
1 cup hot water
1 teaspoon oyster sauce

Heat oil, pepper, salt in wok over high heat. Add shrimp and stir fry five minutes. Add chopped broccoli and water chestnuts. Simmer 2 to 3 minutes. Add sherry and oyster sauce. Combine water and cornstarch. Pour over mixture and stir until gravy begins to boil. Cool 1 to 2 minutes. Serve over rice.

Deb Gee

BAKED FISH   4 servings

2 pounds fish fillets
¼ cup Italian dressing

1 cup bread crumbs
¼ cup Parmesan cheese

Marinate fish in Italian dressing for at least 3 hours. I use a quart size zip bag and keep the marinating fish in the refrigerator. Put bread crumbs in bowl, roll marinated fish in it and arrange on a cookie sheet. Sprinkle with Parmesan cheese and bake in oven at 500° for 15 minutes.

Roy Wiley

PREPARATION FOR SMOKED FISH

3 quarts water
1½ cups ice cream salt
¾ cups sugar

3 bay leaves
2 teaspoons pepper
1 lemon, juice and rind

Soak thawed fish for 1 hour. If fish are frozen, soak for 1½ hours. Remove fish and rinse with cold water. Pat dry and let stand until very dry before smoking.

Note: The process of soaking fish before smoking makes it much better.

Dr. Karl Horn
Moss Point, Mississippi

MUSTARD FILLETS

Fish fillets
Mustard
Salt

Pepper
Biscuit baking mix

Brush fish with mustard until well coated and refrigerate for several hours. Salt and pepper fish; then roll in biscuit mix. Fry fish at 375° until golden brown, drain and serve.

Randy Townsend

GRILLED FISH   6 servings

6 fish fillets (bass, crappie or
* catfish)*
½ cup butter
¼ cup lemon juice
1 Tablespoon Worcestershire

½ teaspoon seasoned salt
½ teaspoon paprika
¼ teaspoon red pepper
Garlic salt to taste

Place fish fillets in a 9x13-inch shallow baking dish. Combine butter, lemon juice, Worcestershire, seasoned salt, paprika and red pepper in a sauce pan and cook until butter melts. Pour over fish and marinate in refrigerator for at least 1 hour. Drain and reserve marinade. Sprinkle fish with garlic salt and place in a greased wire basket. Grill over hot coals 3 to 5 minutes per side. Baste with marinade. Serve with reheated marinade.

Henry McGarrh
Merigold, Mississippi

CATFISH ORLEANS

3 to 4 servings

¼ cup cooking oil
2 large onions, cut in thin rings
2 large bell peppers, cut in
small slices

Creole seasoning
4 catfish fillets

Heat oil in large skillet. Add onions and bell peppers. Cook on high 7 to 8 minutes. Lightly sprinkle creole seasoning on both sides of fillets. Remove onion and bell pepper from skillet. Place fillets in skillet and cook on medium heat 8 minutes; turn fillets, add onion and bell pepper and continue cooking 8 more minutes.

Jim Hunter McCaleb

BOILED CRAYFISH

30 pounds crayfish

Put crayfish in salt water for 10 minutes to burp. Drain and rinse thoroughly. Cover with water and add:

1 box table salt
2 (4-ounce) boxes black pepper
2 boxes crab boil

1 bottle Tabasco
2 (½-ounce) boxes red pepper

Boil for 10 minutes. Turn heat off and let sit for 10 minutes.

Howard Grittman
Drew, Mississippi

MAMAW'S CHILI SAUCE

9-10 quarts

8 quarts of peeled tomatoes
1 cup white vinegar
3 bell peppers, chopped
2½ cups sugar

1 Tablespoon salt
3 onions, chopped
1 jalapeño pepper, chopped

Peel and bring to boil tomatoes in an 8 quart pot; drain with collander. Add vinegar, bell peppers, onions, hot pepper, sugar and salt. Cook 1 hour over medium heat. Can in sterile, hot jars; store until ready to use. Refrigerate after opening. Best on black-eyed peas and okra.

Ben Griffith

DELICIOUS GOLDEN FILLETS   6 to 8 servings

**6 to 8 fillets (bass, crappie, or
    catfish)
¼ cup butter
½ cup bread crumbs
¼ cup Parmesan cheese
½ teaspoon garlic salt**

**¼ teaspoon lemon-pepper
    marinade
½ cup mayonnaise
Juice of one lemon
Paprika**

Rinse and pat fish dry with paper towels. Melt butter in 9x13-inch baking dish. Mix together crumbs, cheese, garlic salt and lemon-pepper. Spread each side of fish with mayonnaise, then coat both sides with crumb mixture. Place fish, single layer in baking dish. Turn over to coat with melted butter. Sprinkle a little Parmesan cheese on top and squeeze the juice of a lemon over all. Sprinkle with paprika. Bake at 425° for 10 minutes or until fish flakes when tested with fork.

Henry McGarrh
(Peter Rabbit)
Merigold, Mississippi

FISH FILLETS IN WINE   6 to 8 servings

**3 Tablespoons butter
3 Tablespoons all-purpose flour
1 (10¾-ounce) can of
    mushroom soup
½ cup white wine**

**2 Tablespoons Parmesan
    cheese
2 Tablespoons chopped parsley
6 to 8 fish fillets**

Melt butter in saucepan. Stir in flour and mix well. Add soup and wine. Cook, stirring constantly, until mixture thickens. Add cheese and parsley. Arrange fillets in a single layer in a 9x13-inch greased casserole dish. Pour sauce over fish and bake at 375° for 20 to 25 minutes or until fish flakes.

Henry McGarrh
(Peter Rabbit)
Merigold, Mississippi

CHICKEN CASSEROLE

4 to 6 servings

4 to 6 chicken breasts (cooked and cut into bite-size pieces)
1 (8-ounce) carton sour cream

1 (10¾-ounce) can cream of chicken soup
Butter crackers (crushed)
½ cup margarine (melted)

Grease a 9x12-inch casserole dish with margarine. Put the cut up chicken in the bottom of the casserole dish. Mix sour cream and cream of chicken soup together and spread over chicken. Sprinkle crushed crackers over sour cream and soup mixture. Pour melted butter over crackers. Bake at 400° for 30 to 45 minutes or until crackers get slightly browned and casserole mixture is bubbly.

Clyde L. Boswell

VERNON SHELTON'S BARBECUE SAUCE

6½ cups

4 Tablespoons butter
2 cups molasses
2 cups water
2 beef bouillon cubes
4 teaspoons salt
Drop of Tabasco

2 onions, chopped
10 or 12 Tablespoons vinegar
2 cups catsup
4 Tablespoons Worcestershire
⅝ teaspoon black pepper

Cook above ingredients until thick. Cool and pour into jar. Will keep in refrigerator for months.

Vernon Shelton
Drew, Mississippi

BASTING SAUCE FOR GRILLED CHICKEN I ✓ ¾ cup

½ cup margarine
2 lemons, juiced and rinds
   grated
¼ teaspoon coarse ground
   pepper

3 dashes garlic salt
4 dashes Tabasco
1 Tablespoon steak sauce

Combine ingredients and simmer 10 to 15 minutes. Wash and dry chicken. Dip in sauce, salt and pepper each side. Cook over hot fire, turning and basting after 20 minutes. Sauce may be used for pork chops or fish.

S.R. "Sonny" Blakeman

BASTE FOR GRILLED CHICKEN II 1⅔ cups

¼ to ⅓ cup oil
1 cup vinegar
5 teaspoons salt

1½ teaspoons poultry seasoning
1 egg, well beaten

Mix the oil and vinegar; add salt and poultry seasoning, stirring well. Add beaten egg and stir until ingredients are thoroughly mixed. Use as baste for chicken being cooked on grill.

Jeffrey Levingston

BASTING SAUCE FOR BARBECUE CHICKEN 1¾ cups

1 cup apple vinegar
¼ cup oil
5-ounces Worcestershire sauce
2 Tablespoons crushed red
   peppers
2 Tablespoons Tabasco

2 lemons, cut in half and
   squeezed
2 Tablespoons prepared
   mustard
2 teaspoons sugar

Combine vinegar, oil, Worcestershire, peppers, and Tabasco in saucepan. Cut lemons and squeeze juice into mixture, then add lemons. In separate cup, combine mustard and sugar and mix well. Add to sauce. Bring to boil and cook 15 to 20 minutes. Makes enough sauce for two chickens. Cook chicken over charcoal, basting with sauce every 15 minutes. Cook over low fire for 1 hour.

Tommy Sledge

MARINATED BEEF TENDERLOIN SUPREME
8 servings

*1 (4 to 5 pound) beef
  tenderloin*
1 teaspoon garlic powder
½ teaspoon black pepper
3 Tablespoons lemon-pepper

½ cup wine vinegar
½ cup Worcestershire sauce
½ cup lemon juice
½ cup soy sauce
⅓ cup cooking oil

Marinate tenderloin in above mixture of ingredients for 24 hours in refrigerator, turning once or twice. Cook over low charcoal coals for approximately 45 minutes for medium doneness while basting with marinate every 10 minutes. (Cooking time will vary with thickness of meat and size of grill.) Remove from grill, slice thick and serve immediately. This meat goes well and baked or stuffed potatoes and a green salad.

Wilson Sledge

PEPPER STEAK
6 servings

*1½ pounds sirloin steak, cut
  in strips ¼-inch thick*
1 Tablespoon paprika
2 cloves garlic, crushed
2 Tablespoons butter
*1 cup sliced green onions,
  including tops*
2 green peppers, cut in strips

*2 large fresh tomatoes,
  chopped*
1 cup beef broth
¼ cup water
2 Tablespoons cornstarch
2 Tablespoons soy sauce
3 cups cooked rice

Sprinkle steak with paprika and allow to stand while preparing other ingredients. Cook steak and garlic in butter until meat is browned. Add onions, green peppers, tomatoes and broth; cover and simmer about 15 minutes. Blend water with cornstarch and soy sauce. Stir into steak and cook until thickened. Serve over beds of fluffy rice.

Jack Machell, Jr.
Sunflower, County

DUCK GUMBO
8 servings

4 mallards
4 medium white onions,
  chopped
3 bay leaves
1 cup chopped green onion
4 ribs celery, chopped
½ cup chopped bell pepper
⅔ cup bacon drippings
1 pint brown gravy, homemade
  or commercial
1 (1-pound) can stewed
  tomatoes

¼ Tablespoon parsley flakes
½ teaspoon thyme
4 cloves garlic, minced
Juice of ½ lemon
¼ pound salt meat
1 Tablespoon Worcestershire
1½ teaspoons cracked pepper
  corns (red)
1 teaspoon Tabasco
1 dash Tabasco
1 dash cayenne pepper
30-ounces fresh okra

In large boiler, boil duck in 4 quarts water with 2 onions and bay leaves for 1 hour. Cool and save broth, debone duck and dice. Sauté onions (green and white), celery, bell pepper, in ⅓ cup bacon drippings. In large boiler, add gravy and tomatoes to these vegetables and simmer 10 minutes. Add ⅓ duck broth and simmer 15 minutes; add parsley, thyme, garlic, lemon, salt pork, Worcestershire, red pepper, Tabasco, cayenne pepper, and rest of duck stock with diced duck. Cook 1¼ hours on meium heat. In skillet fry okra with ⅓ bacon drippings, then add to gumbo and cook for 45 more minutes. Serve with rice.

Mark Pearson

DOVE IN ORANGE SAUCE
6 to 8 servings

12 cleaned and rinsed doves
4 Tablespoons butter

1½ teaspoons salt
2 cups orange juice

Brown doves in butter in heavy skillet. Add salt and orange juice. Cover tightly. Bake at 325° about 1½ hours.

Robert Milbrand

A Man's Taste

BUBBA TOLLISON'S HONEY DUCKS
4 to 6 servings

4 to 6 ducks
2 to 3 cups honey
Salt and pepper

Lemon pepper
Butter

Tear a large piece of heavy-duty aluminum wrap and place one large cleaned duck in the center. Place ¼ cup butter in cavity and sprinkle generously with salt, pepper and lemon pepper. Pour about ½ cup honey on each duck and wrap tightly so juice cannot escape. Bake at 300° for 3 hours. Serve with wild rice.

Bubba Tollison

QUIVER RIVER DUCKS
4 servings

4 ducks
Bacon drippings
Salt and pepper
4 small onions
1 large apple, quartered

4 ribs celery
½ cup Burgundy wine
2 cups chicken broth
1 cup water
16 bay leaves

Rub ducks inside and out with bacon drippings and sprinkle liberally with salt and pepper. Stuff each duck cavity with 1 onion, 1 rib celery, 1 quarter apple, and 4 bay leaves. Place ducks breast down in Dutch oven and cover with broth, water, and wine. Cover and bake 2½ to 3 hours at 300°.

Billy Nowell

SAUCE FOR WILD GAME
1 quart

1 pint cider vinegar
Juice of 3 lemons
1-ounce black pepper
10-ounces Worcestershire sauce

5-ounces Tabasco sauce
1-ounce soy sauce
2 Tablespoons salt
2 Tablespoons sugar

Combine all ingredients and refrigerate. This is a good marinade for wild game or meat. Keeps indefinitely.

G.R. Harden

PEPPER DEER STEAK
6 to 8 servings

2 pounds venison
¼ cup all-purpose flour
1 teaspoon salt
1 teaspoon pepper
3 Tablespoons bacon fat
1 bell pepper, chopped
3 medium onions, chopped

1 stalk celery, chopped
1 Tablespoon Worcestershire
  sauce
1 (8-ounce) can tomatoes,
  chopped
1 (12-ounce) package noodles

Cut venison into serving size pieces; mix flour with salt and pepper. Coat venison with flour; heat 3 tablespoons bacon fat in skillet and brown venison on both sides. Cut up celery, onions and bell pepper and brown. Add Worcestershire sauce, tomatoes, and cook covered 1 to 2 hours or until tender. Cook noodles and serve.

Randy Townsend

DEER OVER RICE
6 servings

4 to 6 venison steaks, sliced
  in strips
Chili powder
MSG
All-purpose flour
Oil
2 Tablespoons butter

1 small onion, chopped
1 (10¾-ounce) can beef broth
  or bouillon
1 (10¾-ounce) can cream of
  mushroom soup
1 (4-ounce) can sliced
  mushrooms

Sprinkle meat with chili powder and MSG. Roll in flour and brown in oil. Remove meat and drain off oil. Melt butter and sauté onion. Add 2 to 3 tablespoons flour for thickening. Stir until browned lightly. Stir in beef broth, soup and mushrooms, blending well. Return meat to skillet and simmer for 1 hour or more. Serve over rice.

Marvin L. Lott

ROY'S CHILI
6 to 8 servings

1 pound boneless venison, coarsely ground
1 pound fresh chuck, coarsely ground
¼ cup vegetable oil
1 cup white onion, chopped
1 large bell pepper, chopped
3 jalapeño peppers, drained and deseeded and chopped
2 cloves garlic, minced
2 (14-ounce) cans skinned tomatoes, undrained and chopped
1 (8-ounce) can tomato sauce
1 cup beer, not light (your brand)
3 Tablespoons chili powder
2 teaspoons sugar
1½ teaspoons salt
2 teaspoons ground cumin seed
8-ounces extra sharp Cheddar cheese, grated

Brown venison and chuck in hot oil in well seasoned 12-inch cast-iron skillet over gas grill, uncovered. Add onion, bell pepper, jalapeño pepper, garlic, and cumin. Cook for five minutes, stirring occasionally. Add remaining ingredients; bring to a rolling boil. Continue to boil, stirring just prior to sticking for 1½ hours or until chili begins to cling to spoon. Remove from direct heat for 5 minutes, covered and unstirred. Serve in bowls, top with grated cheese.

Roy Cole

HOT TAMALE PIE
6 to 8 servings

1 pound ground beef
1 package chili seasoning mix
1 (15-ounce) can hot tamales
1 onion, chopped
1½ cups grated Cheddar cheese

Brown meat in a small amount of oil; drain and add chili seasoning mix. Cut hot tamales into bite-size pieces. Put tamale pieces into 9x11-inch baking dish. Sprinkle chopped onions over this and 1 cup grated cheese. Pour chili mixture over all. Sprinkle with rest of cheese and bake at 350° for 40 to 45 minutes covered with foil. Serve with corn chips and shredded lettuce.

Nevin Sledge

BRUNSWICK STEW   20 to 30 servings

1 (5-pound) beef roast
1 (5-pound) pork roast
1 (5-pound) hen or split chicken breasts
3 pounds potatoes, sliced
3 pounds onions, chopped
3 (16-ounce) cans stewed tomatoes
2 (16-ounce) cans whole kernel corn

2 (16-ounce) cans baby lima beans
1 medium bottle of Worcestershire
1 small bottle of Tabasco sauce
Salt and pepper to taste
Butter if needed for seasoning

Cook all meat until tender (pressure cooker is quickest) and save broth. Remove from bone and put in large pot. Add broth and other ingredients. Cook slowly stirring occasionally 3 to 4 hours.

Danny Abraham

HOT TAMALES   2 to 2½ dozen

Cornhusks or foil for wraps

Filling
1 pound lean ground beef
½ cup chopped onion
2 cloves garlic, minced
1 Tablespoon oil

1 (6-ounce) can tomato paste
3 Tablespoons chili powder
2 teaspoons salt
½ teaspoon red pepper

Lightly brown onion, garlic and ground beef in oil. Add all other ingredients and simmer for 15 minutes.

Mush
1½ cups corn meal
4 Tablespoons all-purpose flour

1 teaspoon chili powder
2 teaspoons salt

Mix the above with 1½ cups cold water. Stir mixture into 2 cups boiling water and cook until thickened. Use corn husks or foil as a wrap. Spread mush on husks, then filling and roll. Fold one end of husk up. Stand tamales with open end up in pan. Add a little water, cover and steam for 1 hour.

Tom Box

RED-NECK SPAGHETTI SAUCE

12-15 servings

2-ounces olive oil
2 onions, chopped
2 pounds ground beef
1 Tablespoon minced garlic
½ cup diced celery
1 Tablespoon parsley flakes
½ cup chopped mushrooms
2 Tablespoons sugar
½ teaspoon black pepper

½ teaspoon salt
1 teaspoon Italian seasoning
½ teaspoon marjoram
4 cups tomato sauce
2 cups stewed tomatoes
2-ounces red wine
8-ounces water
2-ounces Cheddar cheese

Put olive oil, onions, and beef in a large heavy pot. Cook over medium heat until beef is brown. Add the rest of the ingredients and simmer for at least 4 hours; the longer the better. Your may have to add a little more water after a few hours.

F. R. Armstrong
(Mr. Bob E. Que)

WILLIE BYRD'S SPAGHETTI SAUCE

1½ gallons

2 pounds ground beef
½ pound bacon, uncooked
2 large cloves garlic, crushed
2 large onions, chopped
2 (16-ounce) cans spaghetti sauce
2 (6-ounce) cans tomato paste
2 (16-ounce) cans water
1 large bell pepper, chopped
1 (12-ounce) package fresh mushrooms, chopped

2 Tablespoons oregano
2 Tablespoons crushed red pepper
2 Tablespoons black pepper
2 bay leaves
Salt to taste
4-ounces Romano cheese, grated
4 Tablespoons honey

In a large iron skillet, brown ground beef; drain thoroughly, set aside. Slowly cook bacon, reserving drippings. Sauté onion and garlic in drippings until clear. In large Dutch oven add cooked beef, spaghetti sauce, tomato paste, water, bell pepper and mushrooms; simmer on low heat for 1 hour; add all other spices and bay leaves and let slowly simmer for 6 hours, adding Romano cheese gradually during cooking time. Add honey during last hour of cooking.

Bill Powell

ANGEL PIE

4 egg whites   **½ teaspoon cream of tartar**
1 cup sugar

Beat until stiff; spread on floured and greased pie pan; bake 2 minutes at 275° and 40 minutes at 300°. Let cool.

Filling
4 egg yolks   **2 Tablespoon pineapple juice**
½ cup sugar   **1 cup whipping cream**
1 Tablespoon lemon juice

Cook first four ingredients 8 minutes in double boiler; whip 1 cup whipping cream with 1 tablespoon sugar. Spread half of cream in pie shell, put in filling then top with rest of cream. Chill and serve.

Dean Pearman

VERNON SHELTON'S HOMEMADE ICE CREAM   1 gallon

3 quarts sweet milk   **3 Tablespoons all-purpose flour**
3 cups sugar   **Dash salt**
6 eggs, beaten   **1 (5-ounce) can evaporated**
1 Tablespoon vanilla   **milk**

Mix above ingredients, except for vanilla. Pour 3 quarts sweet milk and pet milk into mixture. Cook, stirring constantly until the mixture coats a metal spoon and almost boils. Add vanilla. Let cool. Freeze or chill for boiled custard.

Vernon Shelton
Drew, Mississippi

MIKES MILLIONAIRES

1 (10-ounce) package caramels
2 Tablespoons milk
2 cups chopped pecans

1 (6-ounce) package chocolate
  chips
1 Tablespoon paraffin, shaved

Melt caramels and milk in double boiler. Add pecans and drop by tablespoons onto wax paper. Melt chocolate chips and shaved paraffin in double boiler. Dip caramels and pecan candy into chocolate mixture. Drop on wax paper.

Mike Robbins

SWEET POTATO PIE   2 (8-inch) pies

2 cups sugar
½ cup margarine
3 eggs
2 cups cooked sweet potatoes,
  mashed
1 (5-ounce) can evaporated
  milk of 1 cup homogenized
  milk

1 Tablespoon vanilla
Dash of nutmeg
2 (8 or 9-inch) pie shells,
  uncooked

Cream 2 cups sugar together with margarine; add 3 eggs, one at a time. Add sweet potatoes, milk, vanilla and nutmeg. Bake in uncooked pie shells for 45 minutes at 300°. Remove from oven and sprinkle sugar on top. Return to broiler and let sugar crystalize.

J.T. Pap Stevens
Boyle, Mississippi

CHARLES' POPCORN

1 cup popcorn (unpopped)
¼ cup vegetable oil

4 dashes Tabasco

Mix Tabasco and oil and heat in popper. Add popcorn and pop, shaking.

Charles Lee Jones

Gifts

CIDER BUGS
12 servings

6 oranges
2¼ cups brown sugar, firmly
  packed
12 (1½-inch) sticks cinnamon

12 small whole nutmegs
24 large whole allspices
96 whole cloves

Slice oranges in half crosswise; scoop out pulp and reserve for other uses. Place orange halves, cut side up, on a wire rack on a baking sheet. Bake at 250° for about 2 hours or until dry and hard. Let cool. Pack brown sugar firmly into each orange half; mounding it slightly. Arrange spices in brown sugar to resemble a beetle: cinnamon sticks for bodies, nutmeg for heads, allspice for eyes and cloves for feet.

Note: Cover tightly with plastic wrap and tie with a ribbon. Attach the following directions for use: unwrap beetle and drop into 1½ quarts of apple cider; simmer 30 minutes. Remove orange rind and spices to serve.

Mrs. Billy Nowell (Ann)

BOERENJONGENS

1 cup light raisins
1 cup dark raisins
3½ cups water

2 cups sugar
1 pint (2 cups) whiskey

In large saucepan, combine raisins and water. Bring to boil. Reduce heat, simmer 20 minutes. Add sugar and stir until dissolved. Remove from heat, stir in whiskey. Fill 4 clean, hot pint or 8 half-pint jars with raisin-whiskey mixture; seal. Let stand at least one month.
Serve in tiny cordial glasses with a toothpick for eating raisins. I always make mine at Thanksgiving so it will be ready for Christmas giving.

Mrs. Howard Grittman (Ann)
Drew, Mississippi

KAHLUÁ
7 cups

1 quart water
2½ cups sugar
3 Tablespoons instant coffee

1 Tablespoon vanilla
2½ cups Vodka

Bring water, sugar and coffee to a boil in a saucepan. Simmer very slowly for three hours. Mixture will be very dark and syrupy. Cool. Add vanilla and vodka. Serve as an after-dinner liqueur or over vanilla ice cream.

The Editors

ANTI-PASTA SPREAD

Marinade
⅔ cup white vinegar
⅔ cup corn oil
½ teaspoon dried onion
2½ teaspoons Italian seasoning
1 teaspoon garlic salt

1 teaspoon onion salt
1 teaspoon seasoned salt
½ teaspoon pepper
1 teaspoon sugar
1 teaspoon MSG

Mix all ingredients and bring to boil. Cool and mix with the following vegetables.

2 (4-ounce) cans mushrooms, minced
1 (14-ounce) can artichoke hearts, minced
1 small (7-ounce) jar salad olives, minced

1 small (2-ounce) jar pimento, minced
¼ cup celery, minced
¼ cup bell pepper, minced

Note: This keeps for 3 weeks in refrigerator. This was given to me one Christmas as a gift along with the recipe by Judy McGee. I think of her everytime I make it.

Mrs. Jimmy Goodman (Carolyn)

ANAPASTO

1½ (14-ounce) bottles catsup
5 (3½-ounce) jars pickled
   onions
1 head cauliflower, sliced
3 (4-ounce) cans whole
   mushrooms
1 (16-ounce) can green beans,
   cut
2 cups chopped green pepper
2 cups sliced dill pickles
2 cups vegetable oil

¼ cup sugar
2 cups white vinegar
2 cups stuffed green olives,
   sliced
2 cups sliced carrots
2 cups sliced celery
7-ounces sardines, undrained
4-ounces anchovies, drained
1½ (6½-ounce) cans tuna
1 Tablespoon salt

Drain onions, mushrooms, beans, pickles, olives, Cook all raw vegetables except cauliflower, 1 minute in enough water to cover. Drain well. Add all ingredients in a large dutch oven and cook 20 minutes after it comes to a boil. Put in ½ pint jars and seal. No need to refrigerate until after it is opened.

Mrs. Howard Grittman (Ann)

CREOLE SEASONING

1 (26-ounce) box salt
1 (1½-ounce) box black pepper
1 (2-ounce) bottle ground red
   pepper

1 (1-ounce) bottle pure garlic
   powder
1 (1-ounce) bottle chili powder
1 (1-ounce) bottle MSG

Mix well and use as you would salt.

Note: This is great on hamburgers, steaks and fish.

Mrs. Tommy Naron (Memorie)

Gifts

SEASONED SALT

1 cup salt
2 ½ teaspoons paprika
2 teaspoons dry mustard
1 teaspoon oregano

2 teaspoons garlic powder
½ teaspoon onion powder
2 teaspoons black pepper
1 teaspoon celery salt

Mix and pour into air tight shaker bottles. Decorate with paint pens, attach recipe with a ribbon and give to neighbors, new brides, family and friends.

Mrs. Charles Fioranelli (Vicki)

KOSHER STYLE PICKLES   1 quart

10 cloves garlic
8 whole black peppercorns
Crushed red pepper
1 Tablespoon dill seed

1 pinch alum
1 Tablespoon salt
1 Tablespoon vinegar
1 quart cucumbers

Pack washed cucumbers into quart wide mouth jar. Add above ingredients. Fill to top of jar with hot water. Seal the jar. Put in refrigerator after about 6 to 8 days.

Mrs. Jeff Levingston (Barbara)

K.P.'S CANDIED DILL PICKLES   1 quart

Dill pickles, cut into spears
3 cups sugar
2 Tablespoons pickling spice

¼ cup vinegar
1 clove garlic

Pour sugar, spice, vinegar, and garlic over spears. Stir, cover and place in refrigerator. Ready in 24 hours.

Note: You can use any brand of pickles, or your own homemade dills.

Mrs. Jeff Levingston (Barbara)

OKRA PICKLES
4-5 pints

3½ pounds small okra pods　　　**1 pint vinegar (5% acidity)**
5 cloves garlic　　　　　　　　　**⅓ cup pickling salt**
5 small fresh hot peppers　　　　**2 teaspoons dillseeds**
1 quart water

Pack washed okra into hot sterilized jars, leaving ¼-inch headspace. Place a clove of garlic and a hot pepper in each of the jars. Combine remaining ingredients in a medium saucepan; bring to a boil. Pour vinegar mixture over okra, leaving ¼-inch headspace. Cover at once with metal lids and screw bands tight. Process in boiling water bath 10 minutes.

Note: It works everytime for crisp pickles!

Mrs. Richard Cole (Wendy)

HERBED VINEGAR

1 cup fresh herbs (basil, dill,　　　**1 clove garlic, crushed**
**　tarragon, rosemary)**　　　　　　**1 quart cider vinegar**

Place herbs in a quart jar..Add garlic and vinegar. Seal and let stand 10 days to develop flavors. Pour into small jars or cruets. Add a ribbon, gift tag and label.

Note: You may substitute any herbs of your choice.

Mrs. Charles Fioranelli (Vicki)

STRAWBERRY PRESERVES
6-8 half pints

4 cups berries　　　　　　　**3 Tablespoons water**
5 cups sugar

Put 3 Tablespoons water, 2 cups berries and 2 cups sugar in boiler. Bring to a boil that won't stir down. Cook 3 minutes. Add 3 cups berries and 2 cups sugar. Bring to a boil that won't stir down. Cook 5 minutes. Pour into a flat pan. Stir occasionally until cool. Sterilize jars and lids. Fill jars and seal while jars and lids are still hot.

Mrs. Joe Smith (Bill)

WINE JELLY

¾ cups water, room
   temperature
1 box powdered fruit pectin
4½ cups granulated sugar

1 bottle Rushing Wine (750 ml.,
   25.4 oz.) Red, Sweet White, or
   Rosé

In large enamel kettle, using wooden spoon, stir pectin into room temperature water until dissolved. Bring to a boil over high heat; boil 1 minute, stirring constantly. Add wine, then sugar, stirring constantly, reducing heat to medium. Cook at approximately 200° for 5 to 6 minutes to dissolve sugar. Do not boil. Remove from heat, skim with metal spoon as necessary. Quickly pour into hot sterile glasses. Cover with hot paraffin, or use seal type lids and rings. Serve with meats. Chill before serving. For a milder flavor add water to wine for total not to exceed 32 fluid ounces. A few drops red food coloring added during final cooking stage enchances the color when using red wine.

Mrs. Neil McKenzie (Zekie)

RED HOT PEPPER JELLY

1 cup bell pepper
¼ cup red hot peppers
1½ cups cider vinegar

6½ cups sugar
1 bottle Certo

Wash, seed, and grind peppers (use all juice). Mix all ingredients except Certo in large pan. Boil 7 minutes. Watch and stir. Add Certo and put in sterilized jelly jars.

Note: This is good with meats.

Mrs. Roger Dicks (Sallie)
Merigold, Mississippi

JULIA'S CHRISTMAS BARBEQUE SAUCE 2¾ cups

*2 Tablespoons butter or
   margarine*
6 Tablespoons cider vinegar
¼ cup water
1½ cups catsup
*2 Tablespoons Worcestershire
   sauce*
*¼ teaspoon Tabasco sauce, or
   more to taste*
*1 teaspoon finely chopped
   garlic*

*3 Tablespoons vegetable,
   peanut, or corn oil*
Salt
Freshly ground pepper
¼ teaspoon red pepper flakes
½ bay leaf
2 Tablespoons sugar
1 teaspoon paprika
1 lemon, juiced, quartered

Combine in a saucepan the butter, vinegar, water, catsup, Worcestershire sauce, Tabasco, garlic, oil, salt, pepper, red pepper flakes, bay leaf, sugar, and paprika. Cut juiced lemon into quarters and add it. Heat throughly without boiling. Use to baste chicken, fish, spareribs, etc. as they are grilled.

Note: This sauce will keep for days in the refrigerator if it is tightly sealed.

Mrs. Dana Moore (Julia)

CHILI SAUCE 12 pints

24 ripe tomatoes
*8 coarsely chopped green
   peppers*
8 chopped onions
1 bunch chopped celery
4 cups vinegar

4 cups sugar
6 Tablespoons salt
1 Tablespoon cinnamon
1 Tablespoon all spice
1 Tablespoon nutmeg

Boil all ingredients together until thick. Stir often to keep from sticking. Mash with potato masher and simmer 2 hours or until it is as thick as you like. Pour into sterile jars and seal.

Mrs. John Tatum (Carol)

PICO DE GALLO

1½ quarts

8-10 fresh jalepeño chiles,
 diced
4 large tomatoes, chopped
1 large onion, diced

1 lemon, juice only
1 teaspoon salt
1 teapoon lemon pepper
½ teaspoon cumin

Mix all ingredients and refrigerate. Delicious served with chips as a dip, or add to Guacamole dip to add a zip, or mix with melted processed cheese (to taste). Serve on the side with tacos, meat, or vegetables.

Alice Lee McIntosh

SQUASH RELISH

7-8 pints

12 cups yellow squash, grated
4 large yellow onions, chopped
4 red or green bell peppers,
 finely chopped
5 Tablespoons salt

2 Tablespoons pickling spices,
 tied in a bag
1 teaspoon tumeric powder
2½ cups apple cider vinegar
6 cups sugar

Sprinkle salt over vegetables. Stir. Let sit overnight. Drain. Cover with ice water and let stand 20 minutes. Drain well. Combine pickling spices, tumeric, and vinegar. Bring to a boil. Pour mixture over sugar; stir. Add squash, onions and peppers. Cook 10 minutes. Put in sterilized jars and seal.

Hint: Grating and chopping vegetables in blender saves times.

Mrs. Lannie Mosley (Nancy)

BEST BROWNIES

2 eggs, beaten
1 teaspoon vanilla

½ cup chopped nuts
*2½ cups Brownie Mix

Preheat oven to 350°, grease and flour an 8-inch square pan. In a medium bowl, combine eggs, vanilla and Brownie Mix. Beat until smooth. Stir in nuts. Pour into prepared pan. Bake 30 to 35 minutes, until edges separate from pan. Cool. Cut into 2-inch bars. Frost or sprinkle with powdered sugar.

*Page 371

Mrs. Felix Dean (Rowena)

BROWNIE MIX

6 cups all-purpose flour
4 teaspoons baking powder
4 teaspoons salt

8 cups sugar
1 (8-ounce) can cocoa
2 cups vegetable shortening

In a large (at least 4 quart) bowl, sift together flour, baking powder and salt. Add sugar and cocoa. Blend well. With a hand mixer, cut in shortening until evenly distributed. Put in a large airtight container (like Tupperware). Label with date and store in a cool, dry place. Use within 10 to 12 weeks. Makes about 17 cups of Brownie Mix.

See: Best Brownies and Mississippi Mud

Mrs. Felix Dean (Rowena)

MISSISSIPPI MUD

4 eggs
3 cups Brownie Mix
½ cup margarine, melted
1 teaspoon vanilla
2 cups chopped nuts
1 cup flaked coconut
1 (7-ounce) jar marshmallow
   cream

Chocolate Icing
1 pound powdered sugar
½ cup margarine
6 Tablespoons evaporated milk
4 Tablespoons cocoa

Preheat oven to 350°. Lightly grease and lightly flour a 13x9-inch baking pan. In a large bowl, beat eggs until foamy. Add melted margarine and mix well. Add brownie Mix and blend well. Stir in vanilla. Stir in nuts and coconut. Pour into prepared pan. Bake about 30 minutes, until edges separate from pan. While still hot, carefully spread on marshmallow creme. Frost with Chocolate Icing. Makes 1 large cake.

Chocolate Icing: Put powdered sugar in a medium bowl. In a small saucepan (1 quart), combine margarine, evaporated milk and cocoa. Bring to a boil, stirring constantly. Remove from heat. Immediately add to powdered sugar. Beat until smooth. Pour over cake.

Mrs. Felix Dean (Rowena)

SPICY PECANS (MOM'S SECRET RECIPE)   1 pound

2½ cups pecan halves
1 cup sugar
½ cup water

1 teaspoon cinnamon
1½ teaspoons vanilla
½ teaspoon salt

Heat pecan halves 5 minutes at 375°, stirring once. Butter sides of heavy 2 quart saucepan. Combine sugar, water, and cinnamon. Cook at medium temperature until sugar dissolves and mixture boils. Cook, without stirring, to softball stage. For best results, use candy thermometer. Remove from heat. Beat by hand 1 minute or until mixture becomes creamy. Add vanilla and warm nuts; stir gently until nuts are well coated and mixture is creamy. Turn out on butter platter or cookie sheet. Separate at once using two forks.

Note: This recipe does not double well.

Mrs. Kirkham Povall (Hilda)

SUGARED NUTS   1 pound

1 pound pecans, shelled into
  halves
¼ cup butter

2 egg whites, room temperature
10 Tablespoons sugar
⅛ teaspoon salt

Preheat oven to 325°. Divide butter and melt on two cookie sheets (9x13-inch with ½-inch sides). Remove from oven. Beat egg whites until foamy. Gradually add sugar, 2 Tablespoons at a time while beating at high speed. Add salt and beat until peaks form. Place half of the pecans in each pan and stir to coat with butter. Spread ½ of the egg mixture over each pan of nuts. Coat well. Bake 15 minutes. Stir a couple of times to turn. Cool and enjoy.

Miss Anne Hammett
Greenville, Ms.

ORANGE PECANS

1 cup sugar
½ cup cream

1 teaspoon grated orange rind
1 quart shelled pecans

Cook sugar and cream until soft ball stage. Remove from heat. Add orange rind. Pour over pecans. Separate when cool.

Mrs. Charles Lawrence (Mary Kathryn)

Variation: ½ cup orange juice for ½ cup cream.

Mrs. Mark Routman (Terry)

PEANUT BUTTER

1 pound unsalted peanuts
¾ cup honey
½ cup peanut oil

¼ teaspoon cinnamon
¼ teaspoon allspice
¼ teaspoon nutmeg

Place peanuts in food processor. Using metal blade, grind until smooth. Add honey, oil, allspice, nutmeg, and cinnamon blend until well mixed. Put in bowl and top with extra honey. Let stand 3 hours.

Mrs. David Taylor (Mary)

STAINED GLASS CANDY

3¾ cups sugar
1½ cups corn syrup
1 cup water
Food coloring
1 pound powdered sugar

Oil flavoring-Use one of the following:
1 teaspoon peppermint oil
1 teaspoon clove oil
1½ teaspoons cinnamon oil
2 teaspoons lemon oil
2 teaspoon orange oil

Mix first three ingredients and boil to 300°. Pour in desired food coloring while boiling. Remove from heat and add one of the flavor oils. Have large cookie sheet covered with a thick layer of powdered sugar. Pour syrup over sugar. As edges cool, cut into strips with shears. Then cut strips into bite-size pieces. Sift sugar off and place candy in tightly covered dry container. This makes an excellent gift at Christmas. Put in clear glass container because they are so pretty.

Mrs. Barry Sullivan (Betty)

EQUIVALENCIES AND SUBSTITUTIONS

3 teaspoons = 1 tablespoon
4 tablespoons = ¼ cup
5⅓ tablespoons = ⅓ cup
8 tablespoons = ½ cup
10⅔ tablespoons = ⅔ cup
12 tablespoons = ¾ cup
16 tablespoons = 1 cup

1 cup = 8 fluid ounces
1 cup = ½ pint
2 cups = 1 pint
4 cups = 1 quart
4 quarts = 1 gallon
8 quarts = 1 peck
4 pecks = 1 bushel

No. 300 can = 1¾ cups or 14 to 16 ounces
No. 303 can = 2 cups or 16 to 17 ounces
No. 2 can = 2½ cups or 20 ounces
No. 2½ can = 3½ cups or 29 ounces

1 cup cake flour = 1 cup minus 2 tablespoons all-purpose flour
1 tablespoon cornstarch = 2 tablespoons flour
1 teaspoon baking powder = ¼ teaspoon baking soda plus ½ cup
   buttermilk or sour milk (to replace ½ cup of liquid called for in
   recipe)
1 cup whole milk = ½ cup evaporated milk plus ½ cup water or 1 cup
   reconstituted nonfat dry milk plus 2½ teaspoons butter or margarine
1 cup sour milk or buttermilk = 1 tablespoon lemon juice or vinegar plus
   sweet milk to make 1 cup (let stand 5 minutes)
1 square (1 ounce) unsweetened chocolate = 3 tablespoons cocoa (dry)
   plus 1 tablespoon butter or margarine
1 tablespoon fresh snipped herbs = 1 teaspoon dried herbs
1 small fresh onion = 1 tablespoon instant minced onion, rehydrated
1 teaspoon dry mustard = 1 tablespoon prepared mustard
1 clove garlic = ⅛ teaspoon garlic powder
1 cup tomato juice = ½ cup tomato sauce plus ½ cup water
1 cup catsup or chili sauce = 1 cup tomato sauce plus ½ cup sugar and 2
   tablespoons vinegar (for use in cooked mixtures)

EQUIVALENCIES AND SUBSTITUTIONS

2 tablespoons butter = 1 ounce
1 stick or ¼ pound butter = ½ cup
1 square chocolate = 1 ounce
28 crackers = 1 cup fine crumbs
14 square graham crackers = 1 cup fine crumbs
22 vanilla wafers = 1 cup fine crumbs
1½ slices bread = 1 cup soft crumbs
1 slice bread = ¼ fine dry crumbs
Juice of 1 lemon = 3 tablespoons
Grated peel of 1 lemon = 1 teaspoon
Juice of 1 orange = about ⅓ cup
Grated peel of 1 orange = about 2 teaspoons
1 medium apple, chopped = about 1 cup
1 medium onion, chopped = ½ cup
1 cup whipping cream = 2 cups whipped
1 pound American cheese, shredded = 4 cups
¼ pound blue cheese, crumbled = 1 cup
12 to 14 egg yolks = 1 cup
8 to 10 egg whites = 1 cup

Index

Index

Index

Index

Index

Index

Index

Index

Index

Index

NOTES

NOTES

Temptations
Presbyterian Day School
West Sunflower Road
Cleveland, Ms. 38732

Please send me ____ copies of **Temptations** at $14.95 per copy, plus $3.00 for postage and handling per book. Enclosed is my check or money order for $_____.

Name _____

Address _____

City _____ State _____ Zip _____

Temptations
Presbyterian Day School
West Sunflower Road
Cleveland, Ms. 38732

Please send me ____ copies of **Temptations** at $14.95 per copy, plus $3.00 for postage and handling per book. Enclosed is my check or money order for $_____.

Name _____

Address _____

City _____ State _____ Zip _____

Temptations
Presbyterian Day School
West Sunflower Road
Cleveland, Ms. 38732

Please send me ____ copies of **Temptations** at $14.95 per copy, plus $3.00 for postage and handling per book. Enclosed is my check or money order for $_____.

Name _____

Address _____

City _____ State _____ Zip _____

Reorder Additional Copies